GARY JOBSON'S
CHAMPIONSHIP
SAILING

To Scott: Good luck in the Thistle.

Ja

GARY JOBSON'S
CHAMPIONSHIP
SAILING

The Definitive Guide
for Skippers, Tacticians, and Crew

GARY JOBSON

International Marine / McGraw-Hill
Camden, Maine • New York • Chicago • San Francisco • Lisbon • London • Madrid •
Mexico City • Milan • New Delhi • San Juan • Seoul • Singapore • Sydney • Toronto

BOOKS BY GARY JOBSON

An America's Cup Treasury: The Lost Levick Photographs, 1893–1937

Championship Tactics: How Anyone Can Sail Faster, Smarter, and Win Races, with Tom Whidden and Adam Loory

Fighting Finish: The Volvo Ocean Race Round the World, 2001–2002

Gary Jobson's How to Sail

The Racing Edge, with Ted Turner

Sailing Fundamentals: The Official Learn-to-Sail Manual of the American Sailing Association and the United States Coast Guard Auxiliary, revised and updated

Speed Sailing, with Mike Toppa

Storm Sailing

U.S.Y.R.U. Sailing Instructor's Manual

The Winner's Guide to Optimist Sailing, with Jay Kehoe

World Class Sailing, with Martin Luray

The Yachtsman's Pocket Almanac, revised

The **McGraw·Hill** Companies

1 2 3 4 5 6 7 8 9 DOC DOC 0 9 8 7 6 5 4

© 2004 by Gary Jobson
All rights reserved. The name "International Marine" and the
International Marine logo are trademarks of The McGraw-Hill
Companies. Printed in the United States of America.

Library of Congress Cataloging-in-Publication Data
Jobson, Gary.
Gary Jobson's championship sailing : the definitive guide for
skippers, tacticians, and crew / Gary Jobson.
   p.   cm.
Includes index.
ISBN 0-07-142381-8 (pbk. : alk. paper)
1. Sailboat racing. 2. Sailing. I. Title: Championship sailing. II. Title.
GV826.5.J53 2004
797.124—dc22   2004014536

Photos by Daniel Forster unless noted otherwise.
Line illustrations by Brad Dellenbaugh.

DEDICATION

To my enthusiastic sailing friends:

Norwood Davis
Geoffrey Mason
David Pensky

CONTENTS

ACKNOWLEDGMENTS

In many ways writing a book is similar to a sailing campaign. It takes many people working together to get good results. And, just as a boat under sail needs diligent trimming, so does a work-in-progress.

Some of the material contained here has previously been published in magazines. From *Sailing World* I'm grateful to editor John Burnham for his help fine-tuning my articles. And from my years at *Yachting*, I'm equally grateful to my primary editor Ken Wooton.

I'd also like to thank Kathy Lambert who helped pull much of the material together in Annapolis. It was a big task keeping up with me.

For the trimming section I worked closely with Stu Argo who is one of the best trimmers in the world.

Thank you to Farr Yacht Design for providing the polar diagrams.

I'd like to thank my coach from my Maritime College days, Graham Hall, who encouraged me to develop an organized approach to sailing.

I'm thankful to my daughter Kristi and to Anne Smith for proofreading my early drafts.

Throughout this project, International Marine editor Tris Coburn provided invaluable insight and asked many thought-provoking questions. Thanks to others at International Marine—Molly Mulhern, Janet Robbins, and Margaret Cook—and to copyeditor Cynthia Goss for their hard work making the book read well and flow smoothly.

And finally, I'd like to thank Brad Dellenbaugh for his drawings and Daniel Forster for his photography.

To write this volume I reviewed most of my writings over the past thirty years. It was interesting to see how many good ideas I had when I was young and how those ideas have evolved over time. Like all sailors I keep reviewing my racing techniques to sail better. This book helps me immensely toward this goal.

May it do the same for you.

INTRODUCTION

When I was fifteen, I was invited to crew in the E-scow National Championship. Buddy Melges, who had won a bronze medal at the Olympic Games a year earlier, was one of the participants. He wore a jacket with *USA* emblazoned on the front. I was impressed.

At the start of the first race, Buddy crossed the 85-boat fleet on port tack—a supremely audacious move—and sailed on to win the race. That night I walked down the dock to find him showing some competitors how to trim the jib. They had a sail up on a boat sitting on its trailer, and Buddy was explaining the jib lead system.

I wondered why he would help a competitor, so I asked him. He told me, "The better my competitors are, the better it makes me." That philosophy has stuck with me throughout my sailing career. Thanks to Buddy's example I've tried to be helpful without worrying about what information I might be giving away.

One of the first things we learn about sailboat racing is how vividly the memories of great victories and disappointing defeats stay with us—especially the defeats. We replay the mistakes over and over. It's one of the things that keeps us going back for more.

In the process of writing *Championship Sailing,* I drew on my memories of many races. About halfway through, it dawned on me that I had far more losses to talk about than victories. But win or lose, there are many lessons to review. Like Buddy Melges I haven't worried about giving away secrets. In fact, writing this book has helped me redefine my techniques.

Soon after I started this project I was diagnosed with lymphoma. During nine months of treatments and a long subsequent recovery I was unable to race a sailboat. Visualizing past races was a big help passing the time. And so was writing.

Every day I plugged away. After several months the book started to take shape. And once again I came to the realization that sailing is a uniquely complex sport, and sailors need many attributes in order to enjoy success. My goal through words, photographs, and diagrams is to make racing at the top level understandable and rewarding.

Throughout the book I've used actual races to emphasize points. While I spent days lying in a hospital bed recovering from treatments, I reflected on past races. Every race yielded good material. And I realized that big boats and small boats are equally fun. Even better than the boats are the people you get to know, the places you visit, and the satisfaction of trying your best.

This book is for everyone interested in sailboat racing. From beginning to expert the techniques I've learned apply to all levels of expertise. Take your time reading this book. Think about your own races. My suc-cess is a result of asking questions, taking notes, defining problems, setting goals, and learning from experience. Whether you are a skipper, tactician, or crew member, there's something to be gleaned from these pages.

Sailing is a lifelong sport. The passion stays with you, and many sailors remain competitive in their forties, fifties, and beyond. Regardless of results on the water, the most important thing is to have fun. I hope *Championship Sailing* helps you have more fun out there.

CHAPTER 1

Before the Start:
A Word on Competition and Goals

Competition

A good competitor is a perfectionist. It is someone who constantly strives for improvement by setting specific goals. But, excellence also takes time. Unlike most other sports, sailing will give you that time. While failing knees might keep older players off the football field, age is not a limiting factor in sailing. You will have an entire lifetime to improve. It's no accident that most of our Olympic medalists in 2000 were over the age of forty. These sailors had forty years of mistakes to learn from, and forty years of goals to achieve. Age and perfectionism are a winning combination.

The biggest moment in the America's Cup is the first race. No one knows for sure which boat will be faster. History demonstrates that the first mile will tell the tale. For fans the drama is fascinating, while competitors feel the pressure of the task at hand. The uncertainty keeps everyone on edge.

On the surface, skippers—as leaders of their teams—must exude confidence. But deep down they all have some fear. This fear makes them humble: it's the kind of feeling every racer should have before a regatta.

Having lived through this first-race scene aboard *Courageous*, I could relate to the sailors' emotional struggles during the numerous pre–America's Cup interviews I've done over the years for ESPN. The best answer I received to my standard are-you-feeling-the-pressure question before an America's Cup came from Russell Coutts. His answer was perfect: "Where else would you rather be for these races than on a boat?"

In other words, Coutts knew he could control his own destiny and also have a ringside seat for sailing's most exciting event. The answer also demonstrated to me that Coutts was ready for the challenge.

For Ted Turner, the first race of the 1977 America's Cup seemed like just another day on the water. By sticking with the normal routine of sailing he was able to stay calm. Of course, the crew had been sailing together for months, so the event itself didn't seem much different from the norm.

Every sailor can learn lessons from the masters of the sport. Even superstars learn over a long period of time, for there is no better teacher than experience.

I encourage young sailors to focus more on learning than winning. A learning experience is more rewarding in the long term. Looking back on my own career, I count about seven defeats behind every victory.

Success on the water begins with a winning mindset. Just as you do in life, you make your own choices on the water. But there are always exceptions to the rule. And there are events you can't control. The secret is to play the percentages and make the most of bad situations.

When things go wrong on the racecourse due to bad luck or a poor decision, take the attitude that "just for fun" you are going to work out of the mess. The biggest frustration occurs when you fret about the final outcome. Worrying, impatience, and yelling never solve problems.

To calm nerves, think of past successes. On the course, try to make one gain at a time. Taking a flyer—sailing a long distance away from the fleet—to pass the whole fleet only works about one time in a hundred. To use a football analogy, go for the first down, not the long bomb.

Moments of adversity demand hard thought and innovation. During the race, concentration is the key; focus on one thing at a time and use common sense. Once you have a good idea, go with your instinct and stick with your game plan. Along the way it helps to experiment by adjusting your sails or your course, then observing the results. When things are going well, keep at it. If nothing improves, go back to your original setting or experiment with something else. Be bold.

After a race, the reason for victory always seems obvious. But during the race, it's not always apparent. During the America's Cup trials in 1999, the American entry *Stars & Stripes* was struggling in the first round-robin. For the second round, Tom Whidden—Dennis Conner's longtime tactician and winner of three America's Cup campaigns—was brought in as tactician. He had no magic formula. He simply told the crew to sail conservatively and use common sense.

"We are not going to foul, hit a mark, set a spinnaker prematurely, or jump the line at the gun," said Whidden. His straightforward approach worked. In Round One, *Stars & Stripes* had four wins versus six losses. Round Two produced a 7–3 record. The only change Whidden made was to sail by the numbers (using instruments to determine speeds and wind angles) and not take chances. The crew had been freelancing too much (testing and sailing outside the target boatspeed numbers) and was not sailing in the fastest groove. The time to experiment is during test days.

The start of the America's Cup is the most exciting moment in sailing. No one knows for sure which boat is going to be faster. Here Alinghi *and* Team New Zealand *duel off the starting line of the first race in the 2003 America's Cup.*

Collegiate racing is extremely competitive. The entire fleet will round a mark nearly simultaneously.

But when you are racing, it is better to work with accepted values.

Collegiate sailing is fiercely intense. Every crew is capable of winning a race. Coaches improve the level of competition. As a weekend regatta heats up, boats seem to get closer in speed. A fleet of eighteen boats will often round a mark within 30 seconds of each other. It's very impressive to watch and to experience. To win the college nationals, a fourth-place average will usually prevail. The collegiate champion learns when to take chances and when to be conservative. Learning the difference applies to all levels of sailing. The overriding philosophy is to stay with the pack and not take big risks.

During my college racing career, I realized that the same tactical and boat-handling principles apply to boats of all sizes. In theory, sailing a dinghy is no different from sailing a Maxi boat. The person who helped me understand this was one of America's greatest dinghy sailors, Runyon Colie.

Colie won three college national championships for MIT (1938, 1939, and 1940), the Penguin International Championship (when the class was at its peak), and the E-scow Nationals. Before I headed to SUNY Maritime College, I asked Runnie for the key to his successful college sailing. He said, "The secret to winning is going around the buoys more often than anyone else. When you do it," he continued, "just keep trying to do better." The concept clicked for me. There would be no wasted time. From that point forward, whenever I left the dock, I would be in racing mode.

When I first arrived at college, our coach Graham Hall whistled me off the racecourse after watching me perform a few practice starts. "You will never get consistently good starts by sailing so randomly," he advised. "What you need is an organized approach to a chaotic situation." So with Colie's encouragement to always "race" around the buoys and Hall's organized sailing plan, I started to build my own sailing system. It is this system that I have learned, fine-tuned, and relearned over a lifetime of racing sailboats. There is no magic to winning; small gains and new lessons make the difference. You should develop a system that works for you. Create an organized approach and keep track of what works.

Setting Goals

Winning a race is simply the culmination of a quest to excel that began long before the victory gun. The desire to win drives success, and victory is the result of performing many small things well. The first step to winning is developing a vision— and then using that vision to define your goals.

Goals are important. They might be concrete—faster tacks or faster spinnaker sets, for example—or less easily measured tasks such as understanding how to tune a rig, mastering your understanding of the racing rules, or even having more fun. Spend time thinking about your goals be-

fore deciding what you want to achieve. Talk with other sailors. Once your ideas gel, write them down.

Generate both easily attainable short-term objectives and more difficult long-term goals. Achieving short-term goals helps you measure success, while long-term goals give you benchmarks well into the future. You can even use your goals to inspire others.

Ted Turner always made sure his crew knew why they were there. The most memorable moment came after a bad practice race aboard the 12-meter *Courageous*. We had rounded a leeward mark with the spinnaker still up, the jib still down, and the spinnaker pole in the water. It was ugly. After we cleared away the mess, Ted got everyone into the cockpit and gave a spirited talk on focusing on each job. Along the way he created a reason to win, which was to go for perfection. Ted took the time to explain the overall goal to the entire crew. These moments would always pull the crew together as a team.

Not all goals need to be shared with others. Private objectives are powerful motivators and can provide a special satisfaction when they are reached. Some of my private goals over the years have been to find a way to get along with an unruly crew member, use an event to help promote the sport, and figure out the secrets of my top competitors.

Keep track of your goals by periodically reviewing your progress. Of course, not all goals can be met. Cast away disappointment by finding the lesson in the experience. Listing the reasons for missing a goal helps define problems and builds com-

Matador[2] *crosses the finish line first in Maxi World Championship. There is great satisfaction when a crew wins a race. Immediately after crossing, the next race should become the focus of attention.*

fort and encouragement for the next stage. Remind yourself of your goals by posting them where you can frequently see them, refer to them often, and modify them as needed.

Work your goals into your calendar; having a time frame makes it easier to achieve them. Set daily short-term goals and use one-year or even decade-long cycles for larger goals.

There is no guarantee you will meet every goal, but any progress is good. Patience is the key. You will get great satisfaction from this process—and each success will inspire you to set new, higher goals. In this way, you will continue to improve.

CHAPTER 2

The Sailing Team

Races are often decided by smooth boat handling and precise organization. To win, a crew has to function like a football team and execute maneuvers swiftly and efficiently. In basketball there are five players; hockey has six; baseball, nine; and football, eleven. But in Maxi yacht racing, for example, there are often twenty-four sailors on board. In no other sport do you have to coordinate the activities of twenty-four "players" simultaneously. (Of course, this is an extreme example because while the foredeck on an 80-foot boat will need six people, a 30-foot boat will need only two.)

I have an adage when building a crew for any boat: every crew member you add to a boat squares the potential problems. Therefore, good organization is a key to successful sailing. And this takes practice,

since you must have a plan for each boat-handling sequence. Even a two-person boat needs to be carefully organized.

Learning a crew position requires more than memorizing steps by rote. Executing tasks mechanically works well on paper, but on the water you must stay flexible and time your moves with the rest of your crew and with what is happening on the racecourse. For example, you might have to slow your jib trimming to coordinate with the mainsail trimmer. You have to stay aware of changing conditions, such as the boat's angle of heel or the apparent wind.

But there are certain basics that all crew must adhere to: know your position, be prepared in advance for any maneuver, talk quietly, and keep your weight low and away from the ends of the boat. You can

When an entire crew stands up it cuts down the visibility of the helmsman and shows general disorganization.

always spot a poorly sailed boat because the entire crew will be standing.

When there's a problem on a well-sailed boat, the crew will automatically go to their stations. On a poorly sailed boat, the whole crew dives at the problem simultaneously.

A well-sailed boat is therefore easy to recognize. The crew works in a business-like mode, everyone is poised for the next sequence, and there's no shouting. To see how you're doing, have a spare crew member or a friend who is not racing video one of your races. Include some footage of the class champion too. Review the tape as a group. You may not like everything you see, but you'll have a few laughs and learn something too.

This chapter covers crew organization and the three teams on board: the tactical team, the trimming team, and the foredeck team. On a two-person dinghy, both sailors are part of all three teams. On a bigger boat with, say, five crew you begin to split into separate units. Create a buddy system on board by having two people share each task. If there's a problem, a second person provides backup or can help with a solution. Remember the old saying, "many hands make light work." Together all crew have a common goal: winning. That goal will keep your crew's attention focused on racing hard, for competitive spirit is the lifeblood of sport.

The Tactical Team

The tactical team on most boats is made of the tactician, the helmsman, and the navigator. Every boat with two or more people should always use one crew as the tactician. The tactician is responsible for keeping his or her eyes outside the boat and developing a strategy.

In the America's Cup a strategist is often added to study the big picture or long-term view. Here's a hypothetical situation that you, as tactician, might face: as you round the leeward mark in a fleet of 45-footers, your helmsman is cranky. You lost two boats on the run. He feels unsteady. You ask everyone to stay still and announce your plan to sail up the right side of the course. You calm the crew by forecasting that the boats ahead will soon tack. And they do. Cool! Now you have clear wind, and the boat is quiet. The helmsman is still nervous, so you squeeze his shoulder and ask, "What else can I do for you?" He whispers, "Thanks." A tactician must always be alert and ready with a helpful solution at any moment.

The tactician is the hub around which everything revolves. All top boats designate and empower a tactician. The job can be lonely. When you are behind in a race, expect grousing from the crew. The solution is to run through a list of options and quickly select one.

For example, you might find yourself well behind soon after the start. The tactician is the person who decides whether you'll split from the fleet or stay with a group—even though you are behind. If you split, you might end up even farther behind. Or you could get lucky. The tactician needs to draw on his experience, analyze the wind, and make the call. If crew members get antsy, the tactician needs to settle everyone down and focus on speed.

At times, a tactician can feel like an NFL coach on the sideline when the team is losing: no player gets within twenty feet of a coach when he is angry and things are not going well.

In Newport, during the America's Cup races of the 1930s, 1950s, and 1960s, the navigator played the prominent role. This was by necessity, considering the long courses and potentially foggy conditions. But since the 1970s, with advances in onboard electronics, the navigator spends more time keeping track of performance. The tactician's role has become the strategic focal point.

There are many sailors who feel they excel at the helm, but there are few people who have really developed the art of calling tactics. Anyone can be an expert *after* a race, but *during* a race it takes courage and confidence to make decisions.

As a tactician, you need to stay ahead of the game. Think through all scenarios as one would in a game of chess. The best tacticians absorb all problems so the speed team (helmsman and trimmers) can concentrate on their assignments.

The tactician's tone of voice also carries a lot of weight. Be steady and encouraging. Crews like frequent updates on progress, even if it's bad news. What bothers sailors most are surprises.

Always make the definitive call in precise terms. For example: "We're tacking in two boatlengths," or, "We'll jibe set, sail two minutes, and then jibe back." Precision gives the crew focus and builds confidence. As the situation tightens, your calls must remain accurate. A good time to list and discuss options is in wide-open water, when other boats are not attacking you—not when you're about to round a mark.

Top tacticians do their homework before every regatta, memorizing the race instructions, courses, weather report, sail inventory, crew roster, potential equipment problems, standings, handicap allowances, competition list, radio communications procedures, tides and currents, and learning the waters by studying charts. Tacticians should also make a habit of talking to locals about the anticipated weather, to learn about any possible local nuances.

No detail is too small for a tactician—from when to avoid certain water, to how to engage converging boats. The tactician is usually the one who hands out sunscreen; checks that the crew is wearing the right uniform; decides where crew, as ballast, should sit; or even cleans the helmsman's sunglasses. No job is too big or too small.

The tactician's art takes years to perfect (you'll learn more about that art in the next chapter). I am always learning new ways to improve performance, and I sometimes even relearn lessons. I'm periodically reminded, for example, that different boats have unique wind shadows (blanketing effect caused by the sails and the hull), that the relative speeds of boats changes with the strength of the wind, or that local geographical windshifts in a specific area follow oft-repeated patterns. I sometimes have to smile when I find myself relearning lessons I should already know.

The Trimming Team

Teamwork and collective wisdom are the hallmarks of many sports. Aboard a sailboat, two people working together on the same task can reinforce the mission, eliminate mistakes, and improve efficiency. On the trimming team (composed of those who work the sheets), the trimmer and the grinder must anticipate each other's needs when working with all the sails. On some boats the mainsail trimmer becomes part of the afterguard, since the mainsail trimmer has a huge impact on the steering of the boat. (*Afterguard* is a term defining the people who make the decisions, usually composed of skipper, tactician, and navigator.) Occasionally, it helps to switch positions so trimmer and grinder each understands the other's job. The end result is great satisfaction in handling the sails well.

The grinder doesn't need to be the strongest person on the boat. Speed and endurance are the keys to grinding, not necessarily strength. Here are some pointers for grinders:

❖ Keep the path of your winch handle clear of all obstructions (lifelines, crew, other sheets).

❖ Full revolutions of the winch handle are preferable to a back-and-forth motion, because you can trim more line at a faster rate.

❖ Stand up to grind, keeping your arms rotating below your chest. This gives you the most power.

❖ Stand wide of the winch, allowing your trimmer a clear view of the sail. It also helps to stand facing the sail.

❖ Keep your legs spread about 4 feet apart to distribute your weight for better balance.

The trimmer of this America's Cup yacht works closely with the grinding team. During a tacking duel, efficient trimming saves considerable energy. The grinders appreciate that.

❖ Always use both hands when grinding; two-handed cranks are best (lubricate your winch handles so they spin effortlessly).

❖ The longer the winch handle, the more power you have.

The tailer (also known as the trimmer) should always face both the winch and the sail that's being trimmed, and he must give the grinder room to turn the handle. When tailing, announce your intentions to the grinder: "I'm trimming the jib four inches." By communicating in exact terms (feet and inches), you make your actions easier to understand. Keep your ear tuned to the helmsman. Use as few wraps of your sheet on the winch drum as possible. For normal trimming, use two wraps of the sheet at first, then add more wraps as the sheet tension builds. Wearing gloves saves your hands and gives you a better grip on the sheet.

Anticipate tacks by clearing the working sheet early, so it's free to run. As the boat rounds into the wind, the leeward tailer trims the jib to help force the boat to luff into the wind: tightening the leech helps turn the boat toward the wind. Keep the sails full as long as possible to maintain boatspeed.

Reduce the wraps on your winch on the old leeward side to the bare minimum just before you cast off the sheet. Three wraps will do on most boats; use four on larger boats in heavy air. Use line that is roughened up slightly for better adhesion to the winch drum. (New line tends to be slippery because of the oils used in the manufacturing process. One method of roughening up a line is simply to drag it overboard for a mile; be careful not to drag it too long, or it will begin to fray excessively.)

The casting-off tailer should ease the sail out quickly, but with a steady action. Work the turns off the winch by feeding line out and lifting the turns off the drum, one at a time. Lifting the tail straight up off the drum will cause the line to form a corkscrew, which often gets trapped in the blocks.

Avoid backing the jib when tacking in any wind strength, for this will slow the boat.

To avoid an override on the winch while trimming the new sheet, keep the tail exiting off the drum just below the top of the winch drum, well above the other turns on the drum. As the winch drum turns, the wraps of the sheet work naturally down to the bottom.

An interesting trend first developed by three-time America's Cup winning tailer Simon Daubney of New Zealand is to trim on both tacks. A second tailer is used for maneuvers, but Daubney takes the sheet as soon as the tack is completed. Trimming

The jib of this ocean racer is dramatically backed, bringing the boat to a virtual dead stop. It will take a lot of work for this boat to recover its speed.

the whole time might get tiring, but there is good consistency for the helmsman. Daubney only trims on windward legs. Another trimmer handles the downwind work.

Below are some tips to help you perfect your trimming technique:

❖ The tailer should make long, hard trims on the sheet.

❖ More line is gathered with fewer long trims than with many short trims.

❖ Have a spare short sheet ready in case of an override.

❖ Clip the short sheet on the clew of the sail and use it to trim the sail onto another winch.

❖ Stow winch handles within easy reach of both tailer and grinder.

❖ Remember that the best exercise for trimming and grinding is simply trimming and grinding. The trimming team feels the real power in the sails and should constantly communicate to produce optimum speeds.

The Foredeck Team

To run the bow of a modern offshore racer effectively requires a partnership between the man on the peak, the bowman, and the man at the mast, the mastman. The bowman and the mastman are the foredeck team. (Others from the middle of the boat are in a position to help the foredeck team if necessary during sail changes.) A solid relationship between these two vital crew members contributes to overall teamwork

on board—and the key to success is communication. Anticipation and a step-by-step approach when the going gets rough are also essential.

Bowmen are a special fraternity within the sailing world. Not everyone enjoys working on the bow—where it's wet, cold, and sometimes confusing and dangerous. Bow work requires a special mix of

The work of the bowman is lonely but satisfying. The old adage, "One hand for the ship and one hand for yourself," is certainly true for this position.

physical and mental skills: strength, quickness, agility, and—to be honest—youth.

The bowman has to stay as far forward as possible during a start to observe approaching boats and to gauge distance from the starting line; he then relays this critical information back to the cockpit. Upwind, he has to direct headsail changes. The bowman must also keep sheets and guys orderly, hook up the spinnaker, and direct the bow during jibes. These duties require the bowman's special mental and physical abilities.

Many of the bowman's duties couldn't be performed without the cooperation of the mastman. The mastman needs to keep halyards ready for hoisting; hoist, flake,

Walk Like a Bowman

All crew members should learn the art of walking on deck from the bowman. The goal is to cover a lot of distance quickly without disturbing the boat. Some sailors call this walking with "Jesus feet." In other words, light enough to walk on water.

In choppy waters, pick your moment to move and concentrate on where you're going.

During the 1995 Louis Vuitton Cup Trials, *OneAustralia* skipper John Bertrand ran forward to push the boom out. Distracted at a critical moment, he fell into the water. Fortunately for historians, Mr. Bertrand's error was captured on video; the footage documents the only case on record of an America's Cup skipper going overboard without being pushed!

When working on deck, keep your knees bent so you're prepared to spring into battle: sailors look good when they're poised for action.

and gather sails; clear and coil lines; tend to cunningham and outhaul adjustments during tacks; take care of halyard tension; prepare sheets for any staysails; and pack the spinnaker. The mastman also has to stay aware of the boat's maneuvers and pass along information from the cockpit to the bow.

There are many areas where the roles of bowman and mastman converge, and cooperation should prevail. Just imagine the usual hassles associated with raising a big, heavy spinnaker pole just before a bearaway set, where you approach the windward mark, fall off, and set your spinnaker on the same tack you were on for your approach to the mark. The topping lift has been attached, and the mastman is standing by and ready to hoist. The bowman has attached the guy in the jaws of the pole. Everything is set. The bowman steps aft, the mastman hoists, and the outboard end of the pole gets snagged on a stem-head fitting or comes up inside the bow pulpit. An extra minute taken to work together might have prevented this annoyance. These types of aggravations can multiply—and they can rob a boat of speed.

There are other good examples of the mast-bow partnership, such as the importance of communicating before a spinnaker set. The foredeck team should consult with the afterguard about the specific sail to be used and the type of set that's desired. These partners should also talk about how the set will be done, which halyards will be used, which winches, etc. During setup, the mastman and the bowman should watch each other closely and anticipate each other's moves. For example, if the bowman

Race Day Routine

The following race day routine will help crew members understand their positions and their duties for racing.

Pre-Race

Review list of starting schedule
List goals (your mission statement)
Race with correct number of crew (as specified by your rating)
List pre-race jobs: sails, gear, navigation, and weather
Stick to schedule (this builds morale and enhances the skipper's integrity)

After Leaving Dock

Crew meeting after leaving dock
Review goals
Wear uniform (I consider uniforms an important way to build teamwork and professionalism in sailing)
Reassign specific jobs (anyone who has comments should make them now)
Review safety procedures
Review battle station/regular routine positions
Practice hard for 30 minutes both upwind and downwind
10-minute rest/stretch/final comments

While Racing

Stick to game plan
Stay low—to avoid blocking the view for the rest of the crew
Only one person should speak at a time
Don't get too excited when ahead or behind
Use four-on, four-off watch (for overnight races)
Navigate by piloting—not just GPS
Rotate helmsman on distance races
Keep updating: weather, performance of competition, and your standings
Don't go for gold when behind
Remember winning is playing averages (consistency)
No yelling

Post-Race

Skipper, crew, and coach's comments
Put boat away
Written assessment
Fix broken equipment
Remind crew that post-race behavior counts

---

has gone forward to attach the foreguy, the mastman should make sure he's got plenty of slack. After the spinnaker has been hoisted, the mastman cleats the spinnaker halyard, uncleats the headsail halyard, and goes directly to the foredeck to gather the headsail after it's released by the trimmer.

Once the spinnaker is flying, the bowman and mastman should get ready for the next maneuver. For example, the mastman cleans up around the spar and then prepares sheets for setting a staysail.

Jibes also demand precise coordination between bowman and mastman. The success of the entire procedure rests on the mastman's ability to trip the outboard end of the pole and simultaneously ease the topping lift, thus allowing the bowman to attach the new guy on the opposite jibe. The mastman then rehoists the topping lift—all in one smooth mechanical routine. It takes practice and concentration to get it right. But as a result, the mastman and bowman often become better partners.

The bowman also has to pass information to the back of the boat, and the best way for him to do this is by using hand signals. Before the start of every race, the

Individual Crew Assignments

The individual crew assignments listed below will help every crew member understand his or her responsibilities on board.

One Hour Before Leaving Dock (All Crew On Board)

TACTICAL TEAM (AFTERGUARD)
Stow all personal gear
Review weather
Study starting area and racecourse
Read Sailing Instructions
Watch bill
Post "all hands" station list
Sail inventory cards distributed
Check for amendments to Sailing Instructions
Check all instruments
Power up navigation equipment
Check radios (and batteries)
Review charts
Review meal schedule

SAIL TRIMMERS (MAIN, JIB, SPINNAKER, AND STAYSAILS)
Check sail inventory and stowage
Select sails for start of race
Bend mainsail on boom with battens
Check leads, sheets, and guys
Check and service winches and blocks
Spray tracks
Stow all personal gear
Inspect all sails for telltales and tears
Check masthead fly: see if the angles are correct
Lead mainsail reefing lines

GRINDER
Check and service winches
Check hydraulics to make sure they are working properly. (Hydraulics are often used to adjust the boom vang, the backstay, and sometimes the outhaul.)
Help stow sails
Help bend mainsail on boom
Check bilges
Stow all personal gear

MASTMAN
Help stow sails
Service mast winches
Inspect halyards
Inspect mast, sheaves, and spreaders
Help bend mainsail on boom
Pack spinnakers
Place telltales on shrouds
Stow all personal gear

BOWMAN
Check all halyards
Check spinnaker pole—put on mast with topping lift
Pack spinnakers (recruit help)
Check all sheet and guy leads
Review sail inventory stowage
Assist stowage of sails
Check boat's tools
Check feeder and headstay, spray groove
Stow all personal gear

Below Deck

NAVIGATOR AND/OR MASTMAN
Close and lock all hatches except main and forward hatches
Check fuel, lube, belts, etc., on main engine and generator
Check all batteries
Review availability of food, beverages, and ice
All sails:

❖ In proper bag
❖ Spinnakers in turtles or put in stops—three ends together and labeled
❖ Stowage plan made and posted
❖ Sheets placed on genoa staysail and spinnaker staysail

Check all bilges and bilge pumps
Remove cruising anchor and chain, plus all other cruising gear
Specify place for crew's gear (to be kept at a minimum) including foul-weather gear

After Leaving Dock

SKIPPER HOLDS CREW MEETING
All jobs assigned
Watch routine reviewed if going on long-distance race
All safety requirements, equipment location, and procedures reviewed
"All hands" position reviewed
Strength of competition, the racecourse, weather, and strategy explained to crew—allow time for comments
Review sail inventory
Give reason for performing well in this race
End meeting on positive note
Check in with race committee before start
Record continuous wind readings, direction, and velocity

SAIL TRIMMERS
Sails selected and set
Check jib leads and halyard settings
Check mainsail setting and mast bend
Confirm correct sail for start and always have next sail ready to set

GRINDER
Help set sails
Work with sail trimmers, grinding winches

MASTMAN
Hoist sails
Check mast bend
Stow old sails
Check for lines overboard

BOWMAN
Prepare for next sail change
Keep bow lookout
Coordinate time to start with afterguard

Before Start
Continue with wind readings
Tune up on both tacks and note compass courses
Short speed test with competitor
Make four racing tacks
Tune up on both jibes and note courses
Check for favored end of the line
Check for favored side of course

Sailing to Windward

AFTERGUARD
Helmsman steers and concentrates on speed
Navigator/tactician:
❖ Plot progress on course
❖ Record wind speed, wind direction, course steered, and weather information in log book
❖ Compute apparent wind angle, wind speed, and the course to the next mark
❖ Continuously observe the performance of your competitors using a hand-bearing compass
❖ Play mainsail traveler

SAIL TRIMMERS
Trim sails
Check halyard settings
Check lead positions
Talk continuously with helmsman
Talk with tactician/navigator
Think about next sail
Shift weight in puffs

GRINDER
Trim sails, grind winches
Shift weight with puffs
Stay in tune with trimmer/afterguard discussion

MASTMAN
Back up grinder
Set up halyards for set
Prepare for next sail change
Shift crew weight to windward
Monitor mast bend
Adjust halyards
Haul new sails on deck

After Sailing

TACTICAL TEAM (AFTERGUARD)
Review race
Check on finishing times and results
Check in with race committee
Review broken equipment and assign people to fix

Clean up cockpit area
Shut down electronics
Remove personal gear
Check to see if your boat is involved in a
    protest. If so,
    ❖ Fill out forms
    ❖ Line up witnesses
    ❖ Draw a diagram
    ❖ And most importantly, stay calm

SAIL TRIMMERS
Flake, coil, and stow all sheets, guys,
    blocks, and winch handles
Repair torn sails
Dry out wet sails
Clean up tailing areas
Remove personal gear

GRINDERS
Fold and stow sails
Check and dry bilges
Assist repair of broken equipment
Check and service winches
Remove personal gear

MASTMAN
Help fold and stow sails
Check spar rigging, spreader, sheaves, and
    halyards
Remove personal gear

BOWMAN
Stow all halyards forward
Clean up bow area
Help fold and stow sails
Remove personal gear

bowman and tactician should confirm their signals. The most common technique is to display a thumbs-up when there is no overlap with another boat, and a thumbs-down when two boats are overlapped. A circle motion might signal acceleration. Putting the palm down and raising and lowering the hand would indicate the need to slow down. As for other competitors, the best bowmen ignore them: they see without appearing to look, focusing on their tasks and moving with the quick, sure-footed agility of a ballet dancer. A little aloofness is in order.

On Posture, Clothing, Attitude— and Looking Good

I'm fascinated by the way sailors contort their bodies during a race. For a long time, I wondered if twisting your body out of shape helped or hurt performance. But recently I decided that good posture, attitude, and clothing not only offer greater comfort on the water: they can also increase efficiency and improve speed. Whether I'm right or not, you can have fun with this notion by analyzing what your competitors look like on the racecourse.

When planning your next tactical move, take a quick look at the afterguard of a neighboring boat. Do crew members demonstrate confidence, anger, or frustration? Their body language is your best clue. For example, if the tactician starts repeatedly cleaning his sunglasses, he's hoping for a big shift. When the tactician starts repeating tasks or pacing, he's nervous. When the tactician raises his voice, look for changes. This is a sign that things aren't going well. (If you're nearby, you may not be in such great shape either!)

Hands on the hips are an indication of crew frustration. Body posture is very telling.

When the tactician folds his arms across his chest, things are usually going well. This posture shows confidence. When the arms are on the chest, the tactician is typically looking back at the fleet. But if you see those hands slide down to the hips, there's concern and tension (and it might be time to reevaluate your own strategy). Tacticians are almost always looking forward, at their competitors, when their hands are on their hips.

Hands on the back of the head signal frustration. This is often accompanied by a big sigh. Simultaneously, you may see the rail riders grumbling. If things get worse, the noise dies away entirely—and anyone who speaks can feel as if they are yelling in church. Then again, if you're so close that you can tell no one is talking on board, then you're probably on the wrong side of the course too. Perhaps it's time to throw in a tack.

When you see a full crew standing up, look out! It's a sign of unrest and the sign of a crew populated entirely by chiefs (not to mention the fact that the helmsman has very little visibility). One of the reasons the legendary, undefeated America's Cup helmsman Charlie Barr was successful may have been that he never let his crew stand or speak. (I was on a boat where the tactician was shouting nonstop. It cracked me up when he screamed for everyone to shut up when he was the only one yelling.)

Watch out for sailors who stand in the stern, holding the backstay. It could be they're worried that the mast will fall down if they let go! In fact, this posture usually indicates someone who has no function at all.

I chuckle at the way some helmsmen

tilt their head. By the end of a race they must surely have a sore neck. On a serious note, great helmsmen have a way of leaning forward to "will" the boat to sail faster.

Top helmsmen keep two hands on the wheel at all times. You can balance the pressure of the wheel better with two hands. Steering with one hand can lead to oversteering—and a one-handed helmsman displays laziness. Keep a firm but light touch on the helm. If you are using a tiller or hiking stick, one hand works—particularly if you use your arm as an extension of the hiking stick. Keep your hiking stick at right angles to the tiller.

When you see a helmsman's knuckles turning white from squeezing the wheel too hard, it's a sign. It's time to rotate drivers.

When you're sitting on the rail, remember that your movements are a sign to your competitors. A well-disciplined crew avoids telegraphing upcoming maneuvers to the other boats on the course. When the command to tack is given, sit still until the boat is actually turning. This is the moment to cross the boat.

CLOTHING

Cold, wet sailors tire easily and lose their spirit, so make sure you wear proper clothing. Hats, sunglasses, foul-weather gear, and deck shoes (with socks) improve your performance. I once raced the 600-mile Fastnet (from southern England to Ireland and back) without socks. It rained the entire race, and it took a month for my feet to dry out and warm up. When your feet are warm and secure, you're more effective.

If you see a hat flying overboard, you know that trouble's brewing. Hats only blow off during tense moments: just ask a sailing photographer. Each Mount Gay hat in her collection was usually found just downwind of a leeward mark.

The coolest sailor on the boat is the bowman. He or she always wears the most gear, for the same reason that the cockpit crew are always the last to suit up. At the pointy end, spray tops, foul-weather gear, boots, and harnesses are standard-issue. But staying warm is only part of the point: it's a known fact that the bowman must look good or the whole boat will suffer!

Finally, a crew uniform also helps build team morale and cohesiveness. If your team has a uniform, wear it.

The View from the Rail

Professional racers are always busy, and they never seem to stop trimming, steering, or tweaking. But most sailors spend a high percentage of their time just sitting on the side, or rail, of the boat. Rail sitting can be a magical, Zen-like experience, but it can also be comparable to sitting in an old theater. The seat is not comfortable, and you must wear the right clothes, keep the noise down, and stay awake. When you're on the rail, you never know when spiritual bliss will be shattered by the call to change sails, execute a maneuver, or fix a ripped sail. It is a difficult balance between staying alert and being mesmerized by your surroundings. And the entertainment is often great.

Don't forget that if you're racing, you are always participating. Sitting on the rail requires proper posture; always lean far outboard to give the boat extra stability and righting moment. While you're hiking hard

This crew aboard Chessie Racing *leans forward to maximize stability on the windward leg.*

on small boats or leaning out on bigger boats, you should also be calling puffs, watching for changes in the weather, and studying the performance of the competition.

Your first priority should be comfort, for you might be sitting for a while. I don't like boats with toerails that stick up off the deck. Designers and builders should be sure that deck and hull shapes accommodate rail riders. Protective gear with a padded seat makes a big difference. Along with sunglasses, hat, sunscreen, and reliable foul-weather gear, this type of gear is part of dressing properly.

When you're on the rail, listen to the discussion in the cockpit so you can anticipate the next maneuver. Know which path to take when you cross the deck and develop a protocol of who sits where. If you want to be an instant hero, take the forward spot—particularly when the spray is flying.

The best rail riding is from a trapeze where your head floats above the water. It is quiet out over the water and exhilarating.

Heavier crew members should sit in the middle; older, less agile crew should move aft. If you are expected to block the spray, don't duck; the afterguard gets moody if a little spray touches their boots. If the spray reaches your helmsman's sunglasses, you are really in trouble! The forward-most rail rider is like a secret service agent: he must be ready to throw his body to protect his leader from spray.

Riding the rail can become monotonous, so use your imagination to pass the time. I recall doing this on an uncomfortable ocean race from Miami to Jamaica. As the first signs of twilight appeared on the horizon, ex-NFL player Larry Mialik started comparing the shapes of the clouds to animals. The ploy helped pass the time on a long, rough ride.

I love watching water go by. If you have to sit to leeward on a light-air day, the leeward rail is a great spot. Everything seems faster and more exciting down there. I especially like to study approaching waves. How will the boat respond? Will the helmsman and trimmers keep the boat from slamming and pounding into the waves? If you are on the rail sailing downwind in big seas, be ready to pull your feet in. Many boots have been washed away while surfing.

The hours on the rail are a great time for philosophical discussion. But keep your voice down (use the tone of a golf announcer). And naturally, it's taboo to yell at another boat.

The best rail riding is on a trapeze, like those used on 420s, 470s, and some catamarans. Your head floats above the water, and you feel like you're flying. The worst rail riding is on boats where your feet are tucked under a hiking strap on the boat's bottom and you sit in a droop hike position. The energy used to burst out of this position for a tack is the equivalent of Michael Jordan starting his dunk at the head of the key. Once a bulky crew settles in, you need a good reason to tack.

After watching round-the-world sailors stack gear and sails on the windward rail, fill water ballast tanks, and even sleep on the rail, I wonder if they would be better off hooking up some trapezes. Maybe in the future these offshore boats will be fitted with racks like those fitted to smaller boats (like the one shown opposite). Imagine ocean racing on a trapeze with your feet several feet from the hull. It would be a strenuous ride—but definitely a fast one.

Savor your time on the rail.

CHAPTER 3

The Art of Calling Tactics

Serving as the tactician is not for the faint of heart. The pressure is always on, and the person in this position must be a quick learner, aware of every detail as the eyes and ears of the boat, a strong leader, and the crew's spiritual motivator. Calling tactics is an art and a challenge. But when the tactician sets the pace and makes the right calls, the end result is nothing short of heroic: a boat will perform better and the racing will be more fun for everyone.

Establishing the Tactician's Role

The first step is to establish with the owner/skipper and the crew that the tactician's job actually exists. If you are not the tactician, that person should be appointed by the skipper and crew. Confidence in the tactician will build with time. The tactician should work toward being a steady, upbeat influence on the boat and should only speak when he has something to say.

As mentioned earlier, the great America's Cup skipper Charlie Barr (*Columbia*, 1899, 1901; *Reliance*, 1903) had a good routine. He would use one person to issue all commands. Barr never raised his voice. He worked hard to develop a good relationship with the owner, but he was a strict disciplinarian during the race. He demanded perfection. As a skipper in an authoritarian age, he could get away with it. Captain Barr understood that crew discipline and quiet went hand in hand. A tactician's job takes finesse and careful thought. Barr's example is a good one: once a plan is established, let the helmsman and crew execute their jobs in silence.

Three-time America's Cup winning skipper Charlie Barr (right) was a master *at organization and tactical cunning. He passed all his commands through his tactician.* (Edwin Levick)

In 1970, former Star World Champion and Congressional Cup winner Bill Ficker commanded *Intrepid* with an iron hand. Ficker used the talented Steve Van Dyck as his tactician. The Ficker–Van Dyck combination was clever. *Intrepid* was often slower than her Australian rival *Gretel II.* But Ficker and Van Dyck used fine-tuned tactics to win four out of five races. The 1970 America's Cup film featured a revealing segment of Ficker and Van Dyck working together. Both used the same hand motions during a maneuver, which were easily visible to the crew looking from the hatches below. The two sailors were clearly on the same wavelength. I like the quiet efficiency of Ficker and Van Dyck. Watching them in that film

helped me understand the value of a tactician.

In 1974, Ted Turner recruited California ace Dennis Conner to assist him on *Mariner. Mariner* was eliminated early, but Conner was later invited aboard *Courageous* that summer to serve as tactician for Ted Hood. By the time I raced in 1977, the role of the tactician had been firmly established. Turner taught me that the best time to give him advice was when he asked for it. Some helmsmen like to be told what to do all the time; others prefer knowing the available options. The final decision rests with the skipper—whether he is steering or not. But in tight situations, there is no time to run through all options. In times like these, the tactician must make the call.

Brad Butterworth, the winning tactician in the 1995, 2000, and 2003 America's Cup races, demonstrated the value of the tactician's role to millions of viewers around the world. Butterworth wore a microphone during the races, and we got to hear his continuing chatter during the televised races. In contrast, skipper and helmsman Russell Coutts was quiet and spoke in one-word sentences. The two have been racing together for many years in match races and fleet races throughout the world. There were few wasted words.

Still, there were times when Butterworth was dramatic in his calls. Just prior to finishing the second race of the 2003 America's Cup with *Team New Zealand* half a length behind, Coutts decided to luff his archrival. Butterworth uncharacteristically started yelling, "Don't come up! Don't come up! Come down, Russell!"

Coutts was surprised to hear his trusted

Three-time winning America's Cup helmsman Russell Coutts and tactician Brad Butterworth (left) speak in clipped sentences. Through years of working together they have become a tough team to defeat on the water.

tactician's voice rise. Coutts dutifully bore off, headed for the finish line, and preserved the win. Butterworth understood that a variation in his normal monotone could make the difference at crucial times.

Expanding the Tactician's Duties

On a larger scale, a tactician does far more than choose the boat's route during a race. The tactician makes the final sail selection, calls for crew rotation when necessary, and must understand the sailing characteristics of the boat. Practice makes the difference. The tactician should spend time steering to

learn a boat's sailing characteristics. The routine on many boats today is to have the tactician steer at the start and then pass the helm to the skipper for the duration of the race. Many tacticians are dinghy champions and they react quickly to situations. During a start there is little time to explain things to the helmsman; in some cases, opportunities only last a split second. But once a race starts, the small-boat ace might be more valuable looking around to call tactics while the helmsman concentrates on speed.

When practicing, focus on one thing at a time. Make a list and work hard on each item in a set of drills (see specific guidelines for practice sessions in chapter 11). Think back to any experience you had with team sports in school. Coaches begin with the fundamentals, and repetition through drills and scrimmages is the best way to improve. The key component is an individual's desire to excel. A coach can plant the seed, but the player must make that seed grow. This system works in sailing too.

A tactician should set the tempo during maneuvers and gauge his boat's performance against the competition. Understanding the capabilities of the crew is as important as understanding the boat. If a crew is inexperienced, for example, avoid holding the spinnaker until the last second when the bow reaches the leeward turning mark. If your boat doesn't point high, don't pinch and sail too close to the wind. If you are bearing off, remind the trimmers to ease the sails. Don't assume everything will happen as it should.

An important job of the tactician is keeping the helmsman focused. There should be no storytelling, eating, changing jackets, or even looking around while the helmsman is at the wheel. If any changes need to be made, the tactician should control the steering rotation. Helmsmen sail fastest when they have two hands on the

A well-organized crew sits in place and concentrates on his assigned duties. Skipper Ted Turner of Courageous *made sure that every member of the team had a reason to excel.*

wheel, have an unobstructed view, and when they don't talk unnecessarily. Challenge the helmsman to sail faster: urge him to just "will" the boat to sail half a tenth of a knot faster. This technique works.

One helmsman I guided for many years was new at the sport when we met, and he steered mechanically. Even though my hands were not on the wheel, I gave guidance based on my own instinct and the target speeds indicated by the instruments. In time the helmsman improved and was able to spend less time being coached. This helmsman started to understand how the boat responded in different wind strengths. Every coach tries to get his player—in this case, the helmsman—to understand the fundamentals. Eventually they get it.

Some tacticians panic when their boat is behind. A common solution is to take a flyer, or take a long tack away from the competition in the hopes of finding an advantage, such as a windshift or a favorable current. But as we mentioned before, going for the long pass (as in football) is a bad policy. In sailing, taking a flyer rarely makes up for big losses in one move: the odds are too great. It's better to make small adjustments and test your progress. You will quickly learn what works.

If you are the person calling tactics, you make the call. If several options are available, go with your first instinct. Once you've put some time in as a tactician, your past experience should be a helpful guide.

Fine-Tune Your Tactical Technique

With experience, you'll learn to fine-tune your technique as a tactician. Here are some general guidelines on key areas to think about.

A tactician uses many tools (the next section on tools and references has more specifics on how to use onboard tools). The hand-bearing compass is my favorite. By taking bearings on other boats I can tell if our boat is gaining or losing on the competition. Tacking lines drawn on deck are excellent references for judging the layline, the direct course to the mark. On larger boats a laser range finder sharpens distance-

---

Handling an Abundance of Tactical Advice

During one major championship aboard the Maxi *Matador*, we had two navigators on board. They had extremely different approaches. For local knowledge in this Virgin Islands regatta, we had the services of the great cruising author Donald Street. Street knew the waters well and he had made a successful career out of "sailing by the seat of his pants." The second navigator was MIT professor Dr. Jerry Milgram, who predictably took the scientific approach toward racing. As tactician, I struggled to decipher the immense amount of information being passed my way by Street and Milgram. But I came up with a solution that worked.

To avoid confusion, I decided it was best to only get information when I asked for it. Throughout the series I gave each navigator problems to solve. Over the years, I've learned that it's okay for people to give you information. Just remember that you can either use or disregard it.

apart accuracy. I like to sail with a pair of gyro binoculars. These binoculars keep the horizon steady and make it easier to find turning marks and read the wind.

When I call tactics, I like to occasionally take the wheel to get a feel for how the boat is performing. In very light wind, steering helps me figure out where the new wind will build from. I can feel a trend developing at the wheel. Off the wheel, I struggle. Rotating the helm also gives the helmsman an opportunity to look around and appreciate tactical puzzles.

Many match-racing sailors serve as tacticians. But I have noticed that many of these sailors often lock up with one other boat and shift into match-race mode during a fleet race. Match racing another boat in a fleet race is a sure loser. Always sail your own race. Avoid tacking (or jibing) on other boats early in a regatta, for those moves will come back to haunt you. Have you ever raced against an annoying boat that always seems to be tacking on a competitor without reason? In the end, that boat rarely wins.

A tactician's most valuable assets are intuition and common sense. During a Maxi World Championship in St. Thomas, a major squall blew across the course and racing was postponed. I had our crew lower the mainsail and ride out the storm in a nearby cove. Our closest competitor kept sailing. They weathered the squall by reaching back and forth with their mainsail hoisted, and they caused considerable wear on their sails and rig. When the weather cleared, we went back to racing. Two hours later, I noticed that our competitor's masthead crane had snapped off. Being conservative during the storm paid off for our team.

A fluid relationship between tactician and helmsman is key. The sailors in these two positions should talk about tactical situations before sailing, so both parties have a clear idea of the philosophy on board. Ted Turner and I spent many hours talking through every tactical situation we could think of. The types of scenarios to talk about might be how soon to tack after a leeward-mark rounding, when to split from the fleet, when to call for the spinnaker drop, and at what point a jibe set becomes better than a bear-away set. After each race, review your key tactical decisions to gauge how they worked. This discipline will prepare you for your next race.

As the tactician, you'll have different duties and responsibilities during each phase of the race. Break each race down into segments to come up with your own list. For example, during the pre-start you should instruct the crew to back down to clear seaweed off your keel (or centerboard) and rudder, study wind conditions and the race-course to select the favored side of the course, work with the trimmers to select the right sail for the anticipated wind, and finally set the pace on board by making sure your crew understands that you are now in "race mode."

When you return to the dock at the end of a race, you still have work to do. Post-race hours are not a time for relaxing. Check the official scoreboard; race committees don't always get things right. Make note of any modifications to the race instructions if there is a second day of racing. If you are involved in a protest, you, as the tactician, will typically represent your boat at a protest hearing. Every tactician needs a sound knowledge of the racing rules.

The sidebars on the Race Day Routine and Individual Crew Assignments, included earlier in this book (see pages 15–18), will help you review all the tasks that are part of a tactician's typical day on the water.

Onboard Tools and References

Every tactician has an arsenal of onboard tools and references that are used to gather information about the race and the racing area and to give the tactician reference points he may need to make the right decisions on the water. Those tools may be as simple as a chart and a notebook. Here are a few of my favorites:

❖ The hand-bearing compass is a clever tool. It helps tacticians gauge their progress against the competition, determine the bearing to the next mark, and judge whether one boat will cross ahead of another. When I'm calling tactics I keep one on a lanyard around my neck.

❖ Tacking lines are drawn on deck to help you plot a course on the opposite tack. Or, in a close race, tacking lines can help you determine whether your boat is leading or trailing another vessel.

❖ In addition to keeping notes on bearings, I like to keep a running log of the strength and direction of the wind. It's important to see how the patterns change over the course of a day.

I chuckle at large racing boats with onboard computers that factor the exact distance to every mark or have an instant handicap analysis plugged into the GPS. It's a full-time job just monitoring all this information! Sailboat races are won by making the right calls using good old intuition and gut feeling. The most important asset of a tactician is the trust of the skipper and the crew. The key is having a good winning percentage: once you have the confidence of everyone on the boat, your calls will be honored—even if they occasionally don't pan out well.

Complex electronics don't determine your success as a tactician, but there are essential tools and references you will need to have on board. Using these references and understanding all the information about a race is essential:

❖ Notice of Race

❖ Sailing Instructions (with amendments)

❖ Chart of the racecourse area

❖ Weather forecast

❖ Tide and current tables

❖ Handicap rating sheet

❖ Standings (should be updated after every race)

❖ Hand-bearing compass

❖ Notepaper and pencil

❖ Polar diagram/speed prediction table (These are produced from a velocity prediction program, or VPP; designers and sailmakers often have this information. Polar diagrams plot a specific target

Maxi yacht Sayonara *sailing along the coast of southern England on the way to Fastnet Rock.*

speed a boat can sail in different wind speeds and directions. The polar diagram is a good reference to work with. There are times where you can exceed this theoretical number; at other times, you can't reach that speed—but it is a good reference.)

I learned how critical some of these on-board references are at a young age. My earliest memory of racing is when I was seven years old. I was crew aboard a 15-foot sneakbox, and I had three jobs on the boat: to be quiet, to bail water out, and to keep the racecourse chart. We had taken the lead at the windward mark of the first

race in the forty-boat fleet. I had been quiet the entire windward leg and the boat was bone dry. It was a great moment. Then the skipper asked what the next mark of the course was. I reached into my pocket for the racecourse chart, but it was gone. We sailed to the wrong mark and lost the race. I never sailed with that skipper again, but the experience was a good lesson to have the right references on board so you always know where you are heading. I never made that mistake again.

Reading the Sailing Instructions carefully makes a big difference. But even that can be confusing. At the start of the 1999 Fastnet race, aboard the Maxi yacht *Sayonara,* our afterguard became confused. The fleet ahead of us was postponed. The race committee referred to the amendments to the race's Sailing Instructions. Naturally, we didn't have a copy of the amendments on board and no one was sure whether we started next or whether the smaller boats started next. We watched our competitors and simply started the race when they did. Of course, we never let on about our confusion. We finally got a start off but there was a lot of angst in the cockpit. It was clear our crew should have spent more time studying the amendments to the Sailing Instructions.

In another race in Italy, I was racing on board the Maxi yacht *Matador.* We were trailing behind *Kialoa* when we suddenly came across a buoy in the middle of the racecourse. *Kialoa* had already passed this mark to port. We knew from the Sailing Instructions that the mark was irrelevant to the race, but we decided to pass it to starboard. Through the binoculars we could see the crew of *Kialoa* looking back at us intently. There must have been a lot of discussion aboard, because they suddenly tacked around and headed back to the buoy and rounded it the same way we did, to starboard. Clearly, *Kialoa* either didn't have the proper race instructions aboard, or they hadn't read them carefully enough to understand that this particular buoy was not a mark of the racecourse. *Kialoa*'s moment of confusion gave us the lead. It was a humorous incident (as the two boats passed each other when *Kialoa* returned to the mark, no one acknowledged each other's existence). But it was a perfect reminder of the importance of racecourse references.

Don't forget the importance of taking notes. I like to have a waterproof paper booklet (like a product called WetNotes) with me on deck. You can also keep a piece of tape on deck to use with a grease pencil. This works well on fiberglass.

Taking notes of key information helped U.S. Olympic sailors JJ Isler and Pease Glaser capture a silver medal at the 2000 Games. Before the final race in Sydney, USA 470 women's class contenders Isler and Glaser were in a position to finish anywhere from second to eighth place. As a journalist covering the Olympic regatta for NBC, I was allowed access to the boat village. I noticed that Pease Glaser had written on the deck of their boat all the combinations of the boats they needed to beat to win the regatta. The American team got off to a bad start and rounded the first mark well back in the fleet. Methodically, Isler and Glaser worked their way toward the front of the fleet. They paid particular attention to the boats they needed to beat to

win a medal. At the end of the day, they ended up with an Olympic silver medal. Isler and Glaser credited the combinations written on the deck as the reason they were able to keep track of what they needed to do during this complicated race.

The Tactician's Tools

As mentioned above, a hand-bearing compass is an important tool. These compasses are better known as *hockey pucks* because they are round and have a rubber protective coating around them. In recent years, electronic compasses and laser range finders have been useful tools for tacticians on big boats. But the good old hockey puck is a reliable friend, and there are several ways to use it.

DETERMINING GAINS OR LOSS RELATIVE TO ANOTHER BOAT

By using a hand-bearing compass, you can chart the different speeds of two boats sailing the same course. Take a bearing of another boat and jot down the number. Wait one minute before taking a second bearing. The difference in numbers will tell you who is going faster. This exercise can tell you whether your boat is gaining on the competition or losing ground.

A hand-bearing compass can also be used to determine whether your boat will cross ahead or behind another boat. For example, if your boat is converging with another boat on the opposite tack, you can determine if you are on a collision course by using a hand-bearing compass. If you track the other boat with your hand-bearing compass and you seem to be holding a bearing on the other boat, you will likely have a

Gary Jobson uses a hand-bearing compass to assess performance against the competition aboard the 12-meter Courageous. *Ted Turner is at the helm listening to Jobson's report.*

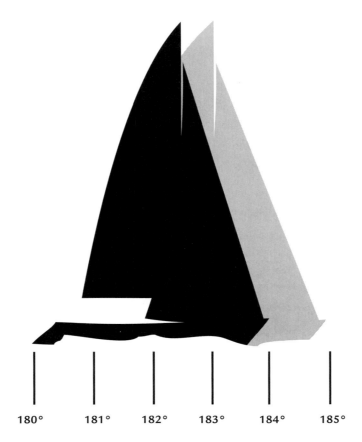

Use a hand-bearing compass to determine if a boat is getting closer. For example, if a boat bears 4 degrees from bow to stern (180° to 184° from bow to stern as shown), it is getting closer if it soon bears 5 degrees (180° to 185°).

collision. If you are on port tack—and you therefore don't have the right-of-way according to the racing rules—you will need to give way to the other boat.

CLOSING OR SEPARATING

A hand-bearing compass can be used to determine whether you are getting closer to or farther away from another boat sailing on the same course. For example, as you sail parallel to the other boat, take your hand-bearing compass and sight the compass bearing to the other boat's bow; then take the bearing to the other boat's stern. Now, factor the difference between those two values. If the bearing to the bow is 184 degrees and the bearing to the stern is 180 degrees, the difference is 4 degrees. Take the same two bearings again in a few minutes. If the bow now bears 185 degrees and the stern bears 180 degrees, the difference has increased to 5 degrees and the boat is getting closer.

Many boats, including dinghies, have

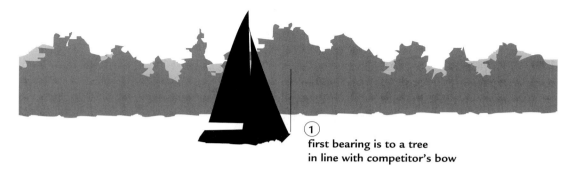

① first bearing is to a tree
in line with competitor's bow

② second bearing reveals that you are gaining distance
(making trees) on your competitor

From your boat, take a visual bearing across the bow of your competitor to the shore beyond (1). If you are gaining distance relative to the trees (or houses and other stationary objects) you are "making trees" (2).

compasses built into their cockpits. These onboard compasses are a good backup to a hand-bearing compass. By taking a bearing of another boat and then looking again a minute or two later, you can determine whether you are gaining or losing. Even if you do not use a hand-bearing compass, you can tell how you are performing against another boat by taking visual bearings on objects in the background. Your bearing can be taken to a point on land, an anchored buoy, or another boat. If you seem to be gaining ground, your boat is sailing faster. This is known as "making trees."

Another method is to stretch out your arm, sticking out your pinkie and thumb and measuring the distance from the water to the top of the mast of the other boat. This is a good way to determine if that boat is getting closer or separating. I do a better job of judging the performance of my boat if I stay in one place to make my observations.

TACKING LINES
Tacking lines are drawn on deck in the area where the tactician works. These are a valuable reference for determining whether other boats are ahead or behind. I recommend drawing them in ten-degree increments. They should be permanently drawn

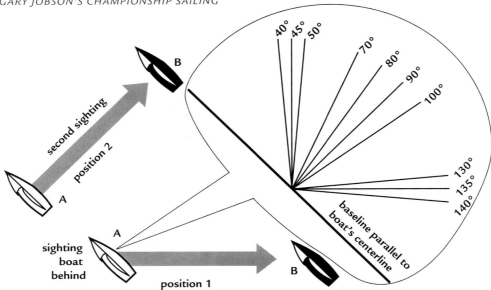

Tacking lines—stationary degree lines marked at various places around the boat (usually near the cockpit)—allow you to determine whether you are gaining or losing on another boat. At position 1, Boat A sights over to Boat B and notes that B is 130° off A's starboard quarter. Two minutes later, at position 2, Boat A takes a second sighting and notes B is now 90° off A's starboard beam. Boat B is gaining on A. Tacking lines can also be used to see if you're in line with stationary objects like rounding marks.

using a protractor. Make the lines long for more accurate sightings. Tacking lines can also be used to determine if you are crossing a boat on an opposite tack or jibe or whether you are on the layline, the direct course to the mark.

The Tactician and Leadership

The key ingredient for winning a race, making a successful passage, or even having an enjoyable day on the water is leadership. A race on board the Maxi yacht *Condor* with Ted Turner drove that point home for me.

Condor began the China Sea Race with a great start. But only a mile later our archrival sailed over us on a close reach and left us in his wake. It was a crushing moment. The crew turned testy, and an argument broke out between two Kiwis at the mast. With 630 miles to go, it seemed like it was going to be a long ride.

Skipper Ted Turner took command. He brought the entire crew back to the cockpit and declared that he guaranteed our boat would pass the competition if the crew performed as he demanded. Turner's message was inspirational; but I thought to myself, "He'll be like Houdini if he pulls this one off." Forty-eight hours later we found ourselves one nautical mile abeam, to windward and ahead, of our opposition as the morning mist cleared. Turner was a hero.

Taking command is a big responsibility—and often a lonely one. Many people would rather not be in charge. For others, leadership is the essence of life and, for these types of sailors, the most rewarding leadership opportunity is on board a boat.

After the fact, a leader can be a hero or a goat. Unfortunately, there is rarely anything in between. Thanks to the experience of racing with many champion skippers over the years, and also having had the command myself from time to time, I've learned many valuable lessons in the art of leadership. Here are some tips on the elements of good leadership:

❖ Once in charge—be in charge.

❖ The fewer words spoken the better.

❖ Consistency and confidence are essential, but avoid arrogance.

❖ Plan in advance. Once a plan is decided, execute it with precision. Let everyone on board know your plan; mistakes are avoided with early preparation.

❖ Hold a crew meeting after leaving the dock. Gather everyone on deck so they can easily see and hear the leader. Prompt attendance is mandatory. Topics should include safety routine, job assignments, a stated purpose for the day, the anticipated weather, the course to be sailed, and any potential surprises that may occur. Discussing situations in advance prepares the crew mentally. It gives the crew confidence that the leader is on the correct course and knows how to handle troublesome situations.

❖ During bad times always remain calm. If the leader is under control, the rest of the crew will follow the example being set.

❖ Although there is strength in collective wisdom, ruling by committee rarely works. Yacht races and naval battles are won by leaders, not committees.

❖ Clear communications make a crew run smoothly.

❖ During the crew meeting publicly state every crew member's job during "all hands." Take the guesswork out of the equation. If events become tense, go back to your normal routine; the crew will feel more comfortable.

❖ Be sure the correct people are resting at the optimum time. Keep a steady pace going and avoid burnout. For example, you cannot have an "all-hands" situation every single hour for two days running. It simply will not work.

When making a decision, a leader should always go with his first instinct. Second-guessing a decision can cause a breakdown in the command structure. Plus, a clear common goal brings a crew together.

Leaders frequently have to balance between selling their ideas and imposing them. Asking for advice ahead of time helps people feel they are part of the decision-making process. But during the heat of battle, there is no time to consult. Take charge. Be authoritative and clear. Hesitation creates uncertainty and undermines confidence.

America's Cup champion Dennis Conner often polls his crew before the start of a race about any ideas people might have on

A Monday-Morning Quarterback

During a regatta in Maine, one crew member constantly questioned the decisions of our afterguard. It was a tough series. The currents in Maine are complex and the wind was shifting dramatically. At times, we looked great; at other times we did not.

After every tack, this crew member on the windward rail sarcastically questioned every call. "Why did we do that?" or, "Well that was a big mistake!" Our afterguard elected to ignore the patter. And as it turned out, we had a good race and finished second. Overnight, I thought about the young man on the rail and what to do about him.

In the next race, the wind filled in well before the start. It was going to be a good day. After our crew meeting (but before the preparatory signal), I invited the young rail rider aft and said, "We have three options. We can sail to the right side of the course, up the middle, or on the left side of the course. Since you seem to have had all the answers yesterday, which side should we sail on? And remember we're in the running for first place for the week—so the decision that you make could make the difference."

The young man stuttered a little bit, sweat started to form on his brow. I just waited. Finally, after a few minutes he admitted, "I'm not really qualified to make this call." At which point I said, "Well, when we do make decisions, it would be helpful if you were supportive as opposed to second-guessing."

We didn't hear a negative word out of him for the remainder of the race.

strategy. But Conner will point out that once the race starts, or after an event has occurred, he doesn't want to hear, "We should have . . . " The time to speak up is prior to the event—and not after the fact. There is no room for a Monday-morning quarterback on board a race boat. But as a tactician, you may have to deal with one; I did (see the accompanying sidebar).

Good leadership is hard. It is learned over time. The best leaders understand all the functions on their boat and the capabilities of their crew. If you declare a common goal and organize the team by giving specific assignments, the crew will naturally want to work together. All naval commanders are taught that you can delegate authority, but you can never delegate responsibility. Understand these principles, and your time on the water will be rewarding.

A final word about building trust amongst your crew. The best way to build trust is to avoid keeping secrets from the crew. And it helps to say nice things about the people you sail with. Word will spread. Everyone responds positively to getting proper acknowledgment for a job well done.

Control the Yelling

When I'm filming a regatta or simply watching one, I find the best viewing place is at the leeward mark. The first boats to round the mark maneuver efficiently and quietly. But the backenders often start yelling as they make their final approach. The scene is both comical and sad. While it's good theater, yelling clearly hurts performance. Why do sailors tend to yell more and more about less and less?

Perhaps yelling is one way a barking

skipper relieves the intense pressure of a long work week. But for the rest of his crew—and for the other boats in the race—yelling is a detriment.

GOOD TYPES OF YELLING

There are times when using a loud, forceful voice can be beneficial. (But make sure you learn to say things in a kind way when you raise your voice.) For example, your crew will hear a loud voice better when it's windy. You can better communicate a dangerous situation to another boat with a loud voice. With a loud voice you can psych up the crew, emphasize urgency, and generate encouragement or enthusiasm.

I was racing off Sint Maarten in the Caribbean aboard the 70-foot *Equation* when I resorted to yelling to get a critical job done quickly. We had rounded the windward mark in fourth place. Just as we set our spinnaker, the wind shifted 50 degrees. The shift made the opposite jibe heavily favored, and the boats ahead didn't notice the big windshift. Uncharacteristically, I screamed my head off to get the crew to execute a quick jibe. The maneuver was completed and we surged into the lead. It was a nice moment, although I regretted yelling afterward. And I said so. We all had a good chuckle about it later.

BAD TYPES OF YELLING

Inappropriate yelling comes in many forms, ranging from a sarcastic comment that deflates crew morale to a boisterous outburst.

During a Maxi race, our tactician screamed at a crew member when the traveler slipped out of his hands and slammed to leeward. As the trimmer worked feverishly to grind the traveler back to windward, the tactician finished his verbal abuse by saying, "If we lose this race by one second, you'll have been the reason!" I later overheard the trimmer tell the owner that he hoped that tactician would not be invited back.

On another boat I sailed on, the crew had fouled a jibe. At the worst moment, the helmsman hollered, "You guys just don't want to win badly enough!"

Screamers are often unaware of how they sound. After a tirade, the crew loses respect. And if the howling starts again, no one will pay attention.

Foul language should never be used. I think too many people are watching the HBO series "The Sopranos" these days and are using the unfortunate language from the show. On a humorous note, I once sailed on a Japanese boat. I asked the crew during a pre-race dinner the worst word you can say on a boat. The answer came back: *bacca*. During the race, I pointed to a winch that had gotten an override and said, "Bacca." The crew recoiled in horror. I later found out that bacca meant foolish. This is the worst thing you can say in Japanese.

STEPS TO CONTROL YOURSELF

Overcoming a habit of yelling is not easy. But there are techniques that can help reverse the problem. The first step is to recognize that there is a problem. I know one sailor who made a tape recording of an abusive helmsman. A few weeks later, he played the tape back on a stereo system at a crew party. Everyone snickered. The helmsman cringed and never yelled again.

On a large boat, when sailors are spread over a long distance, hand signals are a great form of communication. It also helps if the crew at mid-deck relay orders from the cockpit to the bow. This reinforces the message and keeps the noise down.

You can also empower one crew member as the "yelling czar." You can have fun with this. Decide on a penalty for any yellers before the race starts, such as making the offending party wear a "No Yelling" T-shirt. I've sailed on boats where the tactician or an influential crew member used a code word or action to calm a chronic yeller. "Shut up and drive" doesn't work. Try a squeeze on the shoulder along with the comment, "What can I do to help you?" or, "It's time for three deep breaths."

If there are junior sailors on board, it's important to set a good example. Take a young sailor aside after a race and point out the value of quiet. The best crews speak in controlled, one-word sentences. Strive for a businesslike atmosphere sprinkled with encouraging words such as "Good job!" or "Thanks for the help."

When I hear sailors on other boats barking, it actually calms me down, knowing that the other crew is frustrated. When I feel my own blood boiling, I take a deep breath and think first about what I'm going to say. You can also reduce tension by chewing gum, moving to a different part of the boat, cleaning your sunglasses, tacking or jibing, rotating positions, stripping off a jacket to prevent overheating, or even asking for a moment of silence. If a problem comes up, think back to past successes to calm down. Displacement of energy can help reduce the tension.

Too often sailors yell at other crew. Don't yell about something that's personal.

Harsh remarks made on board will linger in the mind of the recipient long after the race is over. If there's a bothersome incident, discuss it off the boat. At the crew meeting before the next race, inform the rest of the crew of the solution you came up with.

America's Cup sailors who are wired up for sound for television broadcasts have learned to improve their behavior. One Cup sailor was amazed at how much negative fan mail he received after his outbursts had been broadcast. He never repeated the mistake.

The test is to ask yourself, "Am I as nice a guy as I think I am?" You can even ask your crew. The way they respond, even if it is diplomatic, will give you a clue about how your behavior is perceived.

A quiet, businesslike crew sails with more class, less crew attrition, and improved performance. It takes work to overcome yelling. But your time on the water will be more enjoyable if tempers on board are controlled.

Overcoming Emotions When Behind

While winning is a function of efficiently executing basic moves, your emotions in the heat of battle will determine your success. One summer I raced three consecutive weekends in back-to-back, two-day J/22 regattas. All three times I found myself down in the standings after racing on Saturday. My crew and I felt like a football team behind by two touchdowns at the half. The question each weekend was, How can we turn the tide in our favor?

The first thing to do—and probably the

On some boats the crews tend to yell more and more about less and less. Yelling into the wind is usually not effective.

most difficult—is to work past your emotions. I do this by evaluating each race and figuring out precisely where mistakes were made. Be honest. Oftentimes, one simple move sets off a series of events.

Second, once you understand what mistakes were made, create a game plan with specific things you can do to improve.

Third, explain to the rest of your crew—before the second day of the regatta—what you will do differently.

And finally, go out and do it!

In those J/22 regattas, each event presented a new problem. Our first event at Fishing Bay, Virginia, was a case of "almosts." We were close to the leaders, but we just kept missing good opportunities. After reviewing the race, our biggest problem was clear: poor starts that forced us to sail in the wrong direction. So at dinner after the first day I congratulated the sailors who were ahead of us in the standings.

A Tactician's Checklist

Here are the key methods and duties employed by a good tactician:

Only one person should be designated as the tactician.

The tactician must have the authority to call for maneuvers and plan the boat's strategy in advance.

Keep your boat in the vicinity of the rest of the fleet; a flyer rarely pays.

Keep your boat in clear wind, particularly after the start.

A good tactician should always anticipate and then verbalize the next move or sail change so the crew is mentally and physically prepared.

Be ready with new ideas on how to improve boatspeed. Make one adjustment at a time.

Know how to judge your boat's performance by watching what other boats are doing.

Make sure you understand the race instructions, the course, and the racing rules. The tactician's job is to keep the team on track.

Keep your crew physically low in the boat and focused on their jobs.

Crews don't like surprises. Early warnings keep everyone organized and avoid mistakes.

Make sure you and the skipper have a clear understanding of the tactician's role on board.

Keep track of wind strength and direction.

Stay calm in the heat of the battle.

A good tactician is prepared to be lonely when the pressure is on.

Congratulate the crew when things go well.

Ask the helmsman to look at the other boat(s) in tight situations.

Discuss tactical options before and after every race.

Avoid getting physically involved in sail handling and boat maneuvers. On larger boats, it's better to watch situations develop and assign someone a task if a problem arises.

Take the helm for a few minutes to understand how the boat feels, particularly in choppy conditions.

Go with your first instinct.

Avoid prolonged silences; this signifies worry to the crew.

Always present options with a clear recommendation.

When possible, give a reason for a maneuver. For example, "We're tacking to avoid a bad set of waves."

Then I quietly resolved that we were going to take the starts and sail to the correct side of the course the following day.

When you're having trouble, go back to your basic routine. For encouragement, think back to a past success. And remember to be consistent and not take major chances.

In the second regatta off Annapolis, we found ourselves a long way back in the standings after some inconsistent sailing on Saturday. Our problems were poor spinnaker work and pinching (heading too close to the wind while sailing to windward). I put a mark on the jibsheet and didn't trim it any tighter than that mark for Sunday's races. We sailed the boat on a lower course, and our plan worked. We were faster, and we came from behind to win the event.

Our third regatta, which was in Baltimore Harbor, was probably the toughest event—emotionally and physically. On Saturday, we had a terrible final race; it was probably the worst race I'd sailed in many years. That night I asked myself why. The first two races should easily have been first- and second-place finishes, but they turned into a fourth and a third because we tried to cover too many boats at once in very shifty winds. The setback caused a chain reaction; we were trying to play two sides of the course simultaneously, and we ended up almost in the back of the fleet. Ouch!

On Sunday, I made a plan to stick to basics. We came back with two third-place finishes and a second. Our turnaround worked and we won!

In reviewing these three regattas, I found four specific ways to improve our standings:

1. Go for a more conservative start. Often when you gun for the absolute best position you risk failure.

2. Don't pinch when sailing to windward; J/22s are boats that must be sailed on a fast course.

3. On the downwind legs, I was trying to sail too low a course. On each Sunday, I steered more on a reach for speed.

4. Even though we were down in the standings, we believed we could win.

Not every boat can always make a comeback. But the key is to work toward improving your sailing every day. Runyon Colie gave me some sage advice before I went off to college, and it still holds up many years later. If you separate your emotions and think about specifics, you'll have a good chance of sailing better.

CHAPTER 4

Strategy at the Start

Winning the start of a race is a huge thrill and it gives your crew a psychological lift. There is a lot of tension during starts. But this is the most important time to stay calm. Edging ahead of the fleet on the first leg takes careful study and methodical planning—and that process should commence well before you begin maneuvering at the starting line. Take the time to make a list of things to do before and during the starting sequence. This might not come easily at first, but eventually you will begin to organize your racing strategies and become a better sailor.

Reading the Wind

The wind is the horsepower you use to sail around the course. Many sailors simply react to the wind once they get onto the racecourse. But studying the wind in advance and understanding how it behaves on the water gives you a valuable competitive edge.

Reading windshifts is key. Anticipating favorable shifts will allow you to sail your boat at a closer angle toward the next mark and therefore cut down on the distance sailed.

Sailors classify windshifts as *lifts* or *headers*. On an upwind leg, a lift is a change in the wind direction that allows you to sail closer to the windward mark. A header forces you to sail farther away from the windward mark. On the downwind leg, the opposite is true: a header takes you closer to the mark; a lift takes you away.

You can also use windshifts to escape from competitors when you are sailing in blanketed wind. If you know the next puff

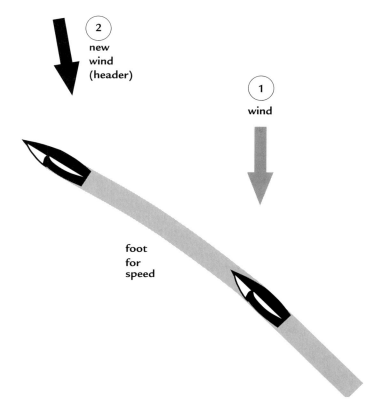

If your next puff of wind is going to be a header, foot off, i.e., head lower than your best upwind course. By footing off slightly and easing your sheets accordingly your speed will increase and you will get to the new wind sooner.

is going to be a header, foot and gain speed to arrive at the header earlier. (I define *footing* as slightly bearing away from the wind to gain speed. This is a subtle action, just one or two degrees.)

If you see a lift approaching, steer a high course to reach the windshift early. You can read a lift or header by noticing the angle of the ripples on the water, by watching the course a windward boat is sailing, or observing the flags on an anchored boat. The stronger the wind, the bigger and closer together the ripples. They look like dark patches. Big windshifts of ten degrees or

more are easy to read because the angle of the ripples change.

Wind patterns vary from race to race. It's important to concentrate on every windshift to understand the trends. These patterns tend to repeat themselves over short periods of time (roughly fifteen minutes). Keep track of these patterns in a notebook. If there is a prolonged new wind direction—i.e., gusts keep coming from the same direction—this means there is a major trend developing in one direction. An oscillating wind shifts back and forth, while a persistent shift generally changes in one direction. If you are racing close to land, windshifts are usually geographic or affected by the terrain. Be flexible and think hard. Accurately reading the wind will give you a big edge over your competitors.

Wind and Weather

Wind is a result of variations in atmospheric pressure or thermal activity, or both. The National Weather Service issues a considerable amount of information to help forecast the wind. NOAA weather reports on the VHF radio also give quality information over a broad region. More specific information can be found on the Internet. Many sailors hire weather consultants to get information. A cheaper alternative is to ask local sailors what they think the wind will do later in the day. If they are not sure of a compass direction, get them to point in the direction they expect the wind to come from.

Most forecasts start with a description of the present conditions (temperature, barometer reading, visibility, cloudiness, wind direction and strength, and precipita-

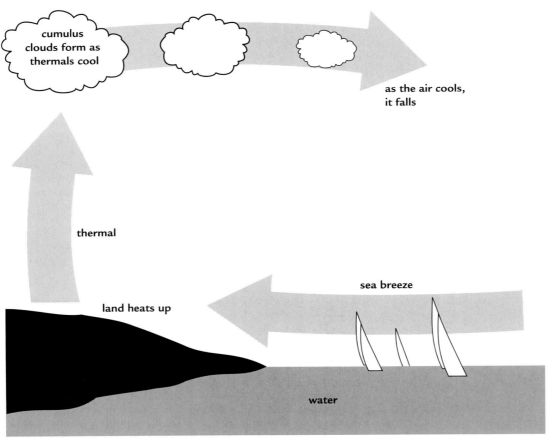

Along the shore, air warmed by the land—called a thermal—rises and the cool air from the sea fills in (known as a "sea breeze").

tion) and follow with a prediction of changes typically expected in the next twelve-hour period. The conditions you experience on the racecourse may be somewhat different from those described in the forecast. But when you begin to notice any of the predicted changes taking place, you can recognize a trend.

For example, if the conditions on the course are partly sunny skies with winds out of the west at 10 to 15 knots and the forecast is calling for increasing cloudiness with winds shifting into the northeast and increasing to 25 knots, keep your eye on the cloud cover. If the sky clouds over, chances are that the forecast is accurate and the wind will shift out of the northeast.

Thermals occur when heated air (such as the air over land in the summer) rises and cold air flows in to take its place. (This cool air flowing in from sea is known as a *sea*

breeze.) As the day wears on, normal thermal winds will shift in the same direction the sun is moving in. When thermal winds build, puffy cumulus clouds appear and move in the opposite direction of the breeze. These clouds, for instance, float seaward during an onshore breeze. The faster they move, the stronger the air circulates. So if those clouds are moving quickly, they indicate that the breeze will soon get stronger.

Wind and Local Geography

If you are racing off the U.S. Merchant Marine Academy at Kings Point, New York, ninety percent of the time it pays to take the left side of the course—regardless of which way the wind is blowing. This is because there is a large hill with buildings that disrupts wind near one portion of the shoreline. I coached the sailing team at Kings

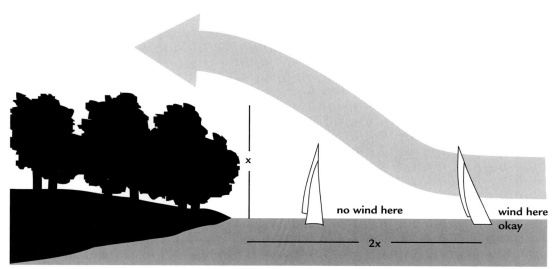

Wind bends around and rises over objects in its path (in this case the shoreline). The wind is disrupted in front of the obstruction at least twice as far out as the object is high. This is known as the snow-fence effect. In this case the sailboat nearer shore will find little wind alongshore in the area in front of the trees, the distance of that area being at least two times the height of the trees.

Point for many regattas before the "go left" revelation struck me. This is only one example of an instance when local geography or objects on or near the racecourse will create predictable winds.

I learned some other important lessons from local sailors while coaching the U.S. Finn team at the pre-Olympics in Tallinn, Estonia. The locals warned me to avoid sailing near anchored boats or close to shore. This is because the wind bends around and rises over objects in its path, which makes the breeze lighter in these areas. When the breeze hits an object, the wind starts to bend at a distance equal to roughly twice the height of the object in its path. For example, if a ship is 40 feet high, it affects the wind at least 80 feet to windward of it. This is called the *snow-fence effect*. If there is a large spectator fleet at the starting line, favor the end away from the spectator boats. The shape of an object affects how the wind bends around it, but wind normally bends equally around both sides. Objects also create a blanketed zone to leeward that is from five to ten times their height. For example, the air to leeward of a 40-foot-high ship could be disturbed for as much as 400 feet.

Using Windshifts to Your Advantage

As a racer, you should have a good sense of how each puff of wind will affect your boat. Timing windshifts will help you calculate their impact. Spend pre-race time recording the intervals between shifts and the variance in degrees. Use this information to anticipate windshifts during a race.

Be careful timing windshifts because it's difficult to determine where you might be in a particular phase. When you round the leeward mark, for instance, it's very hard to know when to expect the next windshift. The safest and most effective way to understand windshifts is to predict the direction and strength of the next puff as it approaches by using the signals available on the water. The ripples the wind creates on the water's surface are good indicators of what the wind is doing—monitor their intensity (darkness) and direction to determine the strength and angle of the new wind.

By looking closely at the water ahead you can often tell how the new wind will differ from your old wind. Check an area five to ten boatlengths ahead every ten seconds. By observing the wind's effect on your sails and your masthead fly (the weather vane flown from the top of the mast) you can develop a sense of whether a lift or a header is approaching. The wind changes at the top of the mast before it does on the water. Patterns repeat. Feel the wind on your neck, face, and ears, being alert to the change in wind strength on your skin. Keep an eye out for flags on boats or buoys. The best method when reading the wind is to compare the course of your boat to other boats. If other boats are sailing a higher course and heeling over more, they most likely have stronger wind and are in a lift.

Secondary sources are also useful guides, including the direction anchored boats are facing (though strong currents may be an influence), smoke from stacks ashore, masthead flies of other boats, birds taking off, the intensity of the sound of the wind, and the direction clouds are moving.

The strongest part of a puff is usually the part just behind the first wind ripples on

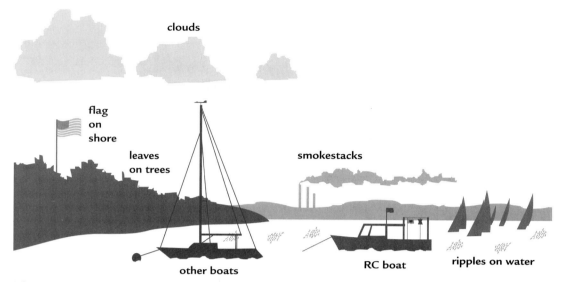

There are many indicators to help you read the wind.

the water. Use this strongest part of the puff to accelerate for speed. Sail two to three boatlengths into a puff before tacking. If you do this, you'll make the best use of the strongest air. You'll also have a better chance of avoiding a false header (a puff of wind that is of brief duration) by sailing these few boatlengths into the puff. If you tack immediately on a puff you predict will be a header, before you are sure of the new breeze's direction, you may find yourself being headed again on the new tack. By contrast, if you are patient, and tack well on a header, you are automatically lifted on the new tack.

In light air, maneuver in lulls when there is little or no air so you get the most speed and distance out of puffs. Once the breeze settles in over 6 mph, use puffs to accelerate for speed. Be sure the new wind-shift or puff is solid before tacking. Stand up to look at the ripples as they appear: stand-

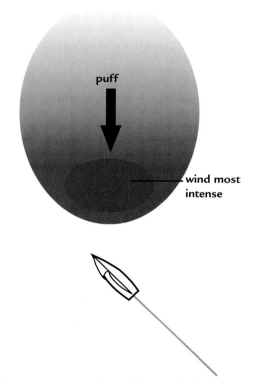

The strongest part of a puff is usually the first part.

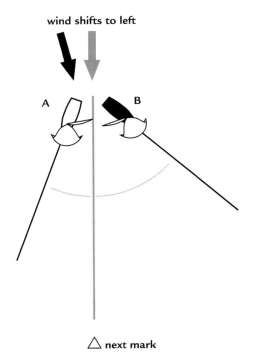

Play the windshifts to your advantage. Your goal is to sail the closer course to the next mark. Keep track of which way the bow is heading compared with your competitors. Boat A is sailing a closer course to the mark because the wind has shifted to the left.

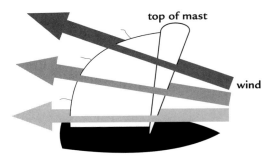

When the wind is either dying or filling in, there is often wind shear—a situation where the wind direction and strength is different at the top of mast from that at the bottom.

ing gives you a better perspective and therefore a better wind reading.

On downwind legs the basic rule is to jibe in the lifts. Sail on the jibe that takes you on the closest course to the next mark. As you get lifted, you will have to sail lower (in relation to the wind) and therefore slower to maintain the same course. It is really a case of simple math: sail on the closest course to the next mark at the optimum point of sail—which is not dead downwind.

Wind shear happens when the wind at the top of the sail is different from that at the bottom. Wind shear occurs most often in a new breeze or in a dying breeze when the wind is light. You can check for wind shear by observing the direction telltales are blowing from the top of your mast to your lower shrouds. Be patient; don't let conflicting wind directions confuse you. Trim the largest part of your sail for the strongest part of the breeze.

Choosing the Best Side of the Course

With experience, you'll learn to determine which side of the racecourse is the best, or favored, side. Developing this skill will help you make early gains in the race and earn you a high place at the first mark. To do this, you'll need a disciplined approach, careful study, and the courage to make the call.

The importance of understanding wind, current, and wave patterns is demonstrated by America's Cup sailors, who go to great lengths to find a competitive edge. Cup teams employ highly skilled weather gurus who analyze weather maps and collect data from weather boats spread throughout the race area. Few sailors enjoy this kind of support, so you'll need to make your own observations. Do your homework both ashore and before the start.

No sailor knows for certain which side of the course will pay. The less certain you are, the more careful you should be about positioning your boat so you can switch sides shortly after the start, if necessary.

Before leaving the dock review all the weather information available from newspapers, the Internet, tide and current tables, and print forecasts. One of the most reliable sources is local knowledge, so take the time to ask the locals about the wind patterns in their area. Unexpected information can be surprisingly helpful. For example, a sheep farm near the America's Cup racecourse in Auckland, New Zealand, was a good place to observe the wind patterns. The wind at the sheep farm filled in about an hour ahead of the wind on the Cup racecourse on the Hauraki Gulf. An observer could give the weather team a handle on what was coming. On one Midwestern lake, cows on the shoreline face downwind. But if the wind is strong, the cows are lined up neatly. In Newport, Rhode Island, dense dew on the grass early in the morning indicates that a strong southwester will fill in.

Once you leave the dock, watch the wind. Keep track of what is happening. Observe changes in the wind by watching other boats on their way out to the course. Take compass readings and write everything down. Well before the start, study the water carefully. Look for dark patches of water. Study one section of the horizon at a time. Stand up so you have a greater height of eye. Use polarized sunglasses because they help contrast the color of the water; let your eyes blink naturally. Watch other boats sailing. If the boats on the left side are heeling more, this indicates more wind.

Split the leg into three sections: left, middle, and right. Look for indicators to help you read the wind on each section: flags, smokestacks, cruising boats, birds taking off, ripples on the water, the direction of anchored boats, and your competitors. Verbalize your findings. Your first instinct is usually correct. After two minutes of study, guess which side of the course seems better.

Prearrange to test the course with one of your competitors. After taking observations, test your ideas by sailing upwind up one side of the course while the competitor you made a prearrangement with sails up the other side. After about two minutes, tack toward each other and note which boat has gained. After crossing, head toward the opposite side of the course for another two minutes. Tack back together and note the difference in position. One boat will most likely have gained on the same side of the course. Return to the starting area and make a second visual observation. Ask yourself whether the wind is any different now.

Of course this technique will help your partner too. If you don't have a partner, simply observe your performance against that of another boat randomly sailing on the other side of the course.

Set up your starting strategy so you head toward your preselected favorite side of the course. If the plan is to sail to the right side of the course, avoid starting on the left side of the line. Keep your information to yourself. Never discuss strategy with your competitors, except for your pre-race testing partner. Sometimes you have to give a little something away to learn something special. After the race, feel free to talk about your experience and what you learned with your competitors— just as Buddy Melges did at the E-scow Nationals.

Few sailors use a disciplined approach when determining their starting strategy. By being organized and methodical, you can gain an advantage. The key is to make a definite decision to favor one section of the course. Once you've decided, go for it. Wind varies in strength and direction. It is better to head for stronger wind than to sail for the next windshift. Stronger wind gives you more speed—and you can always tack or jibe toward the favored side of the course.

The biggest decision after the start is whether to continue sailing in your chosen direction or to switch sides. I always go with

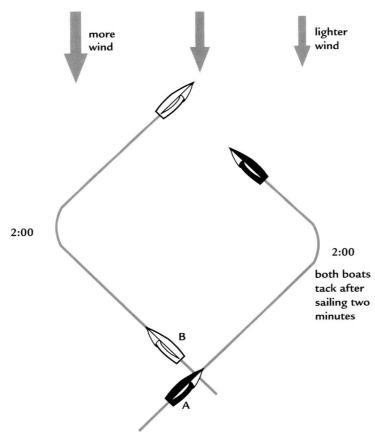

In this case Boat B gains from the left side of the course because there is more wind. Early tuning with another boat helps you determine which side of the course is favored.

my first instinct, but things do change and adjustments are necessary. One crew member should continually analyze whether you are gaining or losing. If you are losing on your present course and you decide to bail out, do this in one motion.

You might consider switching sides of the course if you see a new wind blowing across the course, or if you see that a few boats have made huge gains on one side of the course. But before taking action, ask yourself this question, "Will the new wind still be there when I arrive?" If there is any doubt, avoid chasing wind that may quickly disappear.

If you do decide to switch sides, wait until a boat has crossed just ahead of you or just behind you. This boat will become a blocker as you cross the course. (See page 74 for more information about using a blocker boat.) It's okay to dip (sail) below several boats if you see better wind. Dipping goes against common sense; but if you are certain the opposite side of the course is better, this early loss will translate into a big

gain later on. The biggest mistake you can make at this point is to second-guess yourself and tack back to your original side of the course. You must be resolute.

Later in the race watch for a current shear and/or a major windshift and consider what you learned upwind as you plan to sail downwind. (*Current shear* is a radical shift in the water's direction and speed caused by water flowing in different directions, usually along the shoreline, or as a result of a tide change or different currents colliding.) When you cross a shear, analyze your performance. A difference in the current will often be indicated by debris or irregular, choppy water. You might notice that the shear stretches a long way. Study this phenomenon carefully. If you are suddenly sailing slower than boats on the other side of the current shear, consider changing course.

Some years ago in a Finn Olympic Trials race, I found a current shear halfway up the beat during my pre-race tune-up. On the windward side of the shear, the water

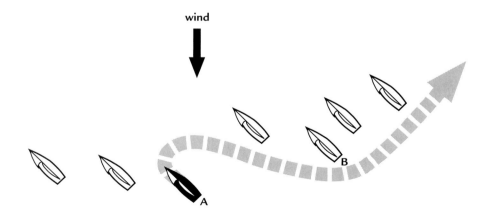

Boat A dips Boat B—tacks and sails behind Boat B—to get to the right side of the course early. Work to get out of a bad position early in the race.

was flowing toward the windward mark. All week long at this regatta, the right side of the course was favored thanks to a big starboard windshift. After the start I headed left and crossed the shear. The entire fleet headed right as usual. I rounded the first mark with a comfortable lead. Early observation and the courage to trust my discovery gave me the edge.

Remember what part of the course was most beneficial on the upwind leg and use this information for the downwind leg. Well before rounding the windward mark, announce where you plan to sail on the run. Ask yourself if you should execute a bear-away spinnaker set or jibe set. If the opposite jibe is favored by 15 degrees or more, a jibe set is a better option. On a course with many boats, it is more efficient to set the spinnaker, accelerate to full speed, and then jibe when your wind is clear of other boats rounding behind you.

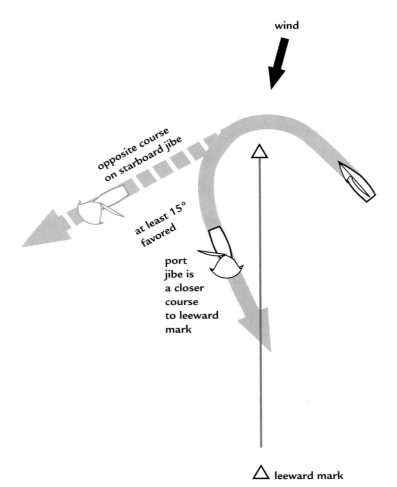

When the opposite jibe is favored on a downwind leg by at least 15 degrees, a jibe set—where you jibe the boat around the mark and hoist a spinnaker on port tack—is the preferred maneuver.

Guidelines for Choosing the Best Side of the Course

Sailors tend to stay in a group when they are winning. If you see a majority of the fleet sailing in one direction, it's an indication that they are sailing to the favored side of the course.

Study the water carefully for more wind. Look for dark patches in the water. Study one section of the horizon at a time. Stand up so you have a greater height of eye. Use polarized sunglasses because they help contrast the colors of the water better. Let your eyes blink naturally.

Watch and observe how the wind affects other boats, even if they are not on your course.

Look for current shears in tidal areas. Once you pass a shear in the water, immediately analyze whether you are gaining or losing to the boats that have not passed the shear.

Remember, taking a flyer rarely pays off.

If you are behind, go for the smaller gain. If you go for a big gain, you risk losing a lot of distance.

Remember which side of the course was favored on the first windward leg and then play that side again, both upwind and downwind.

Avoid switching back and forth between sides of the course.

Keep notes on what happened during the day. Patterns often repeat themselves.

Wind patterns repeat themselves on the water. When you learn what works, put this knowledge into your game plan. Keep notes as reference for future regattas, since geographic patterns stay the same.

A few years ago, I was invited to a college alumni regatta. On the plane ride out I reviewed my notebooks, which were written between 1969 and 1972 during the four times I had sailed in the Timme Angsten Memorial Regatta in Chicago. They discussed how to sail on this body of water. I was pleasantly surprised that my inside information still worked, and I won the regatta. I added a few new passages to my youthful thoughts in case I ever return.

Most sailors react to the wind as it blows across the racecourse. You can consistently improve your results by studying it carefully in advance of the race and making adjustments once the race starts.

Fast Starts

Getting a good start is one of the most exhilarating moments in sailboat racing. With clear wind and a clean pathway, your options are open. You can foot fast or point high. And you can tack at will.

The pre-start seems chaotic because boats are sailing randomly back and forth. The trick to getting a good start is to use an organized approach. The most important time before the start is the last twenty seconds. You must accelerate for full speed, have clear wind, sail as fast as or faster than the boats around you, and have no other boats slowing you down.

Getting into this position takes practice, patience, and persistence. Getting a good start is a state of mind. You must will yourself, your crew, and your boat to get in a good position. I use the word *will* frequently

Getting a good start is one of the most exhilarating moments in sailboat racing. With clear wind you have many options of which way to sail.

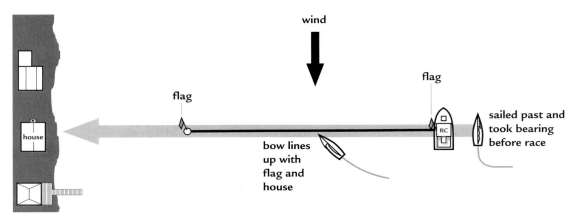

Before the race, take a bearing between an object on shore and the starting line to determine when you are on the line. In this case, when the starting buoy at the port end lines up with the house on the shore, the race boat is on the line.

because it works. Following are a number of techniques I have learned for getting a clean start.

The Pre-Start Tune-Up

Before a race, spend at least fifteen minutes sailing to windward so that you get into the groove of sailing the waves, dealing with windshifts, and hiking hard. I like to leave the dock earlier than most so there is adequate time to practice.

Predetermine your bearings for the starting line so you know when you are actually on the line. Sail to a point *outside* of the committee boat alongside the starting line so that you have both ends of the starting line aligned with a tree (or house or smokestack) on shore. Take note of the bearing along this sight line. Later, as you approach for the start, you will know the exact bearing that puts you over the line.

During the start the crew should stay low and quiet so the helmsman, tactician, and bowman can see and communicate clearly. Work out a system of hand signals in advance so the bowman can signal back to the cockpit when to go for the line, bear off, slow down, speed up, or duck behind a boat if you are overlapped. I recommend a thumbs-up if there is no overlap and a thumbs-down if there is an overlap. Only the helmsman of your boat should hail other boats; random hails from crew members show a poorly organized team.

Starting Techniques

Winning a start gives you a psychological lift. It will give you and your crew the incentive to work harder for the rest of the race. It also gives you clear air and a clear

The bowman uses hand signals to relay boat position and distance relative to the starting line back to the sailors in the cockpit.

pathway so you can look around and pick the best time to tack. These starting techniques work equally well in both dinghies and keelboats. But a keelboat takes longer to accelerate so you need to plan ahead.

The first challenge on the starting line is choosing the favored end of the line. Tra-

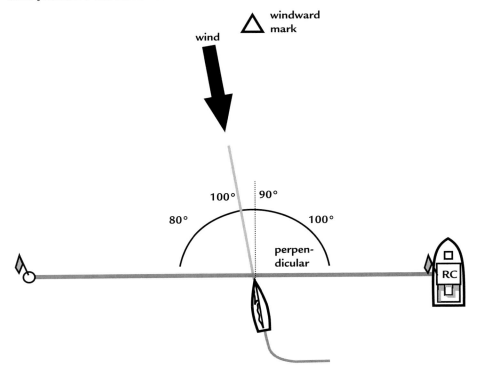

To determine which end of the line is favored, luff directly into the wind, then watch which way the bow points. In this case the bow points 10 degrees toward the port end of the line from the perpendicular, which means the port end is favored.

ditionally, most sailors test this by luffing in the middle of the line and noting which end of the line seems closer to the bow when it falls away from the wind. Although this technique is common and it works, it doesn't take into account current, the direction of waves, and the wind to windward of the line. It's also not particularly good for your sails. The best method to determine the favored end of the line is to sail across the line at one end while another boat is crossing the line at the opposite end. This is best done randomly. I like to sit near the port end and wait until another boat is just about to make a practice start at

the starboard end. At this point I trim in and sail. By noting which boat crosses the other's path first, you can determine which end of the line is favored. It's important to be sailing at full speed and on the wind during this exercise.

In the last race of a Laser North American Championship, four boats would qualify for the World Championship later that year. I tested which end of the line was favored by sailing upwind from either end. I found that the port end was favored by 10 degrees because of a strong wave and current pattern. I ended up crossing the fleet on port tack. What a thrill it was passing

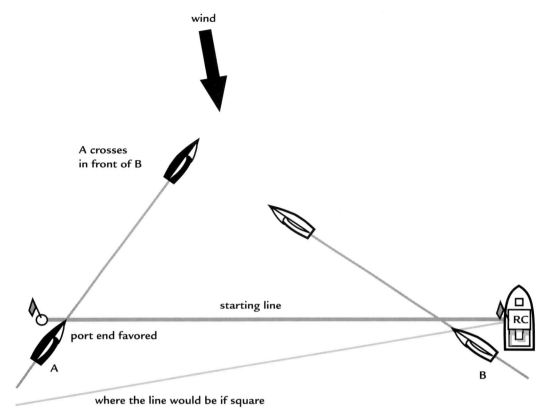

wind

A crosses
in front of B

starting line

port end favored

A

B

where the line would be if square

Before the start, cross the line at one end while another boat is crossing the line at the opposite end. Watch which boat crosses the other's path first—this gives you an indication of which end of the line is favored.

ninety Lasers on that magic start. I went on to win the race and qualified for the Worlds.

The key to any start is to position yourself so you have speed coming off the line. The trick is to maneuver with speed during the starting sequence. The faster your boat is moving, the easier it is to maneuver around other boats. With maneuverability, your options are open. Amazingly, most sailors start a race by sitting on the line luffing their sails, waiting for the gun to go off, and then trimming in at the starting signal.

Or they simply reach down the line and head up at the gun. Both of these tactics are inadequate. Picture two drivers in their race cars. The first driver is sitting on the starting line revving his engine. When the flag goes down, he puts the pedal to the floor and takes off. The second driver has already started his car and his wheels are moving; when the flag goes down, he hits the line at 90 mph. The same idea applies to sailing. You want to arrive at the line at full speed and with more speed than your competitors.

There is really no magic to winning a start. The trick is to consistently get away from the line with clear wind and speed so you pop out ahead of the rest of the fleet. Even if you are sailing a slow boat, you can make consistently good starts if you master one of the following starting techniques.

THE TIMED RUN (VANDERBILT START)

A timed run, when properly executed, brings you to the starting line with speed. This type of start is also a known as the Vanderbilt start because it was developed by three-time America's Cup winner Harold S. Vanderbilt in the 1930s.

Start from the point on the starting line where you want to end up, then head away from that point on a broad reach. Sail a specific distance or time, then maneuver and return to the starting line. For example, for a one-minute timed run, sail away from the line for twenty-five seconds, use ten seconds to tack, then accelerate to full speed on the opposite tack toward the starting line. You should arrive back at the starting line after sixty seconds, just as the race starts.

The timed run works well because most sailboats sail the same speed close-hauled as they do on a broad reach. This is not necessarily true for a planing dinghy, so sailors of planing dinghies have to adjust their timing to allow for the extra speed on a broad reach.

My experience shows that the timed run works effectively on both big yachts and in dinghies. On keelboats, ranging from Etchells to Maxi yachts, the timed run works because it takes a long time for these boats to build up speed. The momentum of a prop-

erly executed timed run is therefore a great advantage. For the same reason, the timed run also works nicely on a downwind start.

The timed run is most effective on the starboard part of the starting line.

Normally if you run away from the line for one minute, it takes you one minute to return (not counting the maneuvering time). As a rule, work your timed run so that you are maneuvering when no one else is. Instead of the standard two- or four-minute timed run, vary your timing and try a run of a minute and thirty-five seconds, or two minutes and fifteen seconds.

If you encounter congestion, such as a stack of boats, do not take any unnecessary risks by starting in their vicinity. You might decide to start just to leeward of the stack, where you will be assured of clear wind.

Every ten seconds during the starting sequence, the crew should call the minutes and seconds remaining until the starting gun. They should speak directly to the skipper, in a normal tone of voice. In the last minute before the start, I like the time called at five-second intervals.

If your competitors are barging down on you from windward, trying to sail a lower course on your windward side, they have no rights. You have the right-of-way so hail an early warning to them so there is no confusion. Anticipate the situation and don't wait for a collision to occur at the starting gun before stating your rights. If a boat looks as if it is about to tack under your lee bow, discourage it by heading right at that boat and force it to tack away early or, better yet, force it to sail past you and tack later.

If there is a boat ahead of you as you approach the line, don't pass it to leeward un-

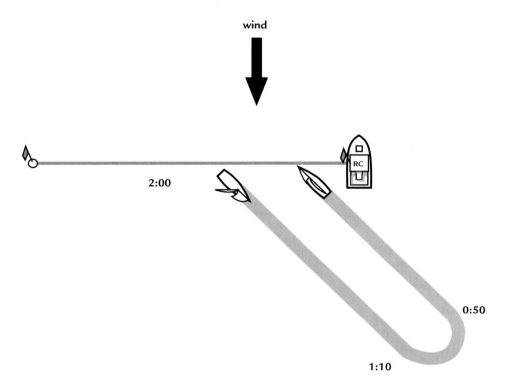

wind

2:00

0:50

1:10

The premise of the timed run is that most boats sail the same speed close-hauled as they do on a broad reach. Here the boat heads away from the starting line at two minutes before the start, tacks after one minute and ten seconds to sail close-hauled toward the line for the remaining 50 seconds until the start.

less you are absolutely certain of breaking through the other boat's lee. If, for example, the boat ahead of you is moving at two-thirds speed with their sails full, it's better to sail to windward. If the boat ahead is parked and stopped with both sails luffing, then pass to leeward.

THE PORT APPROACH

The port approach is a popular starting technique because it is easy to work, particularly at the leeward end of the line. You sail "against the grain," approaching the fleet on port tack, and then tack into a hole on the line. The port approach is successful only if you leave time to maneuver on to starboard tack so you can accelerate to full speed. The trick is to keep your boat moving at maximum speed, and then make a smooth tack into an open position. When you tack for the line, it's important not to tack so close to another boat that they must take evasive action to avoid you.

The port approach is actually a timed run in which you set your boat up to be moving close-hauled at full speed in the last thirty seconds. Find a hole by looking for boats that have been luffing for some time. These boats will have little speed and they won't be able to maneuver when you tack

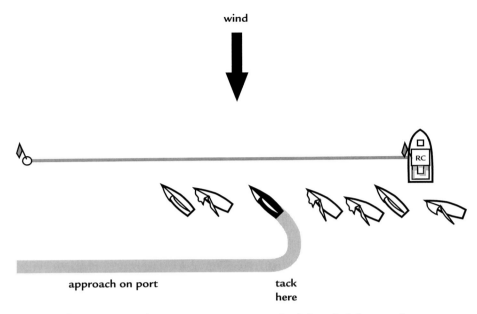

Approaching the fleet on port tack gives you many options. Look for a hole between boats.

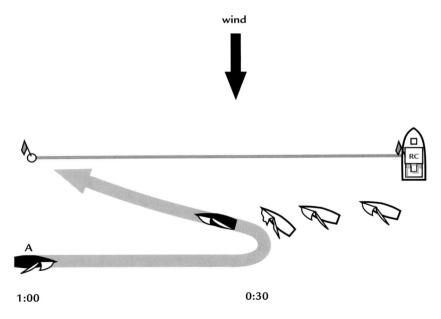

You can use a timed run on any part of the starting line. In this case, Boat A passed the buoy at the port end with one minute to go. After 30 seconds (half the total time to the start) Boat A can safely tack and head for the buoy without being over the starting line.

underneath them. When using the port approach, stay clear of approaching starboard tack boats. The port approach can be used on any part of the starting line. Note how much time you have as you approach the fleet on port. After passing the port end, if half the time to the start goes by before you tack, you know that you will be able to

tack, trim in, and hit the line at full speed before reaching the pin.

THE DIP START

The dip start works well in planing dinghies, particularly when a strong current is running down or through the line, making it difficult to cross the line on star-

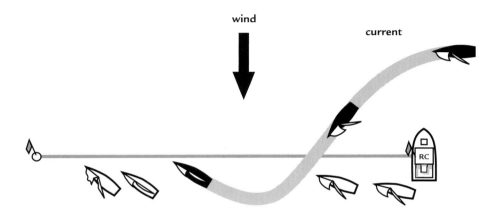

A dip start—approaching on a broad reach, then heading up to close-hauled before the gun goes off—works well in an uncrowded fleet, particularly if the current is running strong down or through the line.

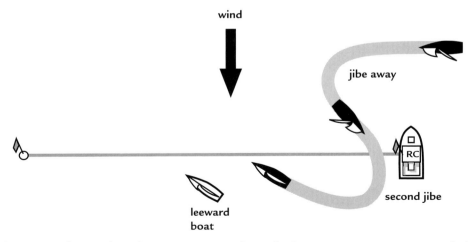

If you're trying a dip start but a boat is setting up to leeward, jibe away, open up some space, jibe back, and you will have room.

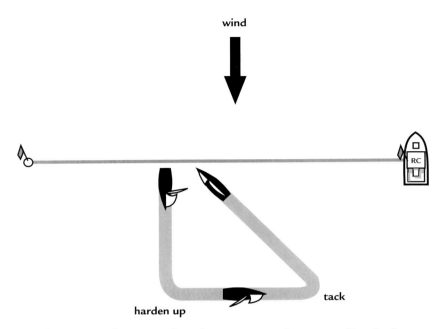

During a triangle start you take up space by sailing in a triangular pattern. No other boats can fill the same space at the same time. This technique keeps your boat moving. With maneuverability you have many options.

board tack. The dip start works best in the middle of the line. Simply sit about five to ten boatlengths to windward of the line, observing where holes develop in the fleet. Approach the line on a broad reach and head up to a close-hauled course about twenty seconds before the gun goes off.

If a leeward boat is preventing you from getting back to the line, jibe to port, sail astern of the boat, and then make your dip. Be extremely careful using this start, particularly if another boat is out to block your return to the line. If a general recall rule is in effect, you must stay below the line one minute prior to the starting gun. In that case, this technique is not an option.

As you dip, round your boat up, keeping it as flat as possible to prevent making leeway. Trim your sails as you round up,

moving the tiller slowly so that you do not lose speed. The faster you spin a sailboat, the faster it will slow down; maintain your speed, make your rounding slowly. The dip start is an effective technique in fast, maneuverable boats—particularly in small fleets that allow ample room to maneuver.

Keep in mind that the dip start takes considerable courage!

TRIANGLE STARTING TECHNIQUES
There are two "triangular" methods of starting. Pick a point on the starting line and then sail from that point directly downwind, harden up, tack, and approach the line at full speed. You are basically sailing a triangle. Your maneuver will clear out a space on the starting line, and you'll end up making room for yourself at the start by sailing this route.

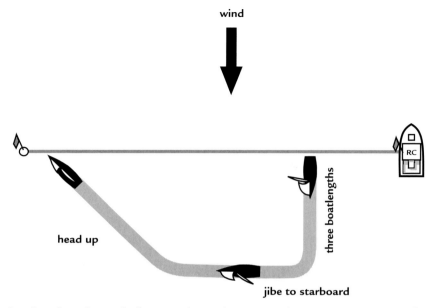

Sail three boatlengths to leeward of starting line. Jibe on to starboard and accelerate to full speed. Then head up to a close-hauled course toward your desired spot on the starting line.

The second triangular approach, which works well for dinghies, is simply to start at the line, sail downwind, jibe on to starboard and sail abeam of the line, then head up and make your approach. This technique will help you start at a particular point on the line while clearing a zone for yourself, which you can sail into, as you make your final approach. Look for a gap in the fleet before making your tack. With both of these techniques, the goal is to be sailing close-hauled, at full speed, and on starboard tack when the gun goes off.

Good Habits for the Pre-Start

Keep your eyes open before the start. Check the wind direction and your compass frequently to keep up with any changes in the wind and to reconfirm which end of the line is favored. If you find that one end of the line is no longer favored, don't be afraid to change your plan. Sail for the opposite end.

If you find that you're going to be over the line early or that you might run into the starting buoy, bail out sooner rather than later. Don't wait until the starting gun goes off to correct your error.

Avoid collisions by maintaining a good lookout during the pre-start. Don't casually cruise around, wishing everyone good luck. The time to be aggressive at the start is when the preparatory signal is sounded. If you see a difficult situation developing with another boat, hail your intentions early so there is no misunderstanding. Dramatic course changes are easily read by competitors, while subtle changes cause confusion. If you find yourself being tailed, shake off

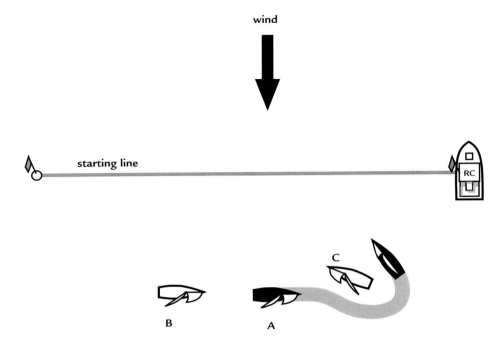

If Boat A is being tailed by another boat (Boat B), use a third boat (C) as a pick to shake the boat tailing you. Boat C blocks B from the tack to leeward of A. Boat A now has a clear lane to the starting line.

the other boat early so you don't end up in trouble. You can make a fast maneuver or borrow the "pick" tactic from basketball. Just as you can "pick" a defender by planting an offense player in the way, you can slow down your sailing opponent by placing an obstruction (another sailboat) between his boat and yours.

Keep your options open during the starting sequence and don't commit to one end of the line or the other until you are absolutely sure which is better. If you think one end is favored and all the other boats are at the wrong end, be a little bit sneaky. Wait until the last minute to sail toward the favored end so no other boat follows you there. If you know you can get away with a port-tack start, don't cross the line six or

seven times on port tack and give away the secret. Wait until the gun goes off to reveal your plan.

By understanding these starting techniques, you'll know in a short time which boats are making good approaches to the line and which boats will have trouble. Avoid starting alongside the fastest boats in the fleet; start near boats you think will be slow coming off the line. But be careful when starting next to slow boats: these same boats might be late for the line.

Starting Techniques in Large Fleets

On crowded starting lines that are favored at the starboard end, particularly in dinghy classes, three or four rows of boats will stack up gunwale to gunwale. Sometimes

Did the leading boat have a better range on the starting line? Or did it jump the gun?

boats arrive on the line as much as two minutes early. In this case the only option may
be, "If you can't beat 'em, join 'em."

When luffing on the line, never let
your boat go slower than your competition. Keep moving fast as you approach
the line. Sail the same course you'll be
heading on after the start, so you won't
have to bear off to accelerate. In a dinghy,
it helps to keep your boat heeled slightly
to leeward. As you trim your sails and flatten the boat out, you create wind in your
sails that gives you some quick acceleration. If your boat is heeling to windward,
it can sideslip and force you to bear off and
heel the boat to leeward before you can
make headway.

Robert Scheidt from Brazil, a multi–
Laser World Champion, has a unique starting technique. He has the ability to luff
slightly beyond head-to-wind, back his
mainsail, lift the centerboard, and slide to
windward. By doing this, he opens a hole for
himself to leeward. In the last few seconds
before the start, he puts his bow down, accelerates, and takes off on a clean start. But
even with this clever maneuver, Scheidt
must be careful. Once he is beyond head-to-
wind he is considered to be "tacking" under
the rules and must stay clear of other boats.

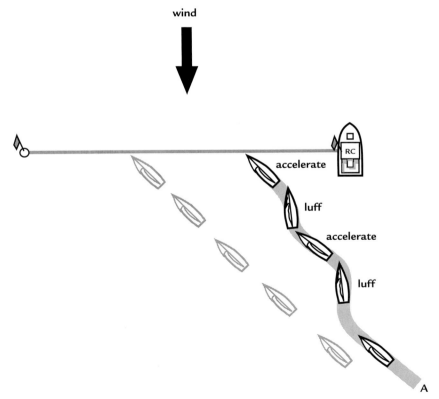

*Crabbing (as shown by Boat A) is alternating between going for speed and luffing up. This helps you accel-
erate and gain windward distance as you approach the line.*

Always fight at the start to be in that first group of boats; you can do it by *crabbing* to windward, just as Scheidt does. Crabbing is a technique where you travel at half-speed and continually luff into the wind, taking bites to windward to stay away from the boats to leeward of you.

Dealing tactically with large aggressive fleets is difficult, but not impossible. The best spots on the line (other than the perfect position, which only one or two boats will be able to attain) are found either just to windward or just to leeward of a *stack*, or group, of boats.

Stacks commonly form to leeward. Typically, one boat luffs on the line; a second boat sails into leeward; and the process is repeated until a stack of ten or more boats is formed on the line. Every skipper is madly trying to avoid a collision; parked boats tend to act like magnets and have little maneuverability.

The best solution is to approach a stack of boats on port tack, sailing against the grain. Holes in the line are easy to find. The key is to pick where you want to make your move and then tack in that spot onto starboard tack. If stacks are forming to *leeward*, this means the stack is shallow. Therefore, you should have room to sail to leeward of the stack to the windward side. After sailing at least two or three boatlengths past the windward boat in the stack, tack to starboard and accelerate. If the stack is *deep* (many boats side by side on the line), then it's best to tack to leeward and ahead of the stack.

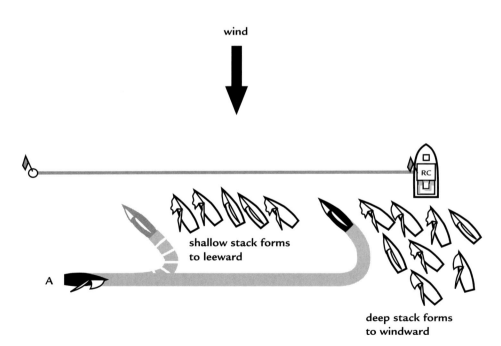

wind

shallow stack forms
to leeward

A

deep stack forms
to windward

When a start is crowded, approach the fleet on port tack. If a stack forms to leeward it will be shallow. Gain advantage by sailing beyond the shallow stack and then tacking to windward before reaching the deep stack.

The start of a large fleet is like a ballet. Every boat is on the line and maneuvering with precision. It is a thing of beauty.

A BRILLIANT STRATEGY

Former College Sailor of the Year Ken Read discovered a clever starting-line trick during the 2003 Etchells World Championship. With 95 boats on the line, the race committee set a mid-line race official boat to help call premature starters over. Read consistently started just to windward of the mid-line boat. As he exited the starting line, he therefore had a clear lane to leeward. Other boats in the area that started to leeward of the race official boat were at least two boatlengths away from Read. This technique allowed Read to sail with more speed for a longer period of time. His position in the middle of the line also provided him options as to which side of the course to head toward. Read went on to win six of eight races. It was a brilliant strategy.

Fast Exits During and After the Start

In every race, there is a one-minute-or-less window of opportunity to make a fast exit off the starting line. This critical time period usually determines your position for the rest of the race. There are several factors to consider during this time:

❖ Sail at full speed at least ten seconds before the gun.

❖ Avoid pinching immediately after the start.

❖ If you are falling into a leeward boat's bad wind, keep your bow down for speed right up to the time you're forced to tack away. Always tack at full speed.

❖ Have one person on the boat concentrate on calling the first tack.

❖ When you tack, don't be afraid to dip a few sterns.

❖ Think speed more than pointing after the start.

❖ Only make one tack in the first two minutes of the race.

❖ If you are blanketed by several boats and you can't tack away, patience often pays off. The boats ahead of you will eventually tack off your wind.

❖ A pre-start tune-up is important so you understand what the breeze is like on that first leg and how to trim your sails for speed. But keep in mind that there is often less wind in the starting area than you experienced farther up the course during your tune-up. You may want to add fullness to your sails for the critical post-start exit and be prepared to flatten your sails later.

❖ If you know you are over the line before the gun, don't wait to circle around and go back to restart. Go as soon as conditions warrant (i.e., you have clear water to maneuver without fouling another boat).

❖ When luffing on the line, never let your boat go slower than your competition.

❖ Keep your boat on the course that you'll sail after the start so that you won't have to bear off to accelerate. Don't give away windward distance. You might need room to foot after the start for acceleration.

One Magic Start

In 1982, I was selected to join *Sailing World* magazine's Hall of Fame. All twenty selectees were invited to sail Etchells in a regatta in Newport, Rhode Island. We had one day to practice. The next day, we were warming up before the first race and all around us were big names—Arthur Knapp, Paul Elvström, Buddy Melges, Dennis Conner, to name just a few. I noticed that the wind was shifting hard to the left with about a minute and a half before the start. I broke off my timed run for the windward end and sailed for the buoy end. The wind kept shifting to the left. With about six seconds to go we tacked and crossed the fleet. It was a magic moment in my sailing career. My crew, Hank Stuart, started reeling off the names: "Okay, we've got Melges by a length. No problem with Stuart Walker. There's Arthur Knapp about two lengths back." My heart started to pound as I thought about all the talent around me. In the back of my head I was thinking, "Why am I even with this crowd?" At that moment, I switched to something that my college coach Graham Hall told me when I was a freshman: "Forget about names of sailors. Only think about sail numbers." So I said to Hank, "I don't want to hear another name during the regatta. Let's just deal with No. 6, not Dennis Conner."

My other crew member, Jud Smith, sensed the nervousness building on the boat, even though we had a nice lead. While looking up at the slot between the main and the jib, he said, "Gary, ease off on the backstay a quarter of an inch." I lifted the pre-stretched line out of the cam cleat, eased it the smallest amount possible, and put the line back in. "That's better now," Jud said, having never taken his eyes off the leech of the jib. I thought to myself, "If this guy can see the difference in trim with that minuscule adjustment, I'm going to be in good shape." It was a great beginning to a magic regatta that Jud, Hank, and I went on to win.

It was a thrill to be included with the world's best sailors at the Sailing World *Hall of Fame Regatta. Shown here from left to right are Dave Ullman, George O'Day, Steve Benjamin, Bruce Kirby, Gary Jobson, Paul Elvström, Bob Bavier, Lowell North, Buddy Melges, Stuart Walker, and Hobie Alter.* (Mitch Carucci)

Gary Jobson and crew in Hall of Fame Regatta. (Mitch Carucci)

❖ During the start, work to position your boat in the front row. Avoid sitting still or you'll be passed.

❖ Communication before the start is critical to attaining the ideal pre-start speed. The only crew talking should be the tactician, trimmers, and skipper. The bowman should communicate with hand signals.

❖ Warn your crew before making a radical turn, so sails can be trimmed accordingly.

❖ To avoid collisions, look constantly to leeward. On big boats, have the bowman call the position of nearby boats.

Starting in Light Wind

Starting in light wind takes finesse and concentration. Keep these things in mind when the breeze goes light at the start:

❖ During the pre-start, always stay on the starting line.

❖ During the pre-start, make the boat sail as fast as possible. Concentrate on speed.

❖ Well before the start, decide which side of the course to head for. Watch for current, wind, and other boats tuning up to help you decide.

❖ Often there's more wind 100 yards to windward of the starting line. Head for the closest puff after the start.

❖ When making your final approach to the line, if there is a boat approaching you on port tack, head directly at that boat. You'll force them to get out of your way. If there's a boat to leeward, slow down early and let it sail away. Don't wait until the last moment.

❖ Get your crew in position and sitting still at least one minute before the start.

CHAPTER 5

After the Start:
Windward and Downwind Tactics

There is a lot of thinking and preparation to be done before you start a race. But once the starting gun goes off, your priorities shift to the next legs of the course and how to find the fastest route to the finish line. This chapter focuses on those legs after the start: how to play the game upwind and downwind, and how to position yourself for a strong finish.

Windward Tactics

Racing upwind is a joy. The apparent wind is strong, the boat is heeled over, and everything feels purposeful.

Sometimes the air at the start is a bit crowded. There are several things you can do to ensure your boat clear air at the start:

1. Tack to port early. Dip sterns and be especially careful of tacking to leeward of a starboard-tack boat. It will be hard to es-

cape later. In a high-performance boat you can generate considerable speed, cross several boats, and be off in clear air very soon after the start. It's better to dip astern and be sure of clear wind and no wake than to risk tacking into blanketed wind.

2. At the leeward end of the line, bear off, and drive for speed to keep your wind clear.

3. Plan your move and stay within the game plan. If you're trying to move ahead, don't tack to cover boats. Play the windshifts. Avoid one-on-one lockups.

4. Stay in phase with the windshifts. Make perfect tacks. Watch the actions of the rest of the fleet. Use this information to your advantage.

5. Keep a good attitude and, just for fun, see how well you can do during the rest of the race.

Once you have cleared out from the confusion of the start, take the time to plan your strategy in wide-open water so when you do maneuver, you can concentrate on boat handling. I like to talk about the tactical options on the windward leg beforehand. By doing that, I feel more comfortable with the plan when it actually takes place.

Keep your wind clear when sailing upwind. Disturbed wind from leading boats can extend as far to leeward as six to eight mast lengths. If you find yourself in an area of disturbed wind, tack away and create your own sailing lane. This takes planning.

When you're playing windshifts, sail into the new wind at least two or three boatlengths before making your tack. This insures that you don't immediately tack out of the new wind. It also insures that the puff is for real. Sometimes the wind just dissipates.

When tacking upwind, I like to use the lead-boat blocker technique. This is effective for boats on port or starboard tack. In football, a runner uses blockers to clear his path. You can do the same in sailing by using one or two boats as blockers to create a clear sailing area. Before tacking, wait until one or two boats have sailed just behind you or just ahead of you. Continue on for five boatlengths before tacking. Maneuver your boat so you're to windward and behind, but clear of the disturbed wind and waves of the lead boats. Now as you cross the fleet, your boat is shielded from boats

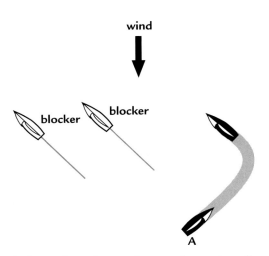

Blockers—here the two boats to leeward—allow Boat A to sail in smoother water and clear wind for a longer period of time. The blockers protect Boat A from any boats approaching from the opposite tack.

approaching on the opposite tack. This technique is effective on boats of all sizes. Using two or more blockers is even more effective. This allows you to sail in smoother water and clearer winds for a longer period of time.

A starboard-tack advantage is an aggressive tactic on the windward leg. Under the racing rules, boats sailing on port tack must stay clear of boats on starboard. Another powerful tactic is using the exhaust from your sails to blanket the wind of your opponents.

There are four ways to tack on another boat:

1. Tack directly upwind of another boat. I find it best to tack slightly ahead of their apparent wind, so there is no opportunity for them to pass you. The boat you have tacked on will either be forced to sail in your bad wind or tack away.

2. Tack directly in front of another boat. This has a damaging psychological effect because the boat you have tacked on must look at your stern all the time. The wind shadow is not as brutal, but there is little chance that you will be passed. This position forces the trailing boat to pinch or bear off and lose considerable distance. Eventually the trailing boat will tack.

3. The third method of making a blanketing tack is a safe leeward position (lee bow, see art below). Instead of crossing another boat, tack to leeward and ahead. This is a particularly good position if you expect the wind to head. However, if the wind is going to lift you, it's dangerous to allow another boat to sit on your windward hip because you will lose distance.

4. The fourth method is covering from behind. If the fleet is heading left and you expect more wind or a favorable windshift on the left side of the course (even if you are behind), cover by tacking and staying to windward and behind the other boats. When the new wind arrives you'll be right in the thick of it and lose little distance, compared with sailing away to the right and losing more distance.

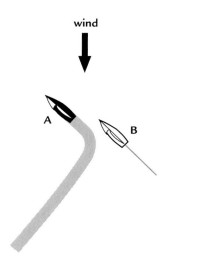

Boat A tacks into a safe leeward position (lee bow). The exhaust from Boat A's sail will slow Boat B down.

Remember that you only want to tack when your crew is prepared and your boat is moving at full speed. There are generally four main reasons for tacking on a windward leg:

1. You've been headed. Sail into the header at least two boatlengths before you tack so that you stay on the new lifted tack longer.

2. You're in blanketed wind. Tack to clear yourself, but be careful that you don't tack into another boat's disturbed wind.

3. To avoid waves, approach them parallel to your course. Many times it's better to tack and ride waves than to smash into them head-on. When you do tack, wait for a smooth spot in the waves. The tactician should make this call.

4. To give room to a right-of-way boat.

5. If you are behind (wrong end at the start, slow speed, missed shift, bad air), make one tack and avoid extra maneuvers to stay clear of starboard-tack boats.

When you're sailing upwind, watch carefully where the fleet is heading. If the majority of the competition is heading to one side of the course, you should be sailing nearby to protect yourself from a big windshift. Sailboats like to stick together in packs.

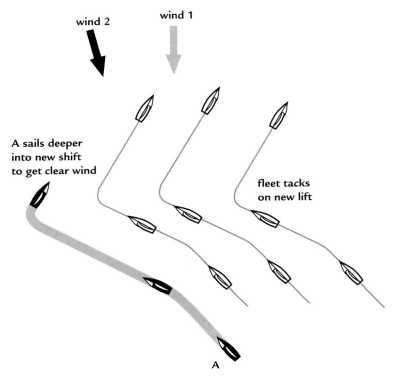

Covering from behind is an effective tactic when you expect more wind or a favorable windshift. Boat A is well behind the fleet. The wind shifts to the left (wind 2). The fleet tacks on to port. Boat A continues on for several boatlengths before making the tack to get clear wind.

It is dangerous to take a flyer. Unless you're absolutely sure that splitting away from the fleet will work, it's better to stay close.

If you're a leading boat and you want your competitors to stay close, keep a loose cover. (*To cover* means to stay with the fleet.) Keeping a loose cover is a defensive strategy where you put your boat in a controlling position between the next mark of the course and your competition. Allow the trailing boats to keep clear wind. By doing this, they won't tack away. Sam Merrick, who raced with me in E-scows, referred to this as "keeping competitors behaving."

Any time you have an opportunity to slow the competition down, do so. Your goal is to gain ground while the competition loses distance.

On the windward leg, situations often develop slowly. Don't try to pass every boat at once. Think in terms of passing one or two boats at a time. Keep working to sail better, improve your boatspeed, and take advantage of windshifts.

HEADERS AND LIFTS

If you see a heading puff ahead, sail fast by bearing off one or two degrees to get to the new header early. If you anticipate a lifting windshift, sail a high course or even tack

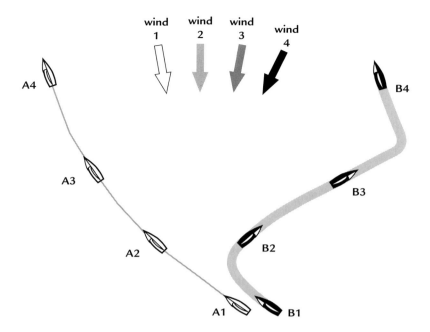

The wind is shifting to the right. Boat B heads to the right side of the course to be on the inside of this persistent shift. This is sometimes known as "sailing around the world" if you are on the outside of the windshift (Boat A).

over to get to the lift sooner. This allows you to sail on the tail end of a fading lift on your original tack before the wind shifts.

If you are sailing in a persistent lift that keeps clocking to the right, for example, there's a danger of being caught "sailing around the world." If you stay on this continual lift, you'll end up sailing a circular path and you'll never quite get to you destination. To get out of this trap, tack to the inside so you are windward of the other boats.

There are times when it is better to sail on a lift and still be in another boat's blanketed wind. This is particularly true on the final approach to the finish, when you're near a windward mark, or when you anticipate an even bigger windshift ahead.

If you're sailing behind a group of boats and they tack on every shift, leaving you in disturbed air, consider tacking away when the group ahead is lifted. But only sail several boatlengths before tacking back to the original course. While you lose distance with the extra two tacks, at least you sail in clear air and eventually stay in phase with the other boats.

CROSSING TACKS UPWIND

When you're crossing boats upwind on the racecourse, it is a cat-and-mouse game to keep other boats from tacking on your wind. To fool a boat into sailing past your wind, sail a high course (5 degrees above normal). The boat ahead will continue sailing until they are on your wind. Once they've passed head-to-wind during their

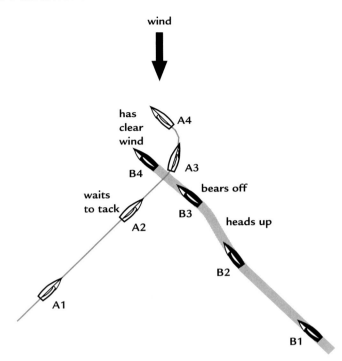

Boat B is being crossed by Boat A. To fool Boat A into sailing past its wind before tacking, Boat B sails a higher course. Boat A waits until it thinks it is in a blocking position before tacking on top. When Boat A tacks (A3), Boat B bears off (B3) to its normal course and now has clear wind.

tack, bear off to your normal course and you'll have clear wind to leeward.

If you want a crossing boat to tack early, sail a low course so the crew believes they are on your wind. When they begin their tack, resume your normal course and you'll have clear wind to windward.

There is a protocol on the water when crossing another boat. If, for example, my crew and I are on starboard and the approaching port-tack boat is not going to make it across our bow, I sometimes wave the port tacker across so I can continue sailing on my desired course. Get the attention of the other crew and hail that they will cross cleanly. Use a hand motion to back up

your verbal hail to reduce confusion. You might have to bear away to let them across. A small loss is better than being tacked on.

There is always uncertainty when two boats meet on opposite tacks. I remember one particular regatta. I was on port tack. I hailed to the starboard tacker, "Am I going to make it?" His answer had a chilling effect, "Well, I don't know." I chuckled to myself and quickly tacked away. It was clear I was going to have trouble with this boat.

I remember a tight crossing situation while racing in a Maxi boat regatta on *Matador*[2]. We were sailing on port tack and trying to cross *Il Moro di Venezia*, *Matador*'s archrival being steered by Paul Cayard. We

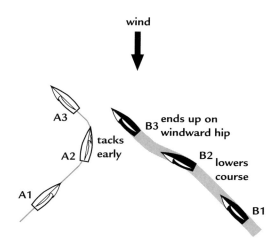

wind

A3

A2 tacks
early

A1

B3 ends up on
windward hip

B2 lowers
course

B1

Encouraging a crossing boat to tack early is an effective maneuver for gaining advantage. Boat A is crossing Boat B. Boat B sails a lower course. Boat A tacks early to try to block Boat B's wind. But Boat B returns to its original course with clear air. Boat A did not notice that Boat B was sailing artificially low.

Matador[2] *and* Il Moro di Venezia *enjoyed an intense rivalry in the Maxi World Championship. The crews spent little time looking at each other.*

just made it across. At that moment I could feel sweat form on my brow. It had been very close. Instead of yelling "Protest," Cayard said, "Nice going, you made it." Cayard proved himself to be an honorable sportsman. A lesser sailor might have taken a cheap shot. The moral of the story is that it's better to give a little room instead of forcing an issue. This keeps everyone out of the protest room. Remember when boats meet, sail at full speed. Bear off a degree or two to accelerate and to make your maneuvering easier.

Be careful when making the final approach to a windward mark. Many helmsmen will pinch their boat to get around the mark. But the problem with pinching is the boat slows down and makes leeway.

I remember sailing a big boat off Miami. Our young helmsman, playing Mr. Macho,

continually sailed higher to fetch the mark. Unfortunately, the current was setting the boat down on the mark. About six boat-lengths out it was clear to me (as tactician) that we weren't going to make it. I suggested making two quick tacks. The young helmsman wouldn't hear of it. We hit the mark on our beam and had to make a penalty turn to absolve the foul. Our young helmsman learned a lesson. After that we made extra tacks to keep out of trouble.

READING WINDSHIFTS
When reading the wind, use the compass as an aid to record the high and low courses on

each tack. For example, on starboard tack you might be sailing at 270 degrees but the wind is shifty and you're able to sail as high as 290 and as low as 260 degrees. Because you recorded your courses you know the wind is shifting through 30 degrees. When the wind gets above or below these numbers, you know there is a new trend developing. For example, the wind might suddenly be moving farther to the right than you had seen throughout the day. When deciding whether to tack or not, wait until you're headed below the average compass course. This helps prevent tacking earlier than necessary. Numbers are valuable references. It is easy to lose track of the changing wind.

In one Block Island Race Week we found ourselves in sixth place after the windward mark. On the downwind leg I noticed the wind trending to the east. I also watched the fleet ahead on their beat to windward and noticed the wind had continued to turn even farther to the east. After the leeward mark I made a firm decision to sail toward the east side of the course, even though the fleet ahead split to the west. The persistent shift arrived. We moved from sixth place to first place. The key to our victory was having the courage to stick with our conviction that the wind was shifting to the east, keeping track of the wind via the compass, and observing how the wind affected the rest of the fleet.

If a boat tacks on your wind while you're sailing across the course to the anticipated favored side, don't tack away. Consider driving through on the leeward side of this boat or hanging in the blanketed wind until the new shift reaches your boat.

Things don't always go according to plan, so you must learn to adjust. Ask yourself, what action will give our boat the greatest gain? If you were heading for a 3-degree windshift, it might not be worth sailing in blanketed wind for a long period of time. But if you see a 20-degree windshift on the horizon with much stronger velocity, then it's worth paying an early price for the long-term gain. Unless the other boat is perfectly situated on your wind, you can hang on for a long time.

COVERING THE COMPETITION

If you're sure the fleet is heading the wrong way and you find yourself on the opposite side of the course, you should still cover from behind. In other words, once you have leverage on the fleet it's best to consolidate your position. For example, if the fleet is heading left and you are on the right side of the course and expecting the wind to shift to the right, it's best to cover the fleet and not risk losing more ground if the right-hand shift does not materialize. If the right-hand shift does come, you will gain and will have protected your position. As mentioned previously, to cover means to stay with the fleet. It's dangerous to split a long way from the other boats. If the wind shifts favorably, you will still gain considerable distance. But if you miscalculate and the wind doesn't shift, at least you won't throw away extra distance. The farther you are from another boat, the more distance you'll gain or lose when the wind eventually shifts.

Try to drive the boats around you to one side of the course. Once you get several boats on the layline their options disappear.

You can do this by tacking on several boats' wind simultaneously or by using your starboard advantage. Blocking another boat's wind is another tactic that slows down the competition or forces them to tack away. Be careful, however, of making too many tacks because you lose distance. Also, if you tack on the same boat repeatedly they may look for revenge in later races. Use your wind shadow wisely when it really counts.

To force a fleet to one side of the course use a combination of loose and tight covering positions. When you cover a boat loosely, you position yourself so you don't disturb its wind. This is when your competitors are sailing in the direction that you want them to. But when you cover a boat tightly, your goal is to force the trailing boat (or boats) to tack away.

You will gain position by sailing to leeward and ahead of a group of boats. If the wind lifts, they overshoot the mark. If the wind heads, they fall into your wind shadow. If the wind stays the same, you are still in a controlling position.

In the beginning of a race or series, you should be more concerned with playing windshifts rather than covering specific

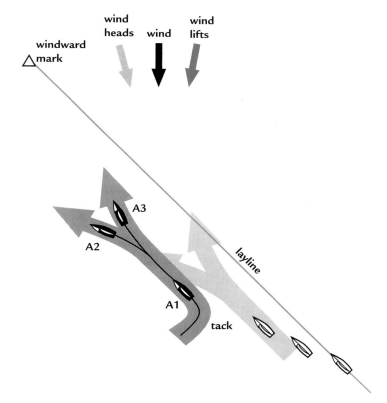

It's possible to gain an advantage by sailing to leeward and ahead of a group of boats. Boat A tacks near the layline from the windward mark. If the wind heads, the boats behind fall to leeward. If the wind lifts, the boats behind overshoot the windward mark. If the wind stays the same, Boat A is still in a controlling position.

boats. Toward the end of a series, your philosophy should change. Protect your position. It's better to make two extra tacks—even if it means you risk losing distance—to guarantee a victory. Don't allow another boat an opportunity to pass. Late in the race it's better to lose some lead and yet stay in control at the head of the pack

If there is a pest covering you on the racecourse, you might consider either a false tack or a half tack.

A *false tack* is when you start turning your boat and the lead boat overreacts and immediately tacks. As soon as you are head-to-wind and you see the boat ahead pass head-to-wind, resume your original course. In match racing, this technique rarely works because the other boat is paying attention. But you can often get away with it in fleet racing.

A *half tack* is where you fill the jib on the new tack but don't come all the way

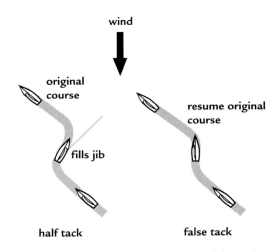

With a false tack a boat pretends to tack by sailing head to wind and then resumes the same course. A half tack is when a boat tacks, fills its sails and immediately tacks back to the original course.

down on your fastest close-hauled course. As soon as the jib fills, turn back onto the original tack. The boat ahead just might continue on for speed, allowing you to get out of phase on the opposite tack. The advantage of a half tack is you don't lose as much distance compared with a false tack.

When trying to force a boat ahead to maneuver, create commotion by hailing loudly to your crew, "Get ready to go about." Or you might ask several crew members to stand up simultaneously, to make it look as if you are preparing to tack. On the other hand, if you don't want the boat ahead of you to know your plan, be sneaky. Avoid telegraphing your next maneuver by tacking your boat while everybody is sitting still.

Watch out for the opposite scenario: a boat pulling a false tack or half tack on you. Watch other boats' actions carefully. Instead of looking at the crew, watch the boat turning against the horizon. I also like to observe another boat's sails. Once you see they are beyond head-to-wind, then it's time to make your own turn. Never turn faster than normal—this helps prevent getting caught by a false tack.

If it's crucial for you to cover another boat and they have faked you with a false tack or half tack, simply continue sailing straight until you are up to full speed. Wait to tack until you are at maximum speed. This keeps you in phase and you won't lose as much distance.

The key to sailing upwind is a positive attitude. If events don't go the way you plan, keep plugging. There are many opportunities to gain. Use common sense.

Look at the performance of your boat compared to the competition. Learn from the trends that have developed throughout the day. Take the attitude that you are never going to give up. Strange things can happen and you want to be ready for any opportunity. Concentrate!

SPLITTING FROM THE FLEET

Whether to stay with a fleet of boats or split in the opposite direction is an important call. If you're behind, the only way you can get an annoying covering boat to tack is to keep splitting tacks. It's dangerous to allow a competitor to sit on your windward quarter for long periods. If the wind heads you, you'll gain. If the wind lifts you, however, you'll lose considerable distance. If you're ahead, make a covering tack to push your competitor closer to the layline, thus taking away his passing room. But keep an eye on the rest of the fleet.

If you find yourself behind and hopelessly out of the race, it's time to go for the gold. Go ahead and do something bizarre, something weird. It is such a thrill when you make an unexpected move work. In a match-race regatta in New York Harbor I was trailing a boat by three boatlengths. The current was running hard against us. As we passed Liberty Island I noticed there was little current on the back side of the island. We jibed off to sail behind the island. It was shallow so we kept the boat heeled over to cross the mud flats. As we came out the other side of the island, our rival was still stuck in the current and well behind. It was a bold move that worked.

Splitting from the fleet should be done with great care. But if you are behind, heading in the opposite direction could give you a chance to catch up later.

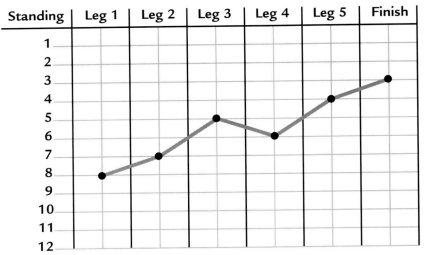

Standing	Leg 1	Leg 2	Leg 3	Leg 4	Leg 5	Finish

Make a graph of your progress on the racecourse. This is a good way to remember what happened so you can focus on improving in the next race.

CHARTING YOUR PROGRESS

To chart your progress in a regatta, make a graph after each day of racing. On the top of the graph, make one column for each leg of the course; on the side of the graph, add a space where you can plot your standing after each leg. Plot your standing at the end of each leg so you can monitor your progress. Plot each race in a different color so you can detect any trends in your performance.

Downwind Tactics

Reaching the windward mark brings with it a sense of accomplishment. Things change dramatically when you sail downwind. On the leeward leg, it is warmer, drier, the boat is upright, it's more comfortable, and it's fast. There is an old expression: "Gentlemen only sail with the wind." It's a nice concept, but racing downwind presents many opportunities to gain ground on the competition.

Before rounding the windward mark, decide which side of the course you're going to favor. The trends on the windward leg give you an idea. Ask yourself these questions: Which side of the course is favored? Is there more wind on the right or the left? Which direction was the wind blowing? If it was favored on starboard going upwind, it will be favored on the port jibe going downwind.

Once you reach the windward mark your priorities, in this order, are:

1. Concentrate on speed.

2. Maneuver into a favorable tactical position.

3. Set new sails.

4. Make minor adjustments to the rig and sails.

5. Spend time on crew comfort, such as passing the water around or taking off foul-weather gear.

It pays to rotate helmsmen on larger boats. But don't just jump off the wheel. Handing off the wheel is like handing off the baton in a relay race. Do this with care. The new helmsman needs to know the course, where the wind is, whether you are in a puff, and the timing of the next jibe. Always hand the helm over when the boat is sailing fast.

One of my more difficult mark-rounding sequences took place during a Liberty Cup Regatta in New York Harbor. The current, as always, was swift. Sailing upwind with the current, it was difficult to bear off around the mark and start sailing downwind. The competition would suddenly be close. It was easy to mishandle the mark.

When the current is strong, as it was in the Liberty Cup Regatta, the helmsman needs to concentrate just on steering and let the crew handle the sails. If the helmsman is also handling the mainsail, be sure to ease it out quickly since the most important adjustment when rounding the windward mark is to dump the mainsail out fast. If the main is over-trimmed, it's difficult to bear off. And you lose considerable distance when bearing off gradually.

The tactician should give the helmsman a compass course or a landmark to steer for after rounding. Take the guesswork out of it. On many downwind legs, boats seem to join in a parade and simply following each other without regard to a heading to the leeward mark.

The next challenge is raising the spinnaker. Don't be hasty on the call. In heavy

This Liberty Cup crew works hard to battle the strong currents of New York Harbor. Lady Liberty keeps a watchful eye over the action.

winds and choppy seas it pays to steer the boat down on course and get the boat upright before hoisting the spinnaker. I've been in many regattas where I've passed boats that have set the spinnaker prematurely and lost speed. Your response is to simply sail over the top, blanket their wind, take the lead, and then set your spinnaker. In light wind, bear away slowly to keep your momentum and apparent wind strength. If you bear off too fast, the apparent wind will diminish quickly and you'll lose speed.

On a larger boat, the foredeck crew should wait for the tactician's call before hoisting the spinnaker. The foredeck crew can sometimes lose tactical perspective. Although their job is to get the spinnaker up and flying as quickly as possible, there are many reasons to delay setting the spinnaker. The tactician should set the pace and make the call.

The Reach Leg

The fastest point of sailing is reaching. It's a shame that the modern trend in racing dictates windward-leeward courses. Reaches seem to be forgotten, and yet there are many opportunities to pass when boats are sailing their fastest. If a group of boats starts sailing high, the question is whether you should stay with the pack, or bear off and sail low. If your boat is last in line, it's better to bear off and sail directly for the mark. But if you're in front of the pack, it's important to keep up by splitting the difference between the course of the boat behind you and your course to the mark.

On a reach leg, sail the course that anticipates the new wind direction. If you expect a header, it's best to sail high early

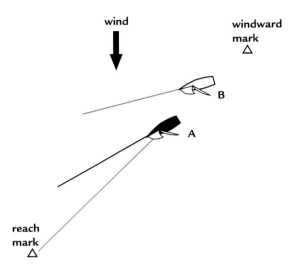

When sailing to leeward, split the difference between your course for the next mark and the course the boat behind is sailing.

and use the header to get down to the reach mark. But if you think the wind is going to lift you, sail a low course early so you sail on a better reaching angle at the end of the leg.

Since reaching is the fastest point of sail, there are large speed differences between boats. Get the spinnaker up and drawing, get the crew to windward, and start sailing fast. If another boat is sitting on your wind, give that boat one hard luff—or simply bear off and sail your own course. The most important thing is to avoid locking up with another boat or even a group of boats.

Keep your wind clear on the reach leg. Watch your masthead fly. This indicates the direction of the *apparent wind*, which is the influence of your boat moving forward on the true wind direction. Apparent wind is farther forward relative to your boat as a result of your boat's forward motion. The masthead fly is a good indicator of whether your wind is clear of windward boats.

When you are behind, your only option is to sail a higher course to make the leeward leg longer and therefore give yourself more time and opportunity to pass. Also, keep the action in the center of the course so you have an option of where to sail. The trailing boat has the advantage of getting a new puff and reacting to windshifts first. A leading boat should drive the action out to the layline.

One of the most famous passes in sailing took place during the 2003 America's Cup. The Swiss challenger *Alinghi* was trailing the New Zealand defender by two boatlengths. *Alinghi* began reaching, and *Team New Zealand (TNZ)* matched her course. *TNZ* had plenty of options to keep *Alinghi*

One of the most exciting moments in America's Cup history took place during the second race of the 2003 match. Here Alinghi, *using a staysail between spinnaker and mainsail, passes* Team New Zealand *to windward.* Team New Zealand *does not have a staysail flying. This could have been the difference in speed between the boats.*

back, including luffing hard, bearing off and splitting the difference between the course of *Alinghi* and *TNZ*'s course to the leeward mark, or simply jibing away. Instead, as *Alinghi* sailed a little higher, *TNZ* matched her course again. Slowly, *Alinghi* began sailing over the top. *Alinghi* set a flatter spinnaker and a staysail and kept sailing a higher and higher course. *TNZ* used no staysail at all and her spinnaker was too full for close reaching. When it was too late, *TNZ* finally bore off with *Alinghi* blanketing *TNZ*'s wind. *Alinghi* surged into the lead and won the race by just seven seconds. *Team New Zealand*'s mistake was playing *Alinghi*'s game, making gradual alterations of course. Tactically, *TNZ* could have sailed a lower course, luffed hard, or simply jibed away. It was also surprising that *TNZ* did not set her staysail.

As you approach the reach mark, fight hard to gain an overlap on the leading boats. But if you just miss getting an overlap it isn't the end of the world. Stay wide and make a tactical rounding so you pass close to the reach mark after your jibe.

Watch the actions of the boats ahead of you carefully. This is where smooth boat handling comes into play. A good jibe is crucial at this moment. If your competition has difficulty jibing, there's a good opportunity to pass. Sail a higher course than the boat(s) ahead of you until you blanket their wind. Make this move dramatic. Small increments invite trouble. If you make a big course alteration when you are behind and to windward, the leading boats may let you go, particularly if they are having trouble filling their spinnakers.

If the wind is building and it's difficult

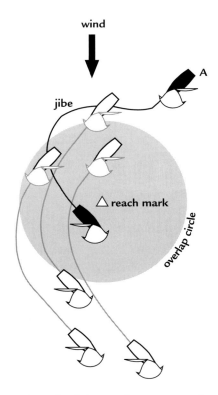

At a reach mark, if the next leg is going to be tight, stay wide early and pass close to the mark as Boat A has. If the next reach leg is going to be broad with the wind well aft, stay close to the reach mark, then make your maneuver ending up wide on the new jibe so you have a better angle toward the leeward mark.

to fly the spinnaker, work to sail a high course early so you still have room to bear off and make it down to the reach mark. If the wind continues to blow harder and you can no longer carry the spinnaker, take the spinnaker down and sail under jib. The biggest mistake on the reach leg is sailing too low a course and then having to work back upwind to round the mark.

Take the current into account. If the current is sweeping you to leeward, sail a few degrees higher. If the current is taking you to windward, sail low a few degrees. Take bearings on the mark compared with the shoreline to determine whether you are being set by the current. If the bearing to the shore stays steady, your course is steady. If you lose bearing, the current is setting you away from the mark. Your goal is to maintain a steady bearing.

If you question whether you can carry the spinnaker on a reach leg, it might be best to first sail with the jib by steering about five degrees high of the next mark. Hoist the spinnaker when you're confident that you can carry it. Plan for the spinnaker by sailing a course higher than the next mark so when you do set you have more room to leeward—this allows you to bear off once the spinnaker fills. Setting the spinnaker in the middle of the leg gives the

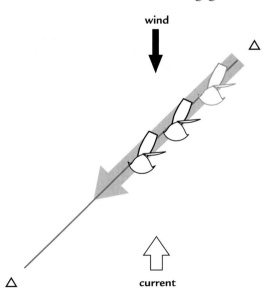

If the current is sweeping you to windward, set a course that is lower than the mark ahead to compensate for set and drift.

crew time to prepare for the maneuver.

Changing spinnakers (also known as a *peel*) must be done with care. Don't let the other boat know you are making a change. As a rule, keep your next sail on deck or at least near a hatch so it's ready to go. Have a second sheet led all the way aft. Taking these early steps will minimize the time needed to change a sail.

Racing aboard *Matador* alongside *Il Moro de Venezia* there was a question of what was the fastest spinnaker. The wind was gusting between 25 and 30 mph. At times the true wind was ranging between 100 degrees and 150 degrees. On the final approach to the finish, which was just 5 miles away (keep in mind, we were sailing at 14 knots), the wind suddenly shifted well aft until the true wind was at 160 degrees. Within seconds *Il Moro*'s crew was popping through every hatch and hauling up a new sail. With a lighter running spinnaker set, *Il Moro* started to gain. By the time we recovered on *Matador*, *Il Moro* had earned a four-boatlength lead that she never relinquished.

After the race I talked to one of *Il Moro*'s crew members and congratulated him on such a fast sail change. He told me they had planned for over an hour to catch us off guard. We weren't ready. They were—and that was the difference in the race. The moral of this story is to be prepared. But don't telegraph your intentions to the competition. We had to give *Il Moro* credit for the gambit.

Some of my most favorite moments in sailing took place on reach legs in heavy wind. In one J/22 regatta, we rounded the windward mark in twentieth place. There were forty boats racing and I wasn't happy. But we got our spinnaker up, put the pole on the headstay, eased the vang on the mainsail, and the boat took off down a wave. Our competitors were having difficulty. There was lots of wind, at least 25 knots. I noticed that boats ahead of us were spinning out or bearing way off to get control of their spinnakers. We maintained a steady course toward the reach mark. By the time we arrived we were in eighth place. Our crew had practiced jibes many times during the summer. We nailed the jibe and continued down the second reach leg. Again boats ahead of us were having trouble. The thing that we did correctly was twist the mainsail aloft by easing the vang so the boat stayed under control. We favored the spinnaker over the mainsail. In other words, the main luffed frequently, allowing the boat to stay under control. This helped me steer a direct course for the leeward mark. By the time we got there we were in third place. It was a big psychological lift for our team.

On a triangular course it pays to sail higher than other boats on the second reach. On this leg it is important to get the inside overlap at the leeward mark. Fight hard! If you are ahead, sail high for a couple of boatlengths before bearing off. This will discourage trailing boats from starting a luffing match. Balance is tricky here because if the fleet is sailing too high on the second reach, it's better to sail a lower course. This is a judgment call. The action of a fleet tends to repeat, so if you are having multiple races and everyone sails very high on a reach leg, you know that the low course will often pay off.

The Run

On the run, there are many opportunities to pass. It's just as important to play the windshifts sailing downwind as it is upwind. Again, the rule of thumb is to jibe on the lifts. If you see a puff of wind passing your stern and not hitting your boat, this is an indication that it's better to jibe onto the other course. This keeps you sailing in stronger wind and on a more direct course to the leeward mark.

In handicap racing, there is often a problem of a larger boat attacking a smaller boat. If you happen to be the smaller boat, it is simply better to let them sail by. If you

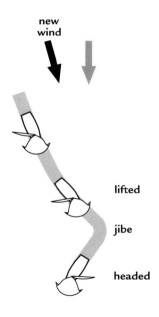

Jibe on the lifts. If the wind shifts aft so that you are sailing the same course at a lower speed, it is an indication that you should jibe on to the other course to sail closer to the leeward mark.

think the larger boat is going to blanket your wind for a long period of time (more than four boatlengths), then simply jibe away. The general mistake in this case is getting into a continual luffing match with a larger boat. You lose distance to the fleet and inevitably you'll still get passed.

There are three offensive weapons to use on a downwind leg:

1. The wind shadow of your sails

2. Starboard advantage

3. Luffing rights

Use these weapons effectively. If you are planning to jibe, for example, position your boat so that your wind shadow is just ahead of the apparent wind angle of a leeward boat. This will force the leading boat to jibe away. If there's an annoying boat just to windward of you, a sudden luff will make

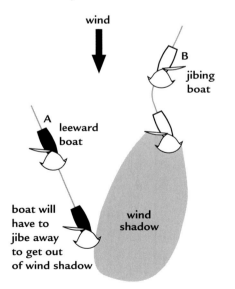

Before jibing, plan your position so your wind shadow is just ahead of the leeward boat. The leeward boat will not sail effectively in this position and will be forced to sail slowly or jibe away.

the windward boat behave in the future. If you plan to luff a boat, make sure that your crew is prepared.

As I've mentioned, don't jibe gradually. Trim your sails as you bear up, be sure the lead on your spinnaker is well aft (you might consider easing the vang off), and turn the boat without warning. The windward boat will get the idea and leave you alone. Jibe at full speed so you turn faster.

Starboard advantage is a powerful tool when sailing downwind. The problem arises when you force another boat to jibe and that boat ends up sitting on your wind. When approaching a boat while on starboard, consider sailing a few degrees high. When boats engage, you always want to be sailing at full speed. Give a clearly stated "Starboard." Try to get the port-tack boat to either cross your stern or jibe early, allowing you to sail in clear wind.

Make your jibes crisp. This is why practice is so important. Use your compass as a reference for the next course to steer. When I'm on starboard jibe I note the course. For example, we are sailing a course of 100 degrees. When I jibe to port, my course might be 40 degrees. This tells me I'm jibing through 60 degrees. If I decide to return to the starboard jibe, I know that my course to steer is 100 degrees. Once back on starboard, you can make adjustments to your course; but at least you have a reliable reference. Both the tactician and helmsman should memorize every new course.

When I am helmsman on smaller boats, especially dinghies, I sometimes test the spinnaker sheet to get a feel of how much I can bear off in the puffs and how much I

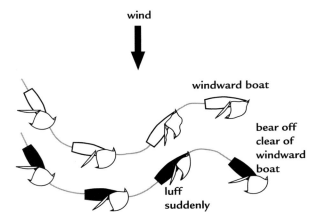

If you have an annoying boat to windward, under the rules you have the ability to luff suddenly directly into the wind. The windward boat will get the message and will stay away.

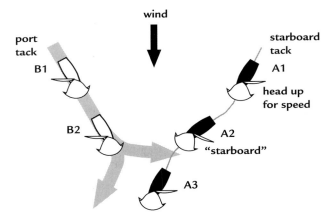

When approaching another boat always accelerate for speed so you have more maneuverability and you are more intimidating. Boat A, on starboard tack, is sailing high for speed. As it approaches Boat B it will try to force the port-tack boat to cross its stern or jibe early.

should harden up in the light spots. Once I get a feel for steering with the spinnaker, then I turn the spinnaker sheet back to the crew to trim.

When you are on a larger boat passing a smaller boat, there's always the question of whether to pass to windward or leeward. Psychologically, the crew on the smaller boat wants the larger boat to sail to lee-ward. If you sail close by, there is the danger of the smaller boat making a hard luff. Therefore, if you are in a larger boat and you plan to pass to windward, start sailing higher about four boatlengths astern. If you see the boat ahead alter course to sail higher, then bear off to pass to leeward. Once you get to the boat's apparent wind on the leeward side, harden up to move

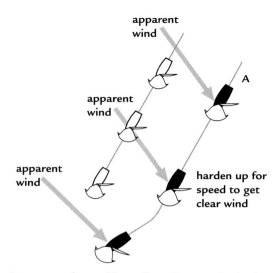

apparent wind

apparent wind

apparent wind

A

harden up for speed to get clear wind

On a run, a leeward boat (Boat A) can sail a higher course to gain clear wind from a boat to windward. Here Boat A has hardened up to move its apparent wind forward. Boat A gives away some of its lead doing this maneuver but won't be passed as long as its wind is not blocked.

your apparent wind forward. Remember you always have the option of jibing away.

On long legs, concentrate on playing the windshifts. Big gains can be made. An important question is whether it's worth jibing on a windshift. On most boats you lose about two boatlengths during a jibe. Ask yourself, will the windshift gain back this distance lost, and then some more? If the wind shifts at least 10 degrees, it's easy to recover lost ground. Windshifts are usually led by a new, stronger breeze. Jibing on a windshift not only shortens your course to the next mark but also keeps you in stronger wind.

One of my favorite tricks on a downwind leg is a fake jibe. This takes considerable coordination by the crew. It works best when two boats are sailing on star-

board jibe. If you are the leeward boat, begin bearing off. Talk through the maneuver in advance but don't let the competition hear you. Make all the motions you normally would. But when the critical moment comes, instead of yelling "trip" to move the pole, yell something else like "pole" or "do it now." But don't actually disengage the pole from the guy. When you see the other boat trip their pole away, resume your normal course. The competition will scramble to return to their original course or be forced to get out of your way since you have the starboard right-of-way. The key to a fake jibe is good communication with the trimmers and foredeck crew.

One of the questions on a downwind leg is whether to *sail by the lee*. You are sailing by the lee when you are sailing downwind and the wind is hitting your sails over the leeward quarter (this point of sail will be covered in more detail in chapter 10). Sailing by the lee can provide an inside overlap on another boat or allow you to bear off and gain distance on a wave without going through a jibe. You should avoid sailing by the lee for a long period of time (I suggest no more than ten boatlengths). Sailing by the lee works if you can gain leeward distance without losing speed. But short bites to leeward can also be quite effective. Taking a bite to leeward is the equivalent of scalloping on a windward leg. (*Scalloping* is the act of sailing a higher course to windward or a lower course to leeward to gain more distance toward the mark. Usually a scallop is a slow turn or arch over six to eight boatlengths.)

In heavy winds stability is reduced when sailing by the lee. I've watched many dinghy sailors capsize to windward when sailing by the lee after being caught off guard by a small windshift. If you are doing this on a bigger boat in heavy winds and the boat starts rolling out of control, the solution is simple: head up and regain balance.

GAINING OR LOSING?

On the downwind leg, it's important to gauge whether you are gaining or losing compared to your competition. It's one way to learn if your strategy of playing windshifts and sailing fast is working. If you're racing on a larger boat, assign one person the job of taking bearings to determine whether you are gaining or losing.

Take a quick line of sight by observing a competitor's mainsail. If you see the forward part of the main, then you're ahead of the boat. If you see the aft part of the main, then that boat is ahead of you. If you see both the forward and aft parts of the mainsail, then your boats are even. As you sail downwind and you start seeing more and more of the forward part of the main, then you're gaining. However, if you start

A Little Help From My Friends

In one Maxi regatta off Miami, I was struggling aboard *Matador²* deciding whether to do a bear-away or jibe set on the downwind leg. The bear-away set was favored by the wind direction but we didn't gain on the boats that consistently jibed to the inside.

In the first two races we rounded the first mark with a comfortable lead. Unfortunately, the lead evaporated because the inside boats gained. Why? At a dinner with my longtime friend Tom Whidden I explained the situation. Tom said he noticed that the boats that jibed inside were getting a favorable set and drift by the current toward the leeward mark. The outside boats, which included *Matador²*, were actually getting pushed away from the mark by the current. In the third race we jibed to the inside and made a big gain. I was grateful to Tom for his observation. Get in the habit of asking your friends for their comments after a race. Of course you will be expected to return the favor by giving your own impressions.

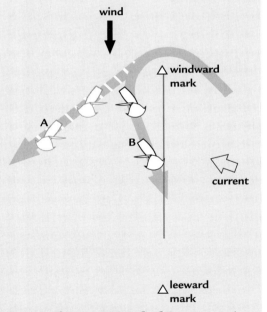

Because of the set and drift of the current, the boat that did a bear-away set at the windward mark (Boat A) is being swept away. The inside boat (Boat B) is using the current to set it on the mark. The boat on port tack arrives at the leeward mark earlier.

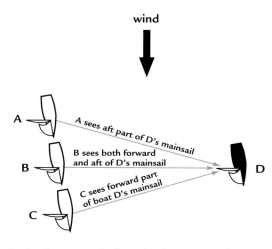

Study the mainsail of another boat to see if you are gaining or losing. If you see the forward part of the boat's mainsail, you are ahead (Boat C is ahead of Boat D). If you seem to be even with the luff and leech, your boats are even (Boats B and D). If you see the aft part of the boat's mainsail, that boat is ahead of you (Boat A is behind D).

seeing more of the aft part of the mainsail, then the other boat is gaining.

Another reference is comparing the progress of another boat with objects on the shoreline. If you seem to be gaining shoreline ahead of another boat, then you are moving ahead. As previously mentioned, this is sometimes referred to as "making trees" because you see trees appearing ahead of the boat you're observing.

DOWNWIND TECHNIQUES

❖ Play the boom vang. Keep the top sail batten parallel to the boom. On a reach leg in heavy air, let the boom ride up to spill wind out of the top of the mainsail. Avoid allowing the boat to heel over too far. Ease the main out in advance of puffs. Use the mainsheet, traveler, and

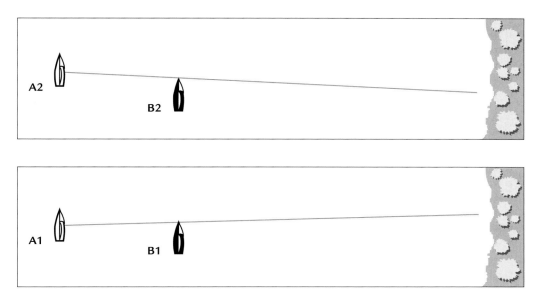

Use objects on shore as reference when comparing your progress to other boats. Here Boat A sights along Boat B to shore, observing that trees on shore are appearing ahead of Boat B. Boat A is said to be "making trees" on Boat B along the shoreline.

vang to keep the boat on its lines. You can also carry a luff in the spinnaker.

❖ On a run, keep a slight windward heel to balance the helm. In heavy wind, keep weight aft. In light wind, move weight forward.

❖ When sailing in wide-open waters, plan your strategy for the next leg.

❖ When you are in close proximity to other boats, concentrate on speed, your position, and your next maneuver.

Tactics for Rounding the Leeward Mark

The most important priority when rounding the leeward mark is getting an inside overlap. (If a windward boat has an overlap on a leeward boat has they enter the two-boatlength circle—an imaginary circle two boatlengths around the mark—the windward boat has the right to all the buoy room needed to pass.) If you are on a racecourse with a gate, then you have an alternative mark to round. (The gate is actually two buoys.) Competitors have to decide which one to round. The idea is to get the fleet to split on opposite courses for the windward leg. It is an interesting tactical choice. The race committee should work to keep both marks square to the wind. The real choice is which side of the

racecourse you want to favor on the next leg and use the gate that sends you off on the desired tack.

If there is just one leeward mark, fight hard to gain the inside overlap. If you miss, slow down and sail wide so that you are sailing close-hauled as you round.

On large boats crews get jumpy as they approach the leeward mark. In many cases they'll take the spinnaker down early. This gives you an opportunity to gain an overlap well outside the two-boatlength circle. If the inside boat takes the spinnaker down too late, there may be an opportunity to round inside. Watch for it.

If you are the boat ahead, however, it's important to establish that boats behind don't have an overlap. Establish this by hailing to the trailing boat, "No room." The

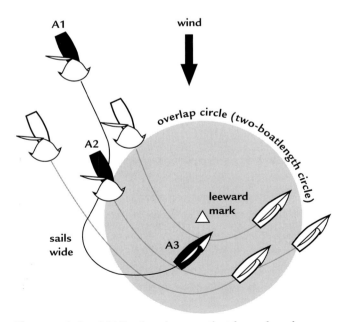

If you are behind (A1), slow down, sail wide, and work to stay on the inside windward hip (A3) of boats rounding ahead of you.

heavier the wind, the earlier you should take down the spinnaker.

As you round the leeward mark, make a tactical rounding. This is where practice is important. Approach the leeward mark on a reach as much as possible. Your priorities are similar to rounding the windward mark: speed first, position second, setting new sails third, minor adjustments fourth, crew comfort fifth. The crew should put on foul-weather gear well before the rounding. You don't want anyone getting off the windward rail to get their gear once you're sailing upwind.

A Close Call

One of the scariest moments I have had while racing was aboard the 54-foot sloop *Jubilation*. We were returning from Block Island and were sailing at 10 knots with the spinnaker up through The Race, the entrance to Long Island Sound. I was at the helm, and the fog was thick. Off in the distance we could hear the horn of an approaching vessel. The sound kept getting louder. Suddenly, a tugboat crossed our bow. Its distinctive red stack blended in with the fog. I had a hood over my head to protect me from the drizzle and mist. As the tugboat passed, I noticed just out of the corner of my eye a large hawser line extending into the water. At this point instinct took over. I turned the wheel hard and jibed the boat away from the tugboat. Our crew thought I'd lost my mind. But I held the wheel tight. After a few moments we could hear the slushing of the bow wave of the towed barge. The barge passed only a few feet away. I turned the wheel and resumed our course. It was a close call with disaster. Luckily, I had seen the hawser as the tug passed or we would have been smashed by the barge. The incident told me that even though we were racing, we should have slowed down by lowering the spinnaker. We should also have taken careful bearings of the approaching foghorn. This moment was a good lesson for all of us to sail more safely in the future. Radar would have been an asset in this situation. In future races I made sure radar was available.

TACTICS FOR ROUNDING THE LEEWARD MARK: A CHECKLIST

❖ Adjust sails, outhaul, downhaul, vang, etc., for the next leg before rounding the leeward mark.

❖ Check the velocity of the wind when approaching the leeward mark so you make the correct adjustments for the windward leg. Choose a new jib early.

❖ Avoid approaching the leeward mark on a dead downwind course.

❖ Approaching the mark on a reach increases the speed of your turn.

❖ Make long pulls on the sheets as you make the rounding.

❖ Keep the boat flat. A heeling boat makes leeway and loses speed.

❖ Avoid getting trapped on an inside boat's leeward quarter. It's better to slow down and round astern.

The Mechanics of Mark Roundings

You can gain considerable distance on your competitors by rounding marks efficiently. You can sail into a mark rounding behind and finish ahead by planning your turn in advance. To achieve this there are several things you must do.

First, learn the optimum turning radius of your boat when you are bearing off, jibing, tacking, and heading up. It's better to turn gradually using less rudder (remember, the rudder can have a braking effect). In most boats any turn requiring a course change of 90 degrees or more will take at least two boatlengths of turning radius. You can turn faster, but your boat will decelerate dramatically. In heavy wind, you are moving faster so the same turn will take even more space.

Almost as important as turning radius is angle of heel. Sailboats have the least resist-

ance to turning when they are on an even keel. At a leeward mark, ease the pressure on the rudder and help the boat steer itself to weather by carrying a slight (about 10 degrees) leeward heel. As you bear off at the windward mark, keep the boat as flat as possible. Learn your boat's correct angle of heel, ideal turning radius, and proper sail trim for maximum boatspeed by practicing mark roundings.

It's helpful to be clear about your priorities in mark roundings. Here's a review. The first priority is boatspeed. Maintain maximum velocity while covering the shortest possible distance. Next comes your position relative to the competition. The third priority is setting new sails. The fourth is

The key to rounding a windward mark is to ease out the sails quickly so the boat stays upright. If a boat is heeling too far, it has difficulty making the turn.

the minor adjustments you'll need to make when you go from one point of sail to another (cunningham, vang, traveler, outhaul, centerboard, and so on). Finally, crew comfort is fifth. Each mark of the course (windward, reach, leeward) presents a different set of problems, but I have found that these priorities hold up well all around the racecourse.

Make sure you know what marks you need to head to. You may think I am stating the obvious, but there are hundreds of cases where leading boats have lost regattas by heading for the wrong mark. You and your crew must continually update where you are in relation to the next mark. Observation is the key. Know what your mark looks like, particularly on bodies of water where more than one fleet is racing at a time. Marks often look the same from a distance, but subtle differences in marks can give you a clue to which one is yours.

Rounding the Windward Mark

Your approach to the windward mark is critical. Most sailors are so anxious to get to the mark, they tack short of the layline and wind up pinching their way to the buoy. Don't make this mistake: it makes no sense to gamble by tacking too soon. Think of the boatspeed you lose by pinching to the mark. If you *overstand* (sail beyond the layline) slightly, you can easily make up the extra distance by footing, or falling off, and gaining speed. Sailing an extra 10 feet before you tack to the mark can make a big difference.

Remember to use a tacking line to gauge the layline. In light air your tacking angle will probably be wider than 90 de-

grees; in strong winds your tacking angle will be narrower than 90 degrees. If you sight the tacking line a few times before the start of a race, you will have a helpful reference during the race (see the discussion on tacking lines on pages 35–36).

If you overstand the mark by, say, one boatlength, you avoid the consequences of misjudgment: a bad tack, an unexpected current, an unfavorable chop, or another boat tacking on your wind. You are always at risk if you tack exactly on the layline, because a header or any of the other possibilities listed above could make you miss the mark. Also, the wind along the starboard tack layline tends to be chopped up by the boats ahead of you. Sail one length beyond the layline and you will have clear wind.

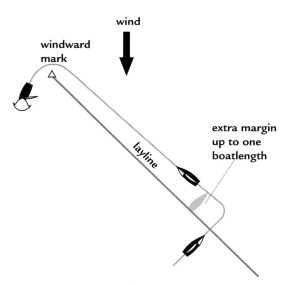

When you make your final approach to the windward mark, overstand—sail beyond the layline—by an extra margin of about one boatlength. This allows for misjudgment, a bad tack, unfavorable current, another boat blocking your wind, or a bad set of waves.

If you see a long line of starboard-tack boats parading on the layline, don't tack early (to leeward and ahead). Wait, look for a hole, and duck in. Be careful not to tack too close to another boat. Make certain to sail well above any of your competitors to give yourself clear wind and maneuverability for the turn around the mark.

Avoid tacking right at the windward mark. If you are coming in on port tack and you must tack to starboard to round the mark, it's best to make your approach five boatlengths or more below the port tack layline to allow time to set the spinnaker up for the rounding. There will be times, however, when this is impossible and you will have to come in right on the mark. If you are behind, you can gain a lot of ground by approaching the mark on port with the advantage of clean air all the way in. But be careful of starboard-tack boats. You are very much at risk when making this maneuver and have few, if any, rights.

You can improve your boatspeed by making only one tack on your final approach to the mark. Repeated tacks slow you down. If you find that you're not fetching the mark, it's better to tack early in wide-open water rather than take a chance in the crowd that converges at the mark.

Plan to make your final approach to the windward mark on the lifted tack. Even still, avoid tacking in the vicinity of the mark. The time saved by avoiding multiple tacks will allow you to concentrate on the mark rounding.

If you're trapped to leeward of several boats, don't wait to tack. Bear off and get clear early. Be conservative and make your move early to avoid trouble.

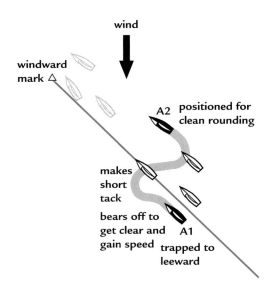

If you are trapped to leeward and behind a group of boats approaching the mark (A1), bear off to get clear ground and make a short tack early. You are then positioned to make a clean rounding (A2).

If you are on port tack (assuming the mark is to be rounded to starboard) and you're barely fetching the mark, slow down by luffing up and let the starboard-tack boat round ahead. Avoid double tacking. Again, make this move earlier so you are accelerating into the turn.

When boats are at close quarters at marks, tempers flare and fouls tend to occur. Try to avoid fouls at all costs. (The section on yelling, in chapter 3, provides advice on controlling tempers on board.)

The boat handling required for smooth mark roundings does not come easily. Make sure your boat is set up properly for the approach by assuring that all lines are free to run as needed. A piece of shock cord across the jaws of cam cleats is excellent insurance against lines getting jammed when you can least afford it. Sheets should be handheld during the approach to the mark to make certain you can ease (or trim) them instantly as you round. Crew motions should be as efficient as possible. Running forward or aft disturbs both the balance and the momentum of the boat.

Before you round the weather mark know your next course. Pick a prominent landmark or steer by the compass to make sure you're headed in the right direction. That youthful experience aboard the sneakbox, when I lost the racecourse chart and we sailed to the wrong mark, has always been with me. Know where you are heading. Don't follow the leader!

Once you have made your approach to the mark, start rounding by keeping your boat flat. One rule of thumb is "keep the boat under the mast." To keep the boat under the mast, dump the main out fast and ease the jib out while rounding. An over-trimmed jib, like your mainsail, will prevent your boat from bearing off. And if you let the boat heel, the centerboard or keel will begin to cavitate (trap air between the water and hull) and your rudder will become ineffective. Keeping the boat under the mast allows you to bear off fast and keeps your boat under control while you increase your speed and lose little distance.

In two-person boats, one crew member must keep hiking during the turn. If both crew are off the rail and have their heads wrapped in halyards and adjustments, they are in for trouble.

Any mark rounding is easier and faster with a slower course change. The faster the change in course, the more the boat will slow down. One way to avoid creating

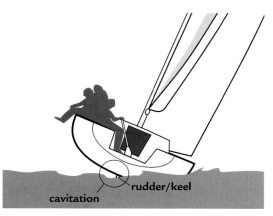

When a keel or centerboard cavitates, the rudder becomes ineffective. Cavitation is when air is trapped between the water and the hull.

pressure on the rudder and rig is to ease off the sails before rounding.

Once you are around the windward mark, make a fast getaway. Head in the direction you wish to sail, haul up the spinnaker, adjust your sails, and work for pure speed. Sailors often arrive at the windward mark, only to relax downwind. That's a mistake: this leg is your chance to get tough and cover as much ground as possible. Your getaway sets the stage for your approach to the next mark.

Rounding Reach and Leeward Marks

As you learned in the downwind tactics section, there are two basic legs after a windward mark: the reach and the run. As a general rule, if you are on a reach, pass boats to windward at the beginning of a leg and pass boats to leeward at the end of a leg. This is because you always want to work toward finishing on the inside at the reach mark. If you are forced to stay on the outside, decide early that you can break the overlap.

If an adverse current is setting your boat away from the desired course, fight the current early in the leg so you have it in your favor at the final approach. The extra speed relative to the turning buoy is helpful at the end of the leg.

When the boats ahead get into a luffing match, dive low to get clear wind and set up for a better angle approaching the next mark.

Marks drift at times and must be reset by the race committee. Never assume you know the location of a mark. Check for it often so there is no mistake.

On spinnaker boats, you'll usually set your spinnaker at the weather mark. If there is a question of whether you can carry a spinnaker on the next leg, remember to round the mark and test the conditions first and observe the boats (if any) in front of you. It's better to set the spinnaker late than to set it and then have to take it down. Wait to haul the spinnaker up until the apparent wind direction is 70 degrees or farther aft. In light winds, avoid setting the spinnaker until your speed stabilizes.

On big boats and small boats, the key to a good spinnaker set is preparation. If the sheet, guy, and halyard are led properly, it's a basic mechanical exercise to haul this sail up. If you are not set up properly, hoisting the spinnaker can be a nightmare. Pre-squaring the pole and pre-trimming the chute to the proper settings for your point of sail help the spinnaker pop out quickly. Avoid trimming until the spinnaker reaches the top of the mast.

After rounding the windward mark on a dead downwind leg, you may need to jibe immediately after the rounding. If you are setting a spinnaker in this situation and it's unclear which jibe you'll sail on, a bear-away maneuver is always preferred. However, if the opposite jibe is favored by 15 degrees or more, it may be useful to do a jibe set. However, a jibe set—where you bear off and jibe—is a big course change of at least 135 degrees. This dramatically slows the boat. The turn is even slower when you go through the process of setting the spinnaker.

Even worse is a tack followed by a jibe set. This is a very difficult maneuver that costs you speed. If you are forced to tack right at the windward mark, it's better to sail a straight course while setting your spin-

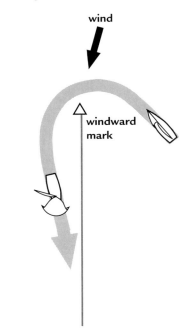

When the opposite jibe is favored on a downwind leg, a jibe set is the preferred maneuver; however, this move costs boatspeed.

naker and then immediately follow with a jibe. The idea is to maneuver at full speed; setting the spinnaker immediately after a tack with a jibe will dramatically slow down your boat.

The jibe mark can be the most exciting of all. I will never forget Laser sailor Craig Thomas approaching a jibe in last place at the U.S. Singlehanded Championship, held on the Berkeley Circle in San Francisco Bay. He picked up every competitor on the course who had already capsized. Fourteen of America's best single-handed sailors had all capsized around the reach mark and sat in the water watching Thomas come flying in. As he went into the jibe he yelled, "Watch this, I'll show you how!"

He certainly did! A full pitchpole flung his body head-first over the bow of his boat

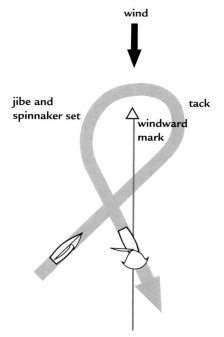

The tack followed by a jibe and spinnaker set is a slow maneuver. This is to be avoided.

in grand style. Needless to say, his performance aroused enthusiastic cheers from those of us who had already capsized. That race was won by the boat that righted itself the fastest. (Thomas went on to win the regatta, and I placed third.)

Jibing is easiest when your boat is moving fast because you have less apparent wind in your sails. Allow a minimum of two to three boatlengths to make your turn while jibing, especially if you're flying a spinnaker. Jibing the chute can be tricky. Jibing around a mark is tougher, but the same rules for a good jibe make for an easy rounding. Square the pole aft as you bear away. If you trip the pole early and fail to continue trimming on the old guy, the chute will be under-trimmed and unstable. The helmsman should think of directing the masthead fly (as a reference) into the chute. As the helmsman turns, the trimmers are briefed to swing the chute as he swings the boat. By doing this, you will jibe without luffing the sail. Never allow both spinnaker clews to be on the same side of the headstay. This invites a collapse (see left illustration next page).

Pre-jibing the main—throwing it from one side to the other before the wind has passed dead astern—allows you to finish the turn earlier, which frees you to concentrate on steering around the mark. This also provides some turning force of its own (via the wind pressure on the sail) and uses less rudder (see right illustration next page).

In heavy wind, trim the main to the centerline prior to a jibe to help your control. If the boat begins to roll, head up 10 or 20 degrees. This puts the water flow on one side of the keel or centerboard and makes

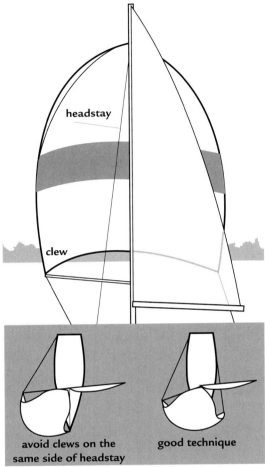

Keep the clews of the spinnaker parallel to the horizon. Don't allow both clews (or clew and tack) of the spinnaker on the same side of the headstay.

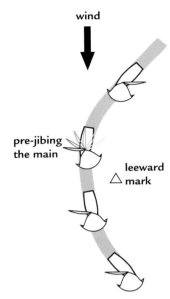

Pre-jibing the main—having the main pass through wind before the hull heads straight downwind—helps you turn the boat without using as much rudder.

steering easier. You can dump the main out quickly to ease pressure if the boat starts to round up.

The *S-jibe* is used to keep a boat under control when you are jibing in powerful winds. In a heavy-air jibe, the main boom comes over with great force. If the main boom goes too far out on the new side, the boat will round hard into the wind. At its worst, this loss of control can cause dinghies to capsize or cause keelboats to broach. An S-jibe helps the boat stay upright and keeps the boat under the mast and in balance.

As you steer into an S-jibe, bear off and keep the boat sailing slightly by the lee. Keep the main over-trimmed or, if you are sailing with a spinnaker, keep the sail on edge by easing the sheet and guy. Then, as the mainsail swings across the boat, steer back in the direction in which the main is going. This change of course reduces the power in the mainsail and keeps the boat from rounding into the wind. As the main fills on the new side, keep it over-trimmed and resume your desired course. Don't begin to head up until the boat is under control (see left illustration page 106). Keep in mind that you need more room for an S-jibe than you do for a conventional jibe.

The S-jibe steering technique helps these J / 24 sailors make efficient maneuvers in heavy wind.

How you round the jibe mark depends on what your new course will be. If your new course is a close reach, steer wide on your approach and round tight to the mark on your turn. This puts you on the weather side of the track to the next mark, and you are free to sail the shortest, fastest reach possible. If you are jibing onto a broad reach, stay close to the mark on the approach so that you are wide on the exit so you'll have a tighter (faster) sailing angle for the next mark (see right illustration next page). Remember to keep your wind clear after you jibe. Take the time to look at the blanketing effect of boats behind you.

Once you complete your jibe, start your getaway by planning your approach to the leeward mark. This is a lot to think about, but practice makes this second nature. If the fleet is heading high, sail below

their course. If you are among the first boats around the mark, you can discourage other skippers from sailing a high course by making a sharp luff and then bearing off to your proper course before another boat has the chance to sail over you (see illustration page 107).

This move enables the competition to sail low, yet they won't be able to break your overlap since they must sail through your lee. And remember that not only is the wind disturbed to leeward, so is the water. Boats make waves. Chopped-up water slows you down. Waves get confused when there are several boats sailing in the same location—definitely areas to avoid.

It's a bad practice to make a reaching leg a continual luffing match. If a boat tries to sail over the top of you, give one sharp luff. Under the rules of racing, the wind-

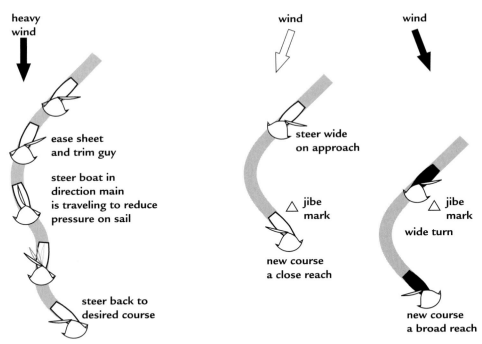

The S-jibe is an effective maneuver in heavy wind. Just as the main is passing over the boat, steer back in the direction the main is heading to take the pressure off the sail. Once the spinnaker is jibed and the boat is under control, steer up to your desired course. The maneuver will resemble the shape of an "S."

At a jibe mark, if the leg is going to be tight, stay wide early and pass close to the mark (left). If the next reach leg is going to be broad with the wind well aft, stay close to the mark, then make your maneuver, ending up wide on the new jibe so you have a better angle toward the leeward mark (right).

ward boat must stay clear of the leeward boat—it's the only protection a leeward boat has against boats sailing over the top. One sharp luff is infinitely better than a series of short and continuous luffs. A windward boat will get the message that you mean business and will stay low.

The leeward mark presents the biggest challenge of all. Because there is so much going on, sailors often forget to keep their boat moving at maximum speed. Approach the leeward mark on as much of a reach as possible to maximize your speed. Also remember that any distance sailed to leeward of the mark is distance sailed away from the

weather mark. Therefore, stay wide (about two boatlengths) of your approach so you can round up right at the mark as you make your turn (see photo page 108).

Keep your boat heeled slightly to leeward (about 10 degrees) to induce the weather helm that makes turning to weather easier. If you heel your boat too much, it will slip sideways. Leeway widens your turning circle and slows your turn.

At the Canadian Olympic Training Regatta Kingston, Ontario (CORK), I was approaching a leeward mark with twenty Finns overlapped and abreast. Realizing that these boats would make a wide pinwheel

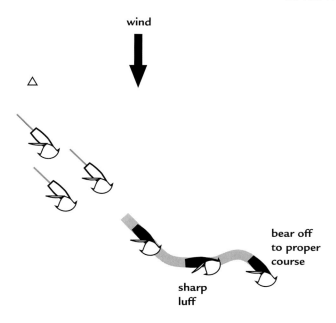

wind

bear off
to proper
course

sharp
luff

leeward mark △

*On the reach leg take a short hitch (luff) to windward to discourage boats behind from continually sailing
a high course.*

around the mark, and being stuck in the
middle, I trimmed my mainsail midships
and slowed down on the final approach to
the mark. Sure enough, the intense battle to
gain the inside position caused the inside
helmsman to forget to put his centerboard
down. His Finn slipped sideways, banging
into every boat. I simply rounded a few
boatlengths later and was instantly twenty
boats farther ahead. Nice! Keeping your
eyes outside the boat helps remind you
where you are.

At the leeward mark, always remember
your position relative to the rest of the fleet.
If you round into a position where you are
to leeward of your competitors, you'll be
blanketed and forced either to slow down
or to tack. Your goal is to round into a spot
on the weather (windward) quarter of the
boat or boats just ahead of you. Here you'll
receive some backwind, but you won't be
blanketed. You'll sail fast enough to pick
the side of the course you choose rather
than being forced to one side to get out of
dirty air (see illustration page 108).

While having an overlapping inside position at the mark is desirable, don't sacri-
fice your overall position to get it. If you go
for an overlap and don't get it, you'll be
high on the mark; you'll then be forced to
make a wide turn, which will put you
to leeward of the boats ahead.

At crowded leeward marks, it's better to slow down early and work to the inside to make a tactical round-ing. At all costs avoid being trapped well to leeward at the mark.

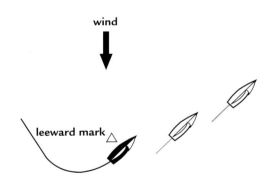

If you round the leeward mark on a boat's windward quarter you have the option of tacking away.

I know this sounds complicated but hang with me. I try to put myself in position to pass boats *after* a mark rounding rather than gambling on passing them *during* a mark rounding. This holds true for carrying the chute until the bitter end. It's better to

take the spinnaker down a little early rather than a little late. Don't give anything away, but you can hurt yourself by taking foolish chances.

Plan your mark rounding in the relative calm of the open water leading up to the mark. Once you've decided not to sprint for inside position, give yourself room to make the rounding that puts you in com-mand once you've passed the mark. Even if you're trapped outside three or four other boats, plan early to assure yourself a wide approach and tight rounding. Even if you must slow down by sailing a greater distance than the boats inside of you, gauge your turn so you can round sharply onto or above the weather quarter of the boat just ahead.

Don't tack right at the leeward mark if you can avoid it. Get the boat up to speed

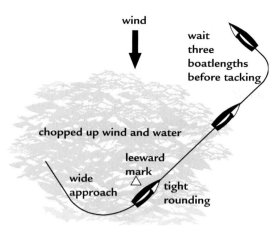

wind

wait three boatlengths before tacking

chopped up wind and water

leeward mark

wide approach

tight rounding

Both the wind and water are chopped up in the vicinity of the leeward mark. Avoid tacking immediately.

before you tack away. Avoid sailing over your own wake or the wakes of the boats still coming downwind.

The tactical possibilities involved in mark rounding are many, and sometimes lots of places can be gained. More often, though, sailors tend to focus on winning the battle at the mark and wind up losing the war at the finish line. Take the tactical advantages when they present themselves but don't forget that keeping your boat moving fast all around the racecourse is the best way to finish at the front of the fleet. Think hard and execute.

Practice mark roundings on your own by setting up a short three-buoy course and sailing it often. Practice makes perfect.

Passing

The most exciting time during any race is when you're in a position to pass another boat. This is also when tension mounts and your concentration peaks. If you're sailing faster, you should be able to sail around your opponent. But there are many special situations to keep in mind when you are trying to pass another boat—or trying to keep another boat from passing you. Following are a number of methods for passing other boats on the course.

There is great psychological value to sailing around a competitor. The frustration you bestow by holding a faster boat in check and behind you can psychologically damage an opponent for an entire series. Passing another boat is also the toughest move in yacht racing. It takes a combination of smarts and extra speed.

How do you get extra speed? When sailing on the wind you can gain speed by bearing off 2 to 5 degrees at the same time as you ease out your sheets. Sailboats increase speed only if the sails are eased out when bearing off the wind. Plan your passing well in advance so you can concentrate on boatspeed. It's critical to watch waves carefully so that you do not slam into one, which stops your boat. Plan on passing in smooth water or during a lifting puff (upwind) where the breeze swings aft and you can use the stronger wind for acceleration.

On downwind legs you can gain speed by heading up at least 5 degrees to a better reaching angle and using puffs and waves for acceleration. The key to getting a boat surfing down a wave (and even the smallest waves help) is to line the boat up perpendicular to the wave direction, and trimming your sails rapidly the instant the wave begins to lift the stern out of the water. Keep the boat on an even keel with no helm pressure. In dinghies it helps to raise the centerboard two-thirds of the way. If there is a lot of pressure on the helm, the course will be unstable and it's hard to get the boat

Actually passing another boat is one of the most difficult moves in racing. Small adjustments can make big differences in speed. Windshifts can be your best friend when trying to pass.

planing. If you're sailing directly downwind, heeling the boat to windward might help reduce rudder pressure.

Sailing is often a game not of brilliance but of the elimination of errors. Most skippers are passed not because competitors have pulled brilliant tactical moves, but because the skippers failed to cover or stay in phase with the windshifts. Or the skippers lost concentration and therefore boatspeed. When you are behind, try to get the competition ahead of you to make extra maneuvers. Boats that maneuver less generally gain distance on the racecourse.

In one Miami–Nassau race on *Jubilation*, we were dueling upwind with *Golden Eagle*. *Golden Eagle* gained substantially by tacking inshore along the Bahamian banks. It be-

came our job to encourage *Golden Eagle* to sail offshore while we headed inshore. We accomplished this by tacking inshore; as expected, *Golden Eagle* tacked to cover. We immediately tacked back and *Golden Eagle* tacked once again, now heading offshore. On *Jubilation* we tacked a third time, which was simply too often for *Golden Eagle* to keep up with. They held on starboard tack for a considerable period with us heading inshore. When both boats tacked again on a converging course several minutes later, *Jubilation* had taken the lead. By making three consecutive tacks, we were able to get *Golden Eagle* off our wind and heading in the wrong direction. The strong adverse offshore current on the outside of the bank cost *Golden Eagle* more distance than our extra tack cost us.

Sailors should take a day out of their racing schedule to observe competitors. I have learned a lot by watching our rivals from the shore or from a powerboat. One move I learned from watching is the half tack, which we discussed earlier (see page 82). This maneuver is used to escape a tight cover from one competitor or a group of competitors.

When you're racing downwind, you can use a half jibe. Instead of swinging the boat all the way up onto a new course or

higher for speed, the second your spinnaker pole is "made" (the word the bowman says when the pole has been swung to the other side and the new guy is in the jaw) or the mainsail swings across and fills on the new side, immediately start jibing back onto the original course.

During half tacks or half jibes, the key is to change course as little as possible so you lose less speed and therefore require less acceleration afterward.

In heavy-displacement boats, double tacks are risky because you lose twice the normal distance following the second tack. If a boat ahead tacks on you, continue sailing on the same tack and coast into the backwind and blanketing zone of the boat ahead. Tack away while the boat ahead is still accelerating. During this maneuver, the

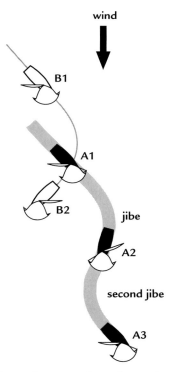

A half jibe—where you jibe and immediately head back in the opposite direction—is used to get another boat off your wind. The boat behind (B1) makes the first jibe (B2) to cover you and you immediately jibe away (A2). They won't expect the second maneuver (A3) of jibing back onto the original course.

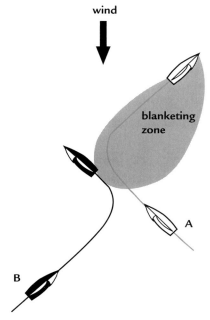

Boat A tacks on Boat B. Boat B sails up to the blanketed zone before tacking away.

wind in your sails will not be affected until you reach the blanketing zone of the leading boat.

Using the half tack while coasting into another boat's wind shadow should be distinguished from a false tack. In heavy displacement boats false tacks rarely work. If you are caught reacting to a false tack of a trailing boat, it's usually better to follow through with a tack than to return to your original course. This is different in smaller boats. False tacks are easier to make in light-displacement boats because they maneuver faster. If a boat ahead of you overreacts to your tack and spins hard, you can get out of phase by returning to your original course (see the illustration on page 82).

Set up for a false tack, a half tack, or fake jibe so you end up on the favored or lifted tack, or the tack heading toward the favored side of the course. The hope is that you confuse your competitor and he sails in the wrong direction. These maneuvers take planning, and it's important not to fake out your own crew. Subtle signals are imperative.

As I mentioned earlier, anytime you plan to tack or jibe, avoid telegraphing your intentions to the competition. Keep yourself and your crew ready and in position when you begin your tack. If your crew stands up, or if you shout that you are preparing to tack, this signals to competitors what you are up to. The automatic response of many sailors is to tack with you if you make a big commotion. Be sneaky on the racecourse.

Although it's difficult to pass a large number of boats at one time, it is possible to pass several boats if they are closely bunched. Avoid sailing near large packs of boats. This only spells trouble and cuts down your options. As we discussed earlier, use other boats on the racecourse as blockers (see page 74).

The most successful offensive move you can make in sailing is to be on starboard tack. As the starboard-tack boat, you have the right-of-way. Use this rule to your advantage, particularly at the final approach to marks or at the finish line. Make your competitors maneuver around you.

On the windward leg, if you are continually gaining on your opponent each time you cross tacks, you should eventually pass. In such a situation, you may be forced to dip under the stern of the other boat if you are on port and your competitor is on starboard. Dipping another boat is a tough maneuver. If you are on port tack with little chance of crossing the right-of-way starboard tacker (and you are afraid to tack to leeward because you might get rolled), it's best to dip. If you notice during the converging that your bow is well ahead of the bow of the other boat, you will need to start your dip earlier. If the starboard tacker is ahead of you, you can hold off dipping until the last moment. The key to a good dip is to change course as little as possible. When your bow reaches the transom of your opponent, you want to be sailing close-hauled and on the wind at a greater speed, anticipating the lift you will receive from the starboard tacker's sails. Be prepared to take a bite to windward as you dip astern.

If you are on starboard tack during a dip and you notice a port tacker dipping you, pick a converging course that is especially

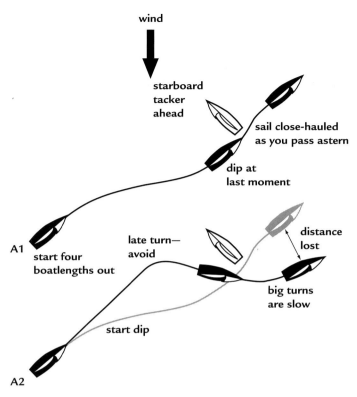

As you pass astern of a boat on the opposite tack, you can actually get a lift off the sails of that boat (A1). Be prepared to take a windward bite. Avoid making a late dip (A2) or you'll lose considerable distance.

fast (5 degrees lower will do). This also brings you together faster and earlier, therefore causing the port-tack boat to make a greater course change. Under the rules, you are not allowed to obstruct another boat from keeping clear, but it is permissible to settle on one course.

During a crossing situation, take continual bearings either with a hand-bearing compass, a compass mounted in your boat, or by simple observations: line up your target with objects onshore to see if you are gaining or losing. When you're gaining bearing you know that you'll cross ahead, but when you are losing bearing you'll cross

behind. When the bearing stays constant, a collision is likely.

A good time to pass an opponent is when they're preoccupied with another boat. In order to find these opportunities, stay away from boats that are in a luffing match, tacking duel, jibing duel, or are close in points in a series. To take advantage of these situations, be sure to stay in phase with the windshifts, keep your own wind clear, and avoid sailing near packs of boats.

The *slam dunk* can be an effective maneuver to trap a boat on your leeward side. The slam dunk works best in winds of at least 10 knots. When you are on starboard tack crossing another boat and want to tack to port, you are in a good position to execute a slam dunk. Although this maneuver works best in keelboats, it is useful on boats of any displacement. Start making your tack just as the bow of the boat you are crossing passes beneath your stern. If you're able to get on your new tack and accelerate before the bow of the now leeward boat lines up with the bow of your boat, you have slam dunked your competitor because you are now sailing on his breeze, and he can't tack away until his bow clears your stern.

Alternatively, the defense for the slam dunk is to tack away immediately if you are dipping just a small amount (10 to 20 degrees). Be sure your bow clears the other boat's stern. Under the racing rules, when two yachts are tacking simultaneously the boat on the other's port side shall keep clear. In this case it would be the boat tacking from starboard onto port that is obligated to stay clear.

If you're making a substantial dip of at least 20 degrees or more, get your boat sailing as fast as possible by easing your sails and accelerating. If the starboard-tack boat begins tacking on top of you, immediately harden up to a close-hauled course or even higher to shoot through to leeward. If your bow ends up ahead of the bow of the windward boat, the windward boat will never have the opportunity to bear off and accelerate. The slam dunk has been thwarted here by a luff on the part of the leeward boat. The temptation for most sailors in this case is to keep sailing on a low course to gain speed after a dip has been made. This opens the door for the windward boat to steer a lower course and accelerate to full speed.

On the wind, if you are a windward boat, taking a dive at the right opportunity will help you sail over the top of a leeward boat. The natural tendency when you're to windward is to sail a continuously high

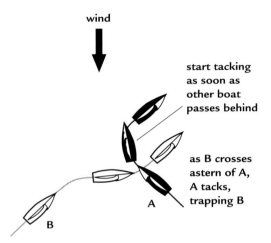

A slam dunk—tacking (Boat A) just as a competitor's (Boat B) bow passes astern—can be very effective to trap a boat on your leeward side.

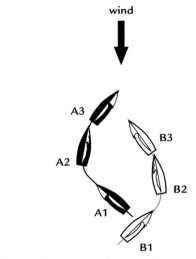

When two boats are tacking simultaneously, the boat on the other's port side shall stay clear. In this case Boat A must stay clear.

course to stay away from competitors' backwind. Don't be afraid of backwind because you always have the opportunity to tack away. I like to bear off for speed and sail over the top of a leeward boat during a smooth spot in the water and just as a puff is getting to my boat. This new puff often forces the leeward boat to round up into the wind and simultaneously slow down. With greater speed, thanks to your acceleration by bearing off, you may be able to ride over the top of the leeward boat. It may take several puffs before this opportunity develops, but angling down on a lower course usually works. Keep in mind that you should keep at least half a boatlength distance from the leeward boat because the rules are not kind to boats in the windward position. Giving the right-of-way to the leeward boat with the ability to luff is the only

protection it has to prevent being passed. Trimmers must work closely with the helmsman in these situations. The rest of the crew should hike hard to keep the boat on its lines.

Tacking or jibing to cover is a golden opportunity for passing other boats. When sailing on the wind, I watch the course being steered relative to the course of the other boats very carefully. For example, if a boat is sailing on my windward quarter, I prefer to wait to tack until the bow of the windward boat is lower than my bow. You will not be closer or have a better opportunity to pass than when a boat is sailing at a lower angle.

It's important to avoid getting so wrapped up with one competitor that other competitors pass you. This is most obvious during a continual luffing match. If you find

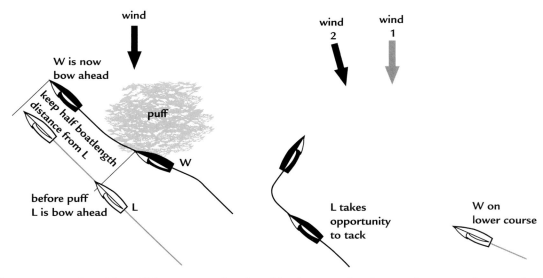

If you are a windward boat (W), you can take advantage of a puff because you get it first. As the wind hits, W bears off for speed and gains forward distance before L gets the new wind.

Watch surrounding boats to determine when to tack. Boat W, sailing on L's windward quarter, is sailing a lower course than L. This provides a good opportunity for L to tack.

that you're close to a pest, jibe or tack away early. Avoid getting close to boats prone to perpetual luffing matches. If the luffing-match problem continues, you might even point it out to the pest after a regatta. They might not like hearing it, but they will think hard about their actions.

After the leeward mark, it's important to get away from other boats and into clear air so you can sail at full speed. Most sailors tend to pinch in the vicinity of other boats. If you find you're sailing slowly around other boats, it's probably best to jibe or tack away even for ten to fifteen boatlengths of distance and then come back again to pass. Don't try to win a battle that is a continually losing effort. I suggest stopping a luffing match when you've lost two or more boatlengths to the rest of the fleet.

At times it pays to take chances, and there's no greater gamble than sailing in shallow water. The penalty, unfortunately, is running aground and losing the race entirely. But there have been many races won by boats willing to hug the shore. It's important to know the tide schedule to the half hour when racing. For example, if the water is 10 feet deep but there is 5 feet of tide and you draw 5 feet, you need to understand where you are in the tide cycle. At high tide you have plenty of water under your boat. But at low tide you are likely to run aground.

Tidal currents change in shallow water first. If there's a strong foul tide in deep water you might find relief along the shoreline. A nautical chart and a fathometer are your best tools.

Getting out of an unfavorable tide produces great rewards. A classic area is along the coast of Florida between Ft. Lauderdale and Miami. There is almost always a countercurrent along the coast, but yachts must be willing to sail in 15 feet of water to catch a favorable current. The current differential is nearly 2 knots between 15 feet of water and 100 feet of water.

In heavier breezes, you can often pass boats that are ahead by being conservative. In order to reduce the chances for a breakdown, it is best to maneuver as little as possible in heavy weather.

If two boats are sailing downwind on

Most breakdowns occur while maneuvering in heavy wind. Be sure your crew is prepared for every action before turning the wheel.

port jibe, the windward boat can force the leeward boat to sail away by suddenly jibing to starboard, forcing the port-tack boat to jibe with haste. Once the boat that was to leeward has completed its jibe, the boat initiating the encounter can return to the port jibe and sail in clearer wind.

If you're on the leeward aft quarter of another boat sailing downwind, you're getting affected by the backwind and waves of that boat and will not be able to gain. It may be best to jibe away for clear wind and smoother water. On downwind legs, you need to watch the apparent wind of other boats and realize that blanketed breezes extend at least six to ten mast lengths away.

One way to pass downwind is by sailing as far as you can to leeward—at least four boatlengths—of a windward boat. Just as

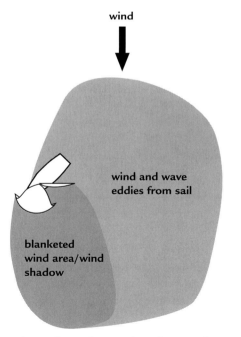

The exhaust from a boat sailing downwind extends both ahead and behind.

wind

wind and wave eddies from sail

blanketed wind area/wind shadow

your breeze falls into the blanketing wind shadow of the windward boat, harden up a good 20 degrees; this pushes your apparent wind forward so that your masthead fly is pointing well ahead of the bow of the windward boat. In this manner you'll be able to shoot through to leeward. The biggest mistake made by boats trying to pass to leeward is staying on a low course for too long and not angling up hard to break through the dangerous wind shadow. You must be willing to give up several lengths to break through. If after a few attempts you are unable to break through, make two jibes to clear your air completely.

In planing dinghies you have a good opportunity to pass on a reach. If you plan to pass another boat on the windward side, give yourself plenty of distance to windward (at least three boatlengths) so you have room to bear off, ride a wave, and sail over the top. Make your move to pass when your competitor has just completed riding a wave, is heading into some bad slop created from a powerboat, or is not watching you. When you are to windward it is easy to watch a leeward boat. The crew on the leeward boat has to turn all the way around to see your actions. Watch carefully for your chance to make a move. If you are sailing in surfing conditions, be careful that the wave you catch doesn't put you way off course. Although you might be sailing fast and enjoying the ride, it does you no good if you are heading away from the mark.

Light-Wind Tactics

Sailing in no wind is frustrating and physically exhausting. You must work hard for every inch gained on the racecourse. Prog-

Patience is the key to sailing well in no wind. Pace yourself. Rotating helmsmen frequently keeps a crew fresh. Big gains can be made in light wind.

ress takes hours, yet any position you've gained can be wiped out with one sudden wind gust from the wrong direction. When there is no wind you might be better off not sailing at all. But in the middle of a race, before the time limit has expired, you'll be working to catch every puff of wind.

When racing in no wind, you need patience. Pace yourself. Many sailors get burned out by trying too hard in the early part of a calm. When you're well behind in a fleet, lack of wind gives you a new opportunity to break the race wide open. Unfortunately, when you have a big lead, the world can cave in on you.

I'll never forget one Fastnet Race some

years ago when I was sailing on the Maxi boat *Condor* with Dennis Conner, Lowell North, and Tom Whidden. *Condor* and our main rival *Kialoa* had established a 100-mile lead over the rest of the fleet. As night fell, with only 60 miles to the finish, we were a mile ahead of *Kialoa*, sailing at 10 knots, and aimed right at the finish line.

I went off watch for four hours and woke up to find *Condor* anchored. There wasn't a breath of wind. Both *Condor* and *Kialoa* sat at anchor for forty-eight hours. The rest of the fleet came up from behind. It was a dismal experience. Finally, the wind did fill. But we finished last on corrected time. And to add insult to injury, *Kialoa* placed just ahead of us.

There are some things you can do to maintain headway when the wind drops. The first is to force the boat to heel to leeward. This keeps the rig out over the side of the boat, which helps maintain some sort of feel on the helm. Because the center of effort of the sail is to leeward of the hull's center of resistance, the resulting force tends to turn the boat to windward. (The center of effort is an imaginary point in a boat's rig that represents the geographic center of the driving forces on the sails. The center of resistance is a similar point on the keel or centerboard that keeps the boat from slipping sideways.)

Heeling helps the sail fill, thanks to gravity. Heeling also helps the draft of the sail stay in position and prevents sail-shape disruption by wave action. Every stray puff gives your boat motion. Keep the boat steady so you build forward momentum. I like one crew to tension the boom so it doesn't bounce around in the waves.

A bouncing boom absorbs a lot of energy from the sails. A steady boom keeps the sail in a consistent shape and the boat goes faster.

It's imperative to reduce your wetted

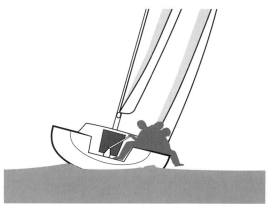

Use crew weight to leeward to induce heel in light wind.

In light wind, move crew weight forward and to leeward to keep the stern out of the water. This reduces wetted surface area, or friction with the water.

surface area, or friction with the water. This can be done in light wind by moving the crew weight as far forward as possible, which lifts the stern out of the water.

As the breeze gets lighter, you should power up your rig and sails. You can do this by making your sails fuller, so your boat has the power to overcome waves. However, if the wind drops to near zero, flatten your sails and move them outboard with the traveler and barber hauler to a close-reaching position.

The theory here is that the wind is so light that sail fullness won't work. Instead the energy in the wind can be extracted by a smaller amount of *sail camber*, the curvature of the sail that generates power. The theory is similar to an aircraft wing where the shape of the wing changes due to its flaps. A sail also changes shape by way of its sail trim. In light wind, upwind, to maintain any chance of headway, the boat must be sailed on a close reach because sailing close-hauled is impossible. When you are reaching, the action of the waves on the boat will be reduced and the sails' shape

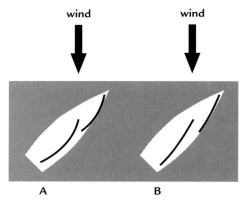

In extremely light wind a flat sail (B) is often more effective than a very full sail (A).

will therefore remain aerodynamic since they will not bounce as much. Experimentation is the key to finding the fastest trim and course.

In light wind remember to have the crew sit very still. Keep the boat heeled over to leeward and keep your crew quiet and conscientious of not losing momentum. When someone has to move, he should glide like a cat. Your crew may sit to leeward to maintain a leeward heel, but the one exception may be the helmsman. He may prefer to sit to windward, where he has a better feel for the boat and the waves. I like to steer from leeward in very light wind. You may also have someone looking toward the horizon for the new breeze. In no-wind races, the winner is the boat that gets the new breeze first. Anything you can do to position your boat toward the side of the course that has the new breeze will help you win the race.

Anticipating and predicting the new breeze is both an art and a science. You should know the official forecast. North America in the summer is often a light-wind area, and consequently some races turn into the proverbial crapshoot. The sailors with local knowledge will have an edge, for they will know the tendencies of the present breeze, the dying breeze, and the new breeze. Keep a notebook of local knowledge where you can record your experience and those of other sailors (particularly the winners). By doing this, you will build up a bank of information on particular areas.

When the current turns against you in light wind, anchoring is an effective tool. Take bearings on navigation aids or landmarks; when you discover you are being set back, gently slip an anchor over the side near the shrouds, where it will not be visible to the competition. Your crew is usually sitting to leeward in these conditions, and the anchor can be handed up on deck unnoticed and set over the side without loud commands. The trick here is to be sneaky (I love that word). Anchoring is legal as long as you drop the anchor straight down. You are not permitted to throw the anchor forward and pull yourself up on the anchor to gain ground.

Your boat will give the illusion of sailing, although you are anchored to the bottom. Everyone else is slipping back while you maintain your distance to the mark, so you actually increase your lead over the other boats. It will appear to the competition that you are sailing directly up current. They, of course, are being swept directly down current. This can lead to a nice gain before they catch on.

If you think you'll need to anchor, it's best to sail into shallower water where the job of setting an anchor will be easier. And

Getting Back into the Game in Light Winds

In an Atlantic Coast Laser Championship—sailed in light winds off Annapolis, Maryland—I finished a dismal thirty-second out of fifty-seven boats in the first race. It was a disappointing finish, but the experience turned into a great opportunity to learn how to sail a small boat in light winds. To add to the challenge, I was heavier than most of the competition. For many, this situation could be considered the ultimate in frustration. But I was able to improve my standing to the top five by focusing on four key techniques: attitude, making boat improvements, learning from the competition, and experimenting. The list below of what I learned may help you next time you are in a similar situation.

Attitude

The biggest hurdle to overcome is an attitude of disappointment. Look at the opportunity to race against light-air speed demons as a chance to improve your own sailing skills. If you don't worry about the outcome of the race, your performance on the water will improve. Many surprising things happen in light air.

Your job is to be in a position to find the favorable wind. In large fleets in light air, there are often big shake-ups throughout the race. With the right attitude you may find yourself in a position to take advantage of these shifts when they occur.

Victory in sailboat racing can come in little ways. Even small improvements from race to race are incentives to work harder.

Don't worry about some boats sailing faster.

Boat Improvements

In light winds, sail as light as you possibly can. Leave everything back on the dock unless you absolutely need it.

Be sure your rudder and centerboard blades are wet-sanded and the bottom is clean before leaving the dock. Always check for seaweed on your blades.

Before the race, tune up with a partner to be sure that you're sailing in the fastest groove. I worked out with two boats. One sailor was my weight and the other considerably lighter.

Learn from the Competition

Don't assume that you're doing everything correctly. Watch other boats to see what you can do to improve. During the Laser Atlantic Coasts, Ed Adams sailed by, noticed my outhaul was fairly tight, and remarked, "Gee, Gary, if you loosened your outhaul I bet you would be faster." I did, and he was right! You really appreciate help. Thank you, Ed.

Jim Brady noticed that my mast rig didn't seem quite right. Back at the dock we did a little work with some gray tape to produce a little more bend in the mast.

I also noticed that the top sailors were all sailing with their travelers all the way down. If the traveler is too high, the leech of the main stalls the wind.

The biggest mistake in light wind is trying to pinch, particularly in short, choppy waves. You must keep your speed up. Foot for speed!

Experiment

Experimentation takes many forms. My advice is to make one adjustment at a time and see if it improves your speed. In light winds, one of the biggest effects on boats of all sizes is the position of crew weight. Look around to see where the fastest sailors are sitting and then try that position. Generally in light wind you want your weight forward and the boat heeling to leeward, although three-time Laser World Champ Glenn Bourke writes in his book, *Championship Laser Sailing,* that actually heeling a boat to windward in light air makes you point higher and go fast. It's an interesting notion that must work well for him, so I gave this technique a try. I was unable to make it work, but I felt better for having experimented. For me, a slight leeward heel is more comfortable.

Experiment with all your adjustments, such as boom-vang tension, sheet tension, and even steering technique. For example you could ease the main, being careful not to allow the boat to bear off. Make small adjustments.

Keep the boat steady in waves by putting your weight against the boom, not necessarily pushing it down but pushing the boom out.

---

there is usually less current where the water is not as deep.

When you're racing in these light-wind conditions, be aware of the physical condition of your crew. It's often hot, and the crew should be adequately protected from the sun. Dehydration is a serious problem. Drink lots of water and avoid soda, which dehydrates you even more.

Keeping the crew's mental condition sharp is very important. You want them to be ready to continue racing when the wind does return. A lunch break or even a swim may be a good idea. You might also send some crew below to nap.

Sailing in no wind is tough stuff. It may be best either to head for the dock and stop sailing, or pace yourself with patience, realizing that anything can happen. Enjoy the experience. An open mind will do the trick.

Fast Finishes

Finishing a race is always emotional. Winning is exhilarating: if you sail past a few boats right at the end of the race, you get a big thrill and build momentum for the next race. If you lose badly, it's a relief to finish. Whether you win or lose, don't allow your feelings to stand in the way of your priorities. Being elated, disappointed,

Gary Jobson (left) and Ted Turner (right) in a close match as they approach the finish line. Plan for your final sprint early to reach the finish line first.

or exhausted is natural. Immediately after finishing there are two attributes to strive for: increased knowledge and eagerness for the next contest.

When you round the final mark and head for the finish, think about your options: protecting your position, being aggressive, or taking chances to pass. At this point it's important to know your race standings. One crew member should add up the numbers. If it's the last race of the regatta and you're losing, it might be worthwhile to take some big chances. Early in a regatta, however, it's better to be conservative. Once you've decided on your philosophy, it's time to go to work.

Approach the finish like a sprinter. Pick up the pace with all the energy you have left. Right at the end, lunge for the line. To be in good position, start preparing for the finish early.

Once the race ends, it's natural to want to relax and savor the moment. But if there is another race scheduled for the day, discipline yourself and your crew to prepare immediately. Pack the spinnaker, reset the rig, and bail out the water. Preparing early lets you unwind at a controlled pace. When everything is cleaned up, then it's time to reflect and think about any lessons that might improve your chances for the next race. This is also the time to eat a sandwich and have a drink.

The Conservative Approach to Finishing

At this point in the race, you are sailing near boats that are similar in speed and, possibly, tactical ability. Try to pass one or two boats at a time.

Avoid getting into one-on-one combat with another boat. Tacking duels drive both boats backward relative to the rest of the fleet. Here is a way to shake off a pest. If a boat tacks on your wind, tack away early and then tack back on the leading boat's hip to discourage them from making a second covering tack.

Immediately after completing your tack, keep your bow down lower than the leading boat until you're sailing at full speed. The leading boat will watch your actions carefully. If you point higher, the leader will immediately tack to cover. If you are angled lower, the leader will likely hold off on tacking.

If you are leading, you can avoid a continuing confrontation by tacking slightly to leeward of the approaching boats and

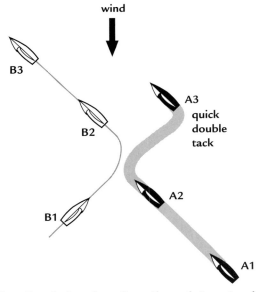

Boat B tacks directly on Boat A's wind. Boat A tacks away early but it tacks back quickly on to starboard to stay with the leading boat and discourage it from making a new tack.

ahead. This might seem like a polite action to your competitor, but it puts you in a commanding position without starting a grudge match.

There is always a question of whether to cover or split. A story told to me by

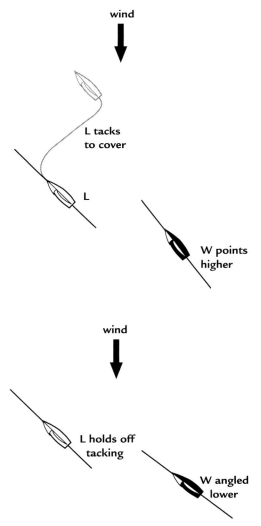

The course of W will help L decide whether to tack or not. If W sails a high course (top), L will tack to cover to windward. If W sails a low course (bottom), L will most likely continue sailing on the same tack.

Conn Findlay, who was crewing for Dennis Conner in the 1976 Olympic Games, is a good illustration of this dilemma. Findlay had won two gold medals and one bronze medal in rowing in previous Olympics. On the last leg of the final race, Findlay was hanging from the wire of their Tempest. Conner wondered aloud if it would be better to protect their position, which would guarantee them a bronze medal, or take some chances by splitting from the fleet. That move might earn them a silver medal, but they'd also be running the risk of losing it all. Findlay's comment to Conner was succinct, "Well, I've got my medals." Conner was sailing in his first Olympics and he took the conservative route. The USA team took the bronze.

In general, to sail a conservative race, avoid experimenting with trim to improve boatspeed. Go with what has worked throughout the race. Build on your experience of the day. You are in a proven groove. Making drastic adjustments will likely backfire.

Think more about tactics than boatspeed. Ask yourself, "What side of the course has been favored? Is the same pattern repeating itself?" Look ahead and ask yourself, "Where is there more wind?" (Remember the techniques for finding the favored side of the course.) This process should only take fifteen seconds or so. As I've repeated frequently, go with your first instinct. Belaboring the issue of which way to sail will cause confusion.

If you're behind, work to keep your boat in the center of the course so your options to sail left or right stay open. On the other hand, if you're leading, push the trailing boats out to the layline to take away any leverage.

There's often a choice of whether to cover the competition or play the windshifts. Picking shifts is tempting, but in doing so, there is no guarantee that you'll gain. The best bet is to try to do both simultaneously.

If you are leading, your first priority is to cover and to only tack at times that are advantageous to you! Wait for a puff, start your turn at full speed, and avoid sailing in disturbed wind.

If the wind is shifty, stay in phase without splitting a long way from the fleet. Again, it's a question of gaining some leverage without losing it all. If I'm

ahead, I like to tack before a boat crosses my stern.

LEVERAGE

The term *leverage* migrated to sailing from the financial world. To gain leverage is to find an advantage. If one boat is directly downwind of another, there's no leverage at all. But if one boat is able to position itself on another's windward hip and the wind lifts, then leverage has been established.

Think of every tactical choice in terms of a percentage chance of gaining or losing. On the last leg I like to stay with high-percentage moves such as staying between the competition and the mark, minimizing tacks, and avoiding big risks.

Taking a chance to gain leverage should be tried only when you're well behind and need a dramatic pass. Unfortunately, the chances of making this work are slim. In these situations I like to take the attitude,

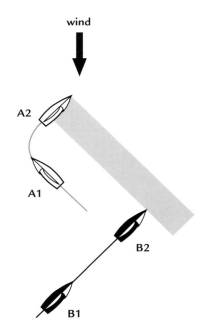

Maintain a controlling position by tacking just ahead of the beam of the leeward boat. Boat A maintains control by tacking before Boat B crosses its stern.

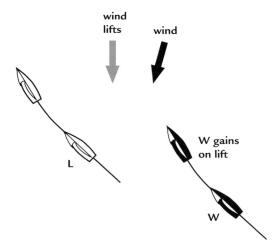

It's important to keep track of what the wind is doing. If a lift is expected, sail to the inside. Here W gains in a lift.

"Just for fun, let's give this a try." You can save yourself considerable angst by not worrying about the outcome.

Sailing with an open mind and with the willingness to experiment, while realizing it could all fall apart, is key. When it works out, there's no greater thrill. As an example, while racing on Long Island Sound our boat was trailing the class by over a mile with 20 miles left of a distance race. The wind was getting light. The leading group of boats stuck together like magnets: no one wanted to split. We took a chance that the wind would die and a new wind would arrive from the north. So we rode the dying southerly toward the north. The wind did die and we waited. After an hour the new wind filled in. Thanks to our northerly leverage we got the wind first, sailed around the fleet, and won. Cool!

When you wrestle with the philosophical question of covering versus gaining leverage, remember that it's hard to actually pass. If you're leading, a trailing boat might catch up but will struggle to sail around you.

Without question the most famous pass happened on the fifth of six legs in the seventh race of the 1983 America's Cup. *Australia II* was fifty-seven seconds behind. *Liberty* had a comfortable lead but the crew was nervous about their speed. So *Liberty* started playing the windshifts without covering. Bad call! *Australia II* simply split, *Liberty* went the wrong way, and the Aussies grabbed the lead. On the final leg, *Australia II* covered every move by *Liberty* all the way to the finish. The lesson is that *Liberty* risked everything to gain leverage. But in doing so, they cut their percentage chances of winning. The door opened and *Australia II* slipped through.

As you near the finish line (within twenty boatlengths), it's okay to make double tacks to cover, even if it means giving away distance. Don't open the door by allowing a competitor to sit on your windward hip or to leeward and ahead. Your goal is to stay directly between the competition and the finish line. Even then, you can be disappointed. In one Liberty Cup match race in New York Harbor our boat was just ten boatlengths from the finish line. Our competitor, Peter Gilmour from Australia, was nicely tucked away twenty boatlengths to leeward. Suddenly the wind stopped. Both boats sat for minutes. Finally, the wind filled from leeward and Gilmour sailed right around us to win the race. We did nothing wrong. Sometimes it is best not to think too hard about a situation like this.

The Aggressive Approach to Finishing

When you must pass other boats to gain points, your philosophy changes dramatically. Even when I'm behind, I like to orchestrate a situation so the lead boats attack each other. Sailors often get weird as they near the finish and they make irrational moves. Often the crew of a boat making a maneuver gets so wrapped up in its own activity that they fail to watch for other boats. You can use this lack of attention to your advantage. Try to tack so a leader covers you without thinking about another boat with the right-of-way. Have a crew member watch closely. Is the leader spending a lot of time watching your boat? This is a sure sign that a leader is nervous. Or do

The most famous finish in the history of sailboat racing was the seventh race of the 1983 America's Cup. Here Australia II *crosses six boatlengths ahead of* Liberty *after two exciting lead changes.*

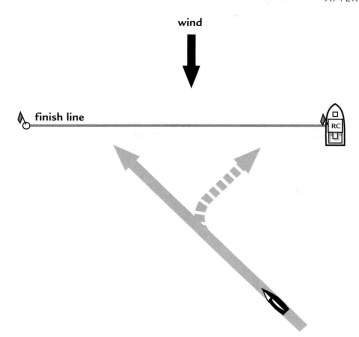

Make your final approach to the middle of the finish line until you know which end is favored. If you head for the middle, you have an option of tacking away if there is traffic with other boats at the line.

they spin the boat too quickly? This is a clue that the helmsman is oversteering. Your chances of passing are encouraging.

It's a great joy to watch a group of three or four boats battle each other, leaving you to sail in clear wind. When boats lock up, someone loses. As mentioned earlier, always stay clear of a pack.

When you are behind, playing wind-shifts is essential. It might be bothersome to have a boat directly upwind, but if they are more than six mast lengths away, their wind shadow will have little effect on your boat. Carefully playing the wind and stay-ing in phase will help you gain extra dis-tance. The tougher part is the pass.

In handicap racing there is a time differ-ence between boats. I like to keep a running tab at turning marks so I can understand if

I'm winning or losing based on time. To help, imagine that you are racing a one-design. If a boat is, say, ten seconds ahead on handicap at the last mark, you need to make up two boatlengths.

As you approach the finish line, keep your boat in the center of the course. You are taking a greater chance when heading to one end of the finish line—approaching the middle keeps your options open. If you are getting pushed to the starboard layline, elongate your time on starboard tack to keep centered (see illustration next page). The same philosophy of staying to the mid-dle to take advantage of options works in football and soccer.

Another question is whether to pass a group of boats all at once or just one boat at a time. The answer depends on your stand-

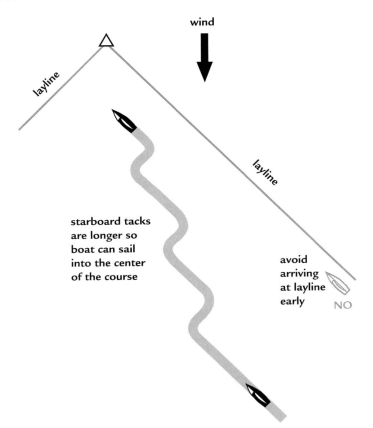

If you are being forced out to a layline, elongate your tacks on starboard to work back to the center of the racecourse.

ings. Early in a regatta, I like to minimize risk. At the end, if I'm down, I go for it. I'd rather end down in the standings after trying hard as opposed to settling for a mediocre finish with no fight. Early in the regatta, I'd rather stay alive to fight another day than risk finishing so poorly that there is no time for recovery.

Closing the Finish Line

By staying focused you can gain a lot of ground (and boats) closing the finish or within five boatlengths of the finish. The techniques are similar to rounding a mark. Speed and position are king.

It is essential to cross the finish line on the favored tack. The closer you sail at a right angle to the line, the earlier you will finish. Flags on the race committee boat tell you which tack is favored. Another way is to simply note your course on both tacks and see which one is at a right angle to the line. This is a judgment call.

Study the finish line to figure out which end is favored. Head for the middle of the line until you understand, for sure, which end is better. Boats that finish ahead will

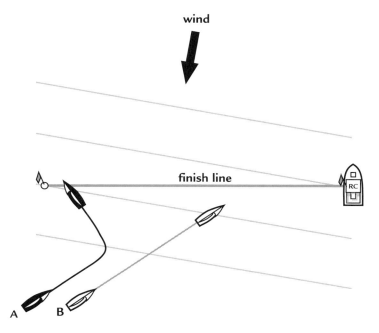

wind

finish line

RC

A   B

Always cross the finish line on the favored tack. Here Boat A's starboard tack (more nearly a right angle to the finish line) is the favored tack.

give you a clue as to which end is favored. Note how close a leading boat is to a right angle of the finish line. Does the boat appear to be sailing straight down the line? If so, this is the unfavored tack. Flags on the committee boat are also helpful clues when looking for the favored end. If the flags are flying to the right side of the finish line, the portside of the line is favored.

If you are sailing upwind, the opposite end that is favored at the start will likely be favored at the finish (see illustration next page). Be careful here because conditions can change. These include the direction of the wind, waves, current, or even the effect of spectator boats milling around to watch. Racing boats that have just crossed the line also have a big effect on the turbulence of the wind and water in the finish line area.

With so many obstacles around the finish, look hard for one final puff of wind. This can be hard to read on the water. I find flags helpful, both in their intensity of flutter and direction. Flags that are high off the water are best. The angle of heel of other boats is another good indicator of puffs. When you see a boat ahead heel over you know more wind is coming.

The most powerful final approach position (upwind or downwind) is on starboard. This forces boats to maneuver around you. For an upwind finish, keep a low course for speed. Many sailors tend to pinch as they near the end of the race.

If two boats are side by side, the final "lunge" (also known as *shooting the line*) could make the difference. The windward boat is in a better position to luff for the

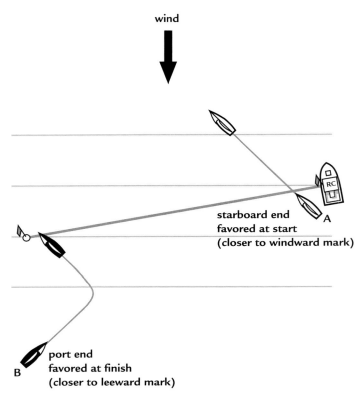

wind

starboard end
favored at start
(closer to windward mark)

A

port end
favored at finish
(closer to leeward mark)

B

If the starting line is used for both the start and the finish, the opposite end will be favored. In this case the starboard end is favored at the start; therefore, the port end is favored at the finish. This assumes that the wind has not shifted.

line, while the leeward boat should go for speed. The problem for the leeward boat is closing the angle toward the windward boat while at the same time losing speed. Shooting the line is a tricky business. It's hard to judge accurately. My motto is, "When in doubt, don't shoot."

It's better to finish at one end of the line because your position is easier to judge. Plus, if you're on the favored end, you will gain boatlengths on the competition. If the line looks even, finish at the end where the line is being called by the race committee. The line caller will naturally have your boat

in the corner of his eye because you're closer. An alteration of course toward the race committee boat helps bring your boat into sharper focus and possibly over the line sooner. You might even make some noise to attract additional attention. A word of caution here: don't overdo it. A helpful reference is to line up the flag with the race official calling the finish. The range closes as you near the line (see illustration page 134).

An alternative to shooting the line is to tack all the way through the wind. Never allow the jib to back. Just as in any maneuver, remember to turn the helm slowly at

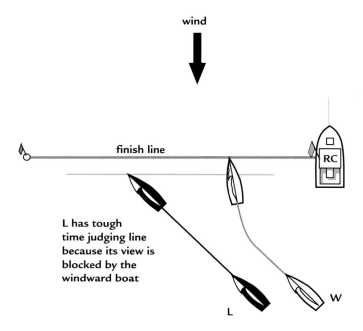

wind

finish line

RC

L has tough
time judging line
because its view is
blocked by the
windward boat

W

L

*Shooting the line is tricky business. As W and L approach the line, W has the advantage because it is in a bet-
ter position to luff, closing the angle with the line. L would have a difficult time judging when to luff and
closing the angle with the line because its view of the committee boat is blocked by the other boat.*

first, trim the sails as you luff, and use your
crew weight to assist in the turn. It is best
to do this at one end or the other because it
is difficult to judge when you are crossing in
the middle of the line. Tack right on the line
to make this tactic work.

One of my most memorable finishes
occurred between the Maxi boats *Matador*
and *Boomerang*. It was an emotionally
charged race. The large spectator fleet
crowded in for a good look. The boats were
even in speed. With ten lengths to go the
bows were also even. The question for us
on *Matador* was, How can we get ahead?

With twenty-four crew on each boat it
was hard to keep everyone sitting low and
concentrating on their own jobs. As the tactician, it was my job to watch *Boomerang*'s

actions. They were to leeward and we were
nervous about a sudden luff. As the line
neared I noticed more of their crew looking
at us. And their foredeck crew moved forward to prepare to drop their jib. This technique is popular on Maxi boats. Lowering
the jib when you luff up reduces windage.
The problem is the crew thinks more about
the sail than about speed. Plus the extra
weight on the bow slows the boat.

Instead of going for a jib drop, we quietly bore off for speed. The combination of
Matador accelerating with *Boomerang* decel-
erating in the last two lengths made the difference. *Matador* won by just two seconds.

On a downwind finish avoid sailing too
slowly on your final approach. In other
words, don't sail a course that is too low.

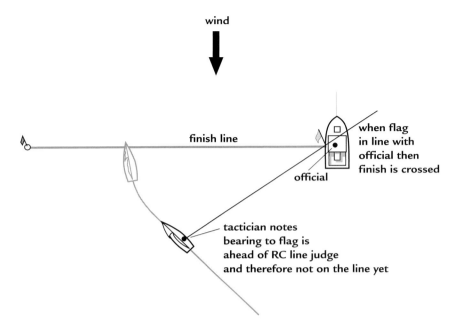

The tactician notes that the bearing to the flag is ahead of the race official and therefore they are not yet on the line. When the flag aligns with the official they will have crossed the finish line.

Maxi yachts Boomerang *and* Matador *finishing bow to bow. Great rivalries bring out the best in everyone.*

More speed pays. Cross the line on the favored jibe, cross at the favored end, don't shoot unless you have a clear bearing of the line, and finish at one of the ends to gain leverage. When sailing downwind, determine the course to take by observing which jibe has a closer to right angle to the line.

Proper etiquette dictates that boats should immediately clear the finishing area so the trailing boats have room to finish. The best action is to sail away at least fifteen boatlengths before dropping sails, congratulating each other, and passing around drinks.

While most top sailors spend time practicing starts, it is equally important to practice finishes. Experiment near a buoy. Learn how much momentum your boat carries in different wind strengths and wave heights. Exciting finishes are the highlight of every sport. You will improve your chances by practicing for the conclusion of the race.

Tactical Tips for Getting Around the Course

As a way to end this important section on how to sail to windward, downwind, and finessing your finish, here are some key tactical tips:

1. Downwind, use a masthead fly to read your apparent wind. Watch the masthead flies of your competitors to see if they are blocking your wind.

2. If you lose distance after crossing tacks or jibes with another boat, have the courage to shift sides of the course.

3. As a rule, always stay on the side of the course where the majority of boats are sailing.

4. When making a maneuver, always know the new course to steer in advance. If you plan a tack or jibe, look at an object on shore, another boat, or the compass as a reference.

5. Recovering from adversity is hard. But in most races you can make one mistake and still do well. Your goal should be to sail better from one race to the next by eliminating little errors.

6. One of the most important maneuvers is dipping a right-of-way yacht. When approaching another boat, always accelerate for speed. If you are on port tack, decide early whether to tack, to lee bow, or to dip. A good rule of thumb is if two-thirds of your boat can make it across usually you can successfully tack to leeward. But when the crossing is close, lee bowing another boat is risky. When dipping, start three or four boatlengths away. Beware of the other boat tacking. Be prepared to come back up on the wind the instant you see the other boat starting its tack. Your goal in dipping is to be close-hauled and sailing to windward the instant your bow passes the other boat's stern.

7. Mistakes to avoid:
❖ Being over the starting line early
❖ Staying in disturbed wind for long periods of time
❖ Sailing on the wrong side of the course after you have lost to the boats on the other side
❖ Getting into a protest
❖ Not communicating the next maneuver to your crew

❖ Trying to play both sides of the course simultaneously by tacking too frequently

❖ Not bailing out of a bad situation at a mark rounding or on the starting line

❖ Not changing helmsman when you're slow

8. When approaching a leeward mark, never allow yourself to sail directly downwind. Always approach the leeward mark on a reaching course.

9. Avoid tacking immediately after a leeward mark so you don't sail back through your disturbed wind and choppy water. Sail at least three boatlengths before tacking.

10. If you are going slow, make a big change such as easing your sails, bearing off for speed, or sailing on the other tack.

11. If you are being covered closely by another boat, the time to get out of phase is to tack when you are faster. Never tack when you are slower than another boat.

12. If you are well down in the fleet, don't try to pass every boat at once by taking a flyer. Flyers rarely pay off. Work on passing one boat at a time.

CHAPTER 6

Racing at Night or in Reduced Visibility

The challenge of racing at night is that your physical senses are dulled, particularly your sense of sight. So much of our ability to sail fast effectively is based on sight: sailing by the telltales, observing the depth and location of sail draft, seeing snarled lines or crossed halyards. When you're sailing at night, it's also hard to see the clouds, the wind on the water, and the course differential of other boats. There are daytime racing situations of reduced visibility—in fog or squalls—that also require a heightened sensory awareness. This chapter provides hints for racing during these times.

Instruments to Gauge Performance

Good instrumentation is a huge asset at night or in reduced visibility. For a racing sailor, critical information includes boatspeed, sailing direction (compass), water depth (depth sounder), wind speed, apparent wind angle, and true wind direction. Here is bit more about each:

Boatspeed indicator: shows you how fast you are moving through the water. I suggest adjusting your instruments on a measured mile so they are accurate.

Compass: keeping a steady course is fundamental. But with tactical considerations and changing winds, your course varies. Keep track with a compass.

Depth sounder: most racing takes place close to land. Keeping track of the water depth is essential.

Wind speed: knowing the strength of the wind insures that you have the correct sail

Racing at night takes considerable discipline. Instruments are particularly helpful at night to keep a boat moving fast. Big gains can be made during nighttime.

up. As the wind speed increases, your boat sails faster. Noting the wind speed over the deck (apparent wind) is your best indicator for selecting the fastest sails.

Apparent wind angle (AWA): I use this indicator to keep me at a consistent angle to the wind. This is particularly helpful if the wind changes direction. While the AWA is the same, the course being steered is different, indicating a windshift.

True wind direction: most instruments will calculate true wind. When the wind shifts more than five degrees, it might be helpful to tack or jibe.

Gather the information you need for that night's racing before darkness falls. For ex-

ample, at dusk take bearings on your close competitors and then keep a bearing log of the position of their lights throughout the night.

The apparent wind angle instrument, along with the compass, are the two most overused instruments by the novice helmsman at night. Neither of these instruments will react quickly enough to allow championship helmsmanship. They should be used only as secondary information sources.

First choices at night for steering references are stationary lights ahead, low stars on the horizon, or even the horizon illuminated by moonlight. The key to effective steering at night is using a reliable reference. These objects are most useful

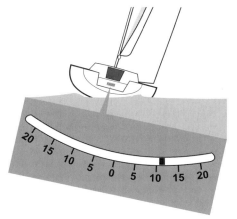

Use an inclinometer at night to determine your angle of heel.

when a wave pushes the bow off course. You can observe this immediately if you are looking ahead through the rigging. But these changes are slow to show up on the compass or the apparent wind indicator. If the night is particularly black, with no reference lights or stars, you probably should tack just behind and to windward of a competitor. By looking to leeward you can see a stern light just behind your genoa and thereby maintain an accurate course. If it is a dark night with no horizon, use an inclinometer to measure your angle of heel.

Onboard instruments and graphs of your performance can give you key information on your performance, which can in turn help you make the right decisions on the racecourse.

VELOCITY MADE GOOD

Velocity made good (VMG) both to windward and to leeward is a valuable reference at night *and* during the day. Sometimes though, racers rely more on this information at night or in times of restricted visibility. VMG is the answer to the age-old question whether you should point the boat close to the wind or foot the vessel for faster speed through the water. The correct answer is the course that gives you the best VMG. You can read the VMG on an instrument that makes this calculation. When in doubt it's better to sail fast than to point too high, especially at night.

VMG is also helpful during downwind sailing. Remember that sailing directly downwind may not necessarily give you your fastest VMG. You rarely sail a true downwind course. Boats usually jibe through 40 to 90 degrees, depending on the strength of the wind.

VELOCITY PREDICTION PROGRAM

A *velocity prediction program (VPP)* for your boat is extremely important. A velocity prediction program is used to develop a polar diagram, a graphical reference of the theoretical speed a sailboat should achieve in different wind speeds and angles to the wind. The idea is to understand the optimum course to sail for a given wind strength and direction. During the day you can have a good seat-of-the-pants feel for different sailing angles. By watching the competition you can determine your correct angle. At night you don't have this advantage, but the polar diagram created by the VPP can be used as a reference to help find the optimum downwind course and speed that will get you to the next mark in the minimum amount of time. By using a programmable calculator that provides your VPP or even several trial-and-error vector plots, you can determine the right sailing angle. Make a careful note

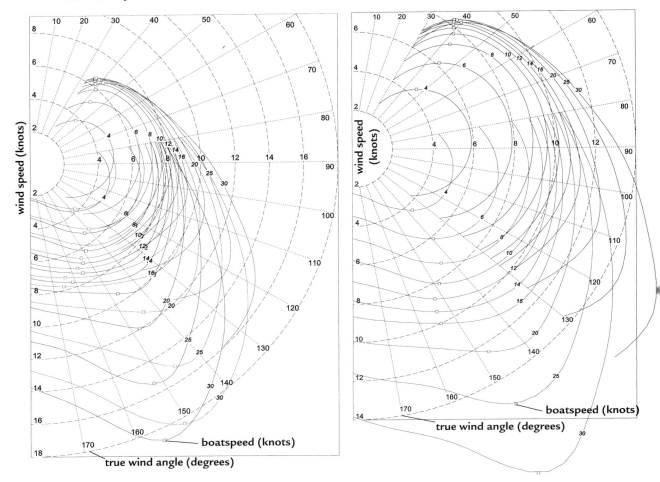

Polar diagrams for a Mumm 30 (left), a 52-foot one-design racing yacht (right), and a 40-foot one-design (opposite). These are available from boat designers, or you can create your own. The polar diagram is a graphical representation of a boat's performance across a range of wind speeds and true wind directions. Optimal upwind and downwind conditions are marked as small rectangles on the boatspeed contours for each wind speed. (Copyright Farr Yacht Design, Ltd.)

of your daytime performance and use the information at night. Using a VPP is not an exact science, rather it is a reference to experiment with.

You can develop your own polar diagram by actual experience or get the information from a designer or sailmaker, or even purchase a VPP from a design office.

But remember these are only references. Many times you can sail faster than your predicted performance such as in smooth water, as a result of brilliant steering, or when there is more wind aloft.

To create your own numbers, make a graph for every knot of wind speed along the side of the paper; along the bottom add

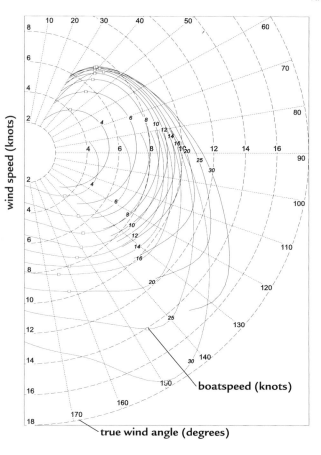

boatspeed (knots)

true wind angle (degrees)

one strong suggestion I have is to name a safety officer. This may be the skipper, or it may be someone else with safety experience and knowledge. It is helpful when one person is thinking about safety and is conscious of when to recommend putting on life jackets or safety harnesses, or when to reduce sail.

Safety on a boat at night (and during the day) is simply a good, solid dose of common sense, awareness, anticipation, and prevention. Sometimes, however, tragedies happen at sea. The tragedy I witnessed in May 2002 on Long Island Sound (see sidebar next page) caused a great deal of reflection and generated important lessons on how to sail safely.

LIGHTS

On most racing boats there never seem to be enough powerful flashlights or enough spare batteries on board. A disposable waterproof light is a good tool, and each crew member should have one in his or her pocket. Another reason to have one in your pocket is in case you go overboard. The ability to shine a light toward your potential rescuers could save your life.

There should be one very powerful spotlight on board that plugs into the boat's power supply. The light can shine down through the water or out across the night. It can be used to find unlighted buoys or for emergency situations.

Use a simple plastic universal joint to clamp a small flashlight to one of the forward stanchions angled at the sails. After tacking to windward, the flashlight should be redirected on to the jib telltales. Having a light on the telltales is extremely effective

space for every knot of boatspeed. Note your performance. Over time, these numbers will indicate your actual performance. For example, in 10 knots of breeze your boat might average 6.8 knots. Should you sail the rhumb line with the wind at 170 degrees apparent? Or should you reach up to 135 degrees apparent with a dramatic increase in speed? The VPP will give you the answer based on wind velocity.

Safety

The need to take responsibility for safety on board remains with the skipper. However,

Tragedy: Man Overboard

(Written with Peter Isler)

Sailing—like many other active, outdoor pursuits—can sometimes be hazardous. That's part of life, but it should not discourage us from racing. As sailors, we have a responsibility to prepare our crews, boats, and ourselves to react swiftly and efficiently during an emergency. Of course, the reality of an actual experience is always tougher than the theory.

None of us aboard *Blue Yankee* had experienced a man-overboard situation in thirty-three years of ocean racing. But on Friday night, May 24, 2002, soon after the start of the Block Island Race, our bowman Jamie Boeckel was injured and knocked overboard by a broken spinnaker pole during a sail change. The memory of the incident will stay with us forever. There are always lessons to be learned in the aftermath of a tragedy. The memory of Jamie Boeckel is best served by helping to prevent future catastrophes. We hope our experience will serve as a guide for sailors finding themselves in a similar situation.

Prior to leaving the dock for the start, *Blue Yankee*'s owner Bob Towse held an in-depth, thoughtful meeting covering safety and strategy. We discussed our man-overboard procedure, the need to wear life jackets, the location of safety equipment (a list was posted), and communication procedures. Following the session we headed to the racecourse anticipating a good race.

Blue Yankee won the start and set a fast pace. Just after sunset, 25 miles from the start, the wind increased to 32 knots. During a spinnaker change the boat rounded up. Standing on the pulpit, bowman Jamie Boeckel struggled to release the shackle holding the old spinnaker. The two spinnakers luffed violently. The pole broke and hit Jamie hard. He went into the water.

As he slid past the leeward rail, crewman Brock Callen noticed that Jamie was unconscious. With the boat sailing at 13 knots, Brock dove in. Neither was wearing a life jacket.

Brock reached Jamie in seconds and tried to revive him. Meanwhile the crew worked hard—dousing the two spinnakers (made difficult by the broken pole slashing across the foredeck), lowering the mainsail, alerting the U.S. Coast Guard about the situation, and motoring back to the crew in the water.

The water temperature was only 53°F. We found Brock near the man-overboard gear but Jamie was missing. Brock reported that he held Jamie up for a few minutes but eventually he sank. Brock was near shock when he was pulled back aboard *Blue Yankee*.

Five boats retired from the race to assist us when they heard our call on VHF channel 16. At least fifteen additional boats also came to our aid. The Coast Guard and Bridgeport (Connecticut) police arrived within fifteen minutes of our call. We were impressed by the quick response. The authorities arranged for a helicopter to search as well.

At midnight the Bridgeport police boarded *Blue Yankee*. They were businesslike yet cordial while taking statements and names and surveying the scene. After an hour and a half, *Blue Yankee* was released to return to her berth in Stamford. Just before departing Sergeant Wolfe said, "I hope this incident won't discourage any of you from racing in the future." It was a soothing comment at a time when we were feeling considerable anguish.

Reflecting on the tragedy we developed a list of thoughts and recommended procedures for ourselves and others in similar situations. We encourage all sailors to think through, in advance, what they would do. We hope these thoughts are helpful.

❖ Be considerate of others and their safety. Be prepared to lend a hand whenever it is needed.

❖ Make sure the entire crew understands the operation of lifesaving/man-overboard gear (i.e., how to deploy it quickly). Also make sure the location of all safety gear (life jackets, radios, etc.) is clearly understood by all.

❖ Make sure the entire crew understands the boat's man-overboard procedures (i.e., shout "Man overboard!," spot the victim, deploy lifesaving gear, etc.). The crew must also be assigned set positions in the case of an emergency.

❖ When performing a difficult sail change, like a spinnaker peel, bear away enough so broaching is not a concern, especially if it is necessary to lock off one spinnaker sheet to free up the primary winch.

❖ Wear your life jacket any time you like, and certainly when operating on deck at nighttime or any time the conditions warrant. Expand the window of what you consider to be "life jacket" conditions and spread that attitude among your crew. If your life jacket is so uncomfortable or unwieldy that you choose not to wear it when you should, then get a new life jacket—one that you will wear—even if that means sacrificing some flotation performance.

❖ Carry a pocket strobe or at least a waterproof flashlight at night.

❖ Have a big knife in a sheath readily accessible in the middle of the boat.

❖ Have some sort of GPS operable from on deck with an easily operated man-overboard button to save the location of an incident.

❖ Do all you can to keep the victim in sight—assign one crew member this duty. If it's night, the man-overboard gear should have an operational light to make for an easier return.

❖ Get the boat turned around as fast and effectively as possible. Usually that means dropping headsails, but not always. It may mean cutting away sails, but not always. Each situation is different and requires cool assessment. The worst thing you can do is panic. For example, after dropping headsails, the crew of our boat took an extra few seconds to ensure all ropes were out of the water before engaging the engine. To get a line wrapped up in the propeller would incapacitate the engine and severely limit the boat's ability to return.

❖ If there are problems, make an emergency call on VHF channel 16 immediately. There are lots of boats out there that could help, and many are monitoring this channel.

❖ Any time you hear of (i.e., on the VHF radio) or see a dangerous situation on the water, stop whatever you are doing and do all you can to help. Every boater on the water has a responsibility to themselves and each other. Maritime attorney Lars Forsberg explains that there is no legal obligation to help another boat in distress but that it is morally correct to lend assistance. The exception is when a vessel is involved in a marine casualty. And then: "The master or individual in charge of a vessel involved in a marine casualty shall . . . render necessary assistance to each individual affected to save that affected individual from danger caused by the marine casualty, so far as the master or individual in charge can do so without serious danger to the master's or individual's vessel or to individuals on board."

❖ During sail changes and maneuvers the most experienced sailors (watch captain, skipper) should watch the evolution carefully and point out solutions to problems as they occur (no yelling).

❖ Maneuvers should be discussed in advance, particularly the course to steer or a course of action if something goes wrong.

These crews—wearing life jackets and safety harnesses—are prepared for rough seas.

in helping the helmsman keep the boat in the groove. The telltales should be different colors and different heights on both sides of the jib. Telltale windows are commonly used. If you plan on buying new sails, order telltale windows. They can also be installed into your current sails in the off-season. The most effective arrangement is to use two or three windows spread along the length of the jib luff.

The Watch System

Another key to sailing at night is the watch system. In recent years the full-court press where nobody sleeps/everybody works has been popular. Sometimes this watch system can win a race—particularly a short one with a lot of sail changes, spinnaker reaching with staysails, or varying conditions. Obviously it's not good for longer races. The biggest mistake in distance races is burnout from staying up all night.

The standard watch system of four-on and four-off is most common, as is the slight variation of three-on and three-off. There are "Swedish" systems that use four-,

five-, and six-hour periods to divide up the twenty-four hours in a day, with the shorter watches taking place in early morning hours when it's supposedly harder to stay awake. Most of these systems have an odd number of periods, so on longer passages of several days or a week or more each person changes his routine in a three-day cycle.

In the recent round-the-world races, a watch system has been used where one-third of the crew is on deck, one-third is below, and the other third is on continuous standby. In other words, the standby crew's foul-weather gear is on and they are ready to come up on deck. But they stay below, out of the wind and spray; they only go up on deck as needed.

On larger boats, a rotating watch system can be effective where every hour an additional one or two crew members are brought up on deck to replace one or two who are then sent below. This way, the crew is not split into groups but the watch system keeps rotating fresh people on deck. This system takes considerable discipline to use, but it can be effective.

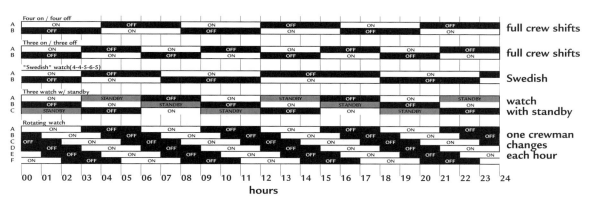

There are many variations for a watch-standing routine. The most popular is a four-hour-on and four-hour-off system (top). Also shown are the three-hour-on and three-hour-off system, the Swedish system, a watch system with one part of the crew on standby, and an hourly rotation system.

Friendly competition between the two watches—such as which had the greater distance sailed—boosts morale and makes races more interesting. It seems as if races always are lost on "the other watch." I find it helpful for watch captains to observe the routine on the other watch. Sometimes little tricks can be learned.

If you are part of the crew for a distance race, plan to be on deck at least five minutes prior to your watch to acclimate and to discuss the boat's situation with the person you are relieving. Look carefully at the GPS and charts before coming on deck. As you go off watch, communicate the current plan and all important information to the oncoming watch. Keep the log book up to date and listen to weather forecasts. Know what sails might be used next. Never relieve an off-going watch late. The whole system will break down.

There are also systems that segregate the afterguard (helmsman, tactician, navigator, owner, etc.) from the deck crew. The crew will stand four-on and four-off watches while the helm is rotated. Perhaps a four-hour trick is too long for a helmsman, even if he feels comfortable. A pair of helmsmen might go for an hour apiece by relieving each other. Then they would be relieved for the next two hours by another pair.

When choosing the best watch system for your boat, pick a system that will get the most out of your crew in the time needed to successfully complete the race. You may want to combine two of these watch systems in one race. Oftentimes, a standard watch system is sandwiched between two periods of full-court press at the start and finish of a long race.

There are two reasons why most boats go slower at night. The first is that practice is not conducted with the entire crew. To avoid this it's important to have the entire crew show up for a practice. The second is that practice is always conducted during the day, when everything is easily seen. To practice for a long race where you'll use a watch system, break your crew into watch sections and practice as small teams, and sneak in one practice at night, if possible. The maneuvers you will need to practice are: reefing, changing sails, tacking, setting the spinnaker, jibing, and taking down sail. If you conduct these types of practice sessions, you'll be way ahead of your competition. Few sailors practice in this way.

Using Common Sense

Finally, good common sense is an important part of any sailor's night-racing strategy. Pay attention to basic crew needs, such as keeping warm, preventing seasickness, staying awake, etc. It's important to realize that most people underestimate the magnitude of change when the sun goes down. Even in the middle of the summer, it can get cold racing a sailboat at night. Hot drinks and snacks should be available to the crew on deck throughout the night. People susceptible to seasickness should take active measures against the problem. (I have had good success with prescription antinausea patches.)

A skipper and his boat are only as good as his crew. A successful night-racing skipper realizes that darkness poses some special problems, particularly in the area of crew performance. He realizes that the boat can't be sailed in as narrow a groove as it is during the day. He realizes that his people aren't going to be as sharp, as awake, or as competent as they are during a day race. The night-racing skipper should be demanding, but he should allow a wider latitude and sail more conservatively and safely at night. This attitude will help a boat and its crew reach a higher potential during the dark portions of the race.

Mishaps can occur at any time. A well-organized crew practices and prepares for safety procedures and maneuvers.

CHAPTER 7

The Race Committee and Protests

The race committee and the jury are the authorities of the racecourse. As a racing sailor, you will deal with both of them. Hopefully, you won't deal with the jury overseeing protests too often. In this chapter we'll examine how both of these groups work so you know what to expect from each.

The Race Committee

During the 1995 America's Cup, I remarked on an ESPN broadcast that the racecourse was skewed. The windward mark was set perfectly into the wind, but a 0.7-knot crosscurrent forced the race boats to spend more time on port tack.

The next morning, as I made my daily greeting to the San Diego Yacht Club America's Cup race committee, I sensed something was wrong. As I approached the committee boat, the race officials were standing in a line with their backs to me. Two guns were fired; code flag Bravo (protest) was hoisted. And then, in unison, the entire committee mooned me. "Well," I thought to myself, "I guess race committees have feelings too." In the end everyone had a good laugh. But the point was made. It takes good strategic thinking to run a race. Like sailors, officials can make mistakes. And committees must make tough calls without the benefit of being on a sailboat.

Over the past twenty years, race committees have evolved into user-friendly organizations. Fortunately, the days of the stoic race officer refusing to communicate with sailors are over. Today the sailor and the race committee are on a merging course and racing is improving.

The San Diego Yacht Club race committee boat Corinthian *at the start of the 1995 America's Cup.*

There are increasing demands on to-day's race committees, including having to run multiple short-course races, enforcing PFD (personal flotation device) require-ments, safety-at-sea regulations, changing racing rules, video replays, computerized scoring, complex handicap scoring systems, professional sailors, high-budget racing pro-grams, demanding owners, increased me-dia exposure, financial costs, variable wind conditions (global warming), competitive one-design fleets, and overseeing certified umpires who watch every move. (An um-pire is on the water during a race and makes a call on a specific rule at that moment. If one boat is deemed to be wrong, a penalty turn is assessed. A jury conducts a hearing after a race to determine if rules have been

infringed.) All these elements combine to make the race committee's job a tough one.

The skill level of race committees has improved in recent years thanks to the co-ordinated efforts of US SAILING, the Na-tional Governing Body for sailing in the United States, and the more recent influ-ence of professional race officers. Major events such as the NOODs (National Off-shore One-Design regattas), Key West Race Week, the America's Cup, and the Olympics all employ professional principal race officers. Many yacht clubs now employ race managers. Amateur race committees can learn new techniques by studying how the pros operate, since the professionals have the advantage of running frequent events all over the world. Some clubs ask sailors to rotate on the race committee. This gives everyone an appreciation of what it is like to manage a race. US SAILING publishes guidelines on how to be a race officer.

Sailors and regatta organizers need to show their appreciation to race committees. A simple thank-you is a good start. At award presentations, a memento for the race officers, in addition to the sailors, is greatly appreciated. As for race officials, an open mind is important. It helps everyone if officials listen to sailors' requests.

Guidelines for Good Race Committee Work

It takes lots of cooperation and organization to run a smooth sailboat race. Here are some guidelines for race committees:

Timing

Start races on time.

Minimize time between races.

Use short starting sequences. I like three minutes for dinghies and six minutes for keelboats.

Communications

Ask spectator boats via VHF radio to keep their wake down.

Demand that nonstarting classes stay well clear of starting area.

Publish a thorough Notice of Race early.

Technique

Communicate all actions and intentions on VHF radio.

Use code flags.

Fly course flags at both ends of the line.

Use a hand-bearing compass for wind readings.

Send out a chase boat to read currents. Use a current stick next to an anchored buoy.

Move the leeward mark when the wind shifts before the boats arrive at the windward mark.

Use a loud horn or gun.

Use oversized anchor and ground tackle.

Do not delay races by attempting to make courses too perfect.

Scoring

Organize classes in narrow bands of handicap rating.

Test computer-scoring programs before the regatta.

Post provisional scores as soon as possible.

Attitude

Work with sailors and experiment with course configurations.

Invite sailors to serve on the race committee on a rotating basis.

Be sure that every race official has a useful job. Being overstaffed or understaffed produces diminishing returns.

Don't be too formal. Spend time with sailors.

Protests

If you are in the right, there is no reason to lose a protest. This is the philosophy of the International Sailing Federation (ISAF) Rac-

A Brief Note on the Rules

The best way to learn the racing rules of sailing is to get two model boats, sit down at a table, and work through the rules. There are some good books on the market including *Understanding the Racing Rules of Sailing* by Dave Perry published by US SAILING. *Paul Elvström Explains the Racing Rules of Sailing, 2001–2004* (edited by Soren Krause) is another excellent reference, and it includes two small model boats. Frequently yacht clubs and associations hold rules seminars. It is good to brush up every few years. The rules are updated every four years. I suggest keeping a rule book on the boat so you can read about situations immediately after the race if there is an incident. It's also important to have a regulation protest flag on board. I remember getting protested at a world championship some years ago. The protest was thrown out because the protesting yacht did not fly a proper flag. We were lucky.

ing Rules of Sailing and the jury-hearing system: justice should prevail. However, fairness is not automatic. In most instances, you must work for it.

When you are involved in a protest situation and you're in the wrong, it is your responsibility to drop out; make the penalty turn(s), if the racing instructions permit them; or take a percentage penalty. But if you believe you're right, then it's up to you to take the necessary steps to ensure that justice is served.

First, there is no substitute for knowing exactly where you stand in any racing situation, so know your racing rules (see sidebar). Ignorance of your rights and responsibilities or even a moment's indecision can lead to disqualification.

Second, the best policy is to simply avoid getting involved in protests. I have frightening memories of protest presentations in front of the New York Yacht Club's America's Cup Committee. These sessions had all the trauma of oral exams in college!

Despite what I said earlier, no matter how right you think you might be, there is always a chance you might be disqualified because the jury will believe the other boat's story. In judgment situations, slightly different views of the same incident can make it difficult to tell who was really right or wrong. In college I learned that no matter how correct you think you are, you can expect to win (or lose) about half the time. This is not a good percentage.

This is especially true in onus situations. (The "onus" is an obligation or responsibility to stay clear. The boat with the onus has the burden of avoiding a collision.) For instance, you may be positive you completed your tack before the other boat had to alter course, or that you established your overlap exactly two boatlengths from the jibe mark. But the rules say that the onus is on you to *prove* it, which can sometimes be tricky when it's a matter of a few feet or even inches. And don't forget that although most of the rules don't state the onus, some, such as the opposite tack rule, either imply or state that in an appeal, the helmsman who is cutting it close has to prove that he made it. Although it sometimes pays to take a risk, you should fully realize that the consequences might include disqualification, even if you're successful. Most of the time you're better off avoiding questionable situations and deciding the outcome of the race on the remaining legs of the course rather than in the protest room.

However, when you're fouled and you believe that you're right according to the rules, you should protest. Take every precaution to make sure your protest is upheld. Even before a foul, when you see a situation developing, you can improve your chances by stating loudly and firmly what your rights are. Don't be obnoxious or try to intimidate anyone, but such nonmandatory hails could conceivably strengthen your case at a protest hearing. Also, it draws the attention of nearby sailors who might act as witnesses.

If you're fouled, immediately note the circumstances and the pertinent facts: your course and speed and those of the other party, the point of contact, the timing involved, and possible witnesses. Once you've done this, put these facts in the back of your mind until after the finish; your first priority is to get back to the business of racing. As long as you make these few important mental notes, you should be able to recall the complete incident back ashore. Belaboring your protest strategy while still racing will prevent you from concentrating on sailing.

When the foul occurs, you're required to raise your protest flag and hail "protest" immediately. Once that is done, don't talk about it with the other boat. Wait until you finish to go through the incident with your crew.

Planning Your Protest

Once you are ashore, go directly to your rule book. Even if the situation was relatively straightforward, you should read every rule that might conceivably relate. Find the rules that specifically describe the incident. If you can't find the exact application in the rule book, then go to the book of appeals. It's rare that you will you encounter a set of circumstances that is not already specifically covered in the rules or the appeals. One of the most common reasons people lose protests when they are actually in the right is because they enter a protest meeting armed only with an intuitive sense of the situation. This is a mistake. You must prepare.

Put yourself in the other party's position. How is he likely to prove his case? Which of your facts might he possibly refute? What rules might serve his purpose? For example, let's say you are coming into the leeward mark on the starboard jibe; in rounding the mark, you have contact with an outside boat that approached on the port jibe. His only possible defenses are that you established your overlap too late, that you took too much room in rounding, or that there was another boat that prevented him from keeping clear. You should be prepared to counter these attempts with facts and rules that refute his argument.

It is also useful to put yourself in the jury's place. In making a ruling on an incident, what facts are they looking for? What rules might they possibly consider? In a particularly sticky protest, what key points would clear up any direct disagreement between the protesting parties? For instance, you claim you had to alter course for a boat that tacked below you at a weather mark, and the other boat claims that not only had he completed his tack, but also that you altered course down on him in the middle of his tack. To decide this protest, the committee will be interested in where you were at the time he began his tack, exactly when you began to alter course to keep clear, what your relative positions were immediately after the foul, and what the point of contact would have been had you held your course.

Rather than waiting to be questioned about the pertinent facts, you should put everything on the protest form. (The race organizers will have protest forms. A sample can be found in the rule book.) Think carefully about what you want to say before you begin writing. Write a clear, concise, complete, to-the-point description of the incident. Print as neatly and legibly as possible; most committee members won't struggle very long over a sloppy protest form that is difficult to read. Put everything in chronological order; don't tack additional facts on at the end.

Whenever possible, word your description using the phrasing of the rule under which you are protesting. Here is a well-written example:

Thirty seconds before the start, I established an overlap on a parallel course one boatlength to leeward of US1234, who was reaching slowly down the line on starboard. Providing ample room and opportunity to keep clear, I hailed, "I'm coming up," and then began to carry out my luff slowly.

US1234 at first did not respond and then only slowly. After four or five seconds had passed, I hailed again. Then, after another four or five seconds, before reaching a close-hauled course, my starboard side, two feet in front of the shroud, made contact with the windward boat directly abeam of its traveler.

This description immediately tells the protest committee that you have complied with all the requirements of a leeward boat luffing before the start.

Take equal care and pains in drawing your diagram of the incident. Make a trial sketch before putting it on your protest form, making sure that all angles and distances are accurate to the best of your knowledge. In America's Cup trial race protests, we used designers to draw accurate diagrams. Don't forget that the jury will be trying to gain some insight through your drawing. If your boats are drawn in different sizes, or it is difficult to tell which way they are pointed, or the distances and positions are inaccurate, the committee will be misled—possibly to your detriment. Draw a line through the bow and stern of your boats to show their exact headings. You might also find it to your advantage to identify the number of boatlengths to a mark or the number of feet separating boats. When drawing a sequence of positions, identify the time separating each stage of action.

Video is often shot at major regattas. Most juries will accept video evidence for testimony. The best video is directly overhead. Side angles often distort a situation. Be sure to point out video distortions to the jury if they are apparent.

Fill in all the blanks on the protest form accurately, even if you think the information is irrelevant. Include the exact rule numbers under which you are protesting. If it is a relatively straightforward protest, simply state the one rule that covers the situation; don't cloud the issue with a lot of other rules that don't directly apply. On the other hand, if it is a complex situation and you are not sure what rule you should protest under, list all rules and appeals that appear to be applicable.

Witnesses from your own boat tend to be redundant with your testimony. Third-party witnesses give the most credibility at a hearing. It is important that you understand what the witness is going to say before the presentation. The person representing a boat does not necessarily have to be the skipper. As a tactician on big boats, I've often been the one putting together the presentation.

If you have a witness, spend some time talking to him before the hearing. Obviously, it is not ethical to coach a witness on what to say. In fact, this can backfire if the committee's questioning goes beyond your coaching. What you should do is simply listen to the witness's account of the incident, ask him questions that the jury or the other party might ask, and then decide whether he will help or hurt you in a hearing. Sometimes a witness who means well simply does not have a clear picture of the situation. Don't forget that a witness is at a disadvantage in that he may not be present for any of the other testimony. Either because of his point of view or because he was, after all, a disinterested party, a witness's story might not match your own in certain details. In such cases, you are better off letting your account stand on its own, rather than taking a chance that the jury might be misled by an unclear or partially contradictory account of the incident.

Prior to a protest hearing, an arbitration meeting is often set up. This is a popular new trend that juries use to avoid a lengthy hearing. The two parties make a brief presentation. A jury member will listen and forecast a possible outcome. At this point, one of the boats may elect to take a percentage penalty and not risk being disqualified completely after the hearing. This preliminary hearing gives you a feel for how a jury might rule. It is a good innovation and saves a lot of trouble and time. The arbitration hearing takes place back on shore when emotions are not running as high as they might have been on the water.

Conduct at the Protest Hearing

Know your rights. You are entitled to be present during the hearing, you have the right to hear any and all testimony, you may call witnesses, you may question the other party or any witnesses, and you're entitled to a written decision and an explanation of it.

In addition to your rights at a hearing, you also have several responsibilities. Respect both the jury and the other party. Protest hearings and jury decisions are the fairest and most efficient means of deciding disagreements in what is still a gentleman's sport. All involved should act accordingly. Don't speak unless you are spoken to, even though the other skipper may present facts that don't seem accurate to you. It is important to listen quietly until it is your turn to speak. When your turn comes, look directly at the committee and talk *to* them, not *at* them. Don't look down at them or turn away. Respect them as the jury and speak in a positive tone. Be cordial and firm. Don't speak in anger and never use foul language.

When presenting your case, it's important to establish the facts as you remember them and to say exactly what happened. If you are uncertain on a point when questioned, then state that you are not sure. This is much better than trying to come up with some sort of vague answer. Speak in precise terms. For example, "At two or three boatlengths before the mark, we were half a boatlength apart," or "The collision occurred ten seconds before the start." Don't say, "I think there were several boatlengths between us," or "It was about the time the starting gun went off . . . " As with your written testimony, state the facts in the context of the rules.

A good technique is to go back to key points when questioned or when questioning a witness. This is a delicate area. An experienced protest committee knows the rules and doesn't like to be told what is important and what is not—and the committee definitely doesn't like to be told how to interpret the facts.

If the jury is not experienced and is not quite as familiar with the rules as you are, don't hesitate to tactfully point out rules or appeals or facts important to your case that they seem to be overlooking. Before the hearing, try to find out who the jury members are and how experienced they are. During the hearing, try to estimate their grasp of the rules and the situation. The quality and personality of the jury will, to an extent, determine how you present your case.

Once you have given your testimony, don't change your story. The single factor that seems to hurt sailors most in protests is changing testimony halfway through the hearing. Bringing up new information that changes what has already been said merely makes a jury believe that you are not certain of the situation. This is an important point to remember. A protest committee reaches a decision by relating the facts of an incident to what is prescribed by the racing rules. If you cannot get your facts across to the jury, either because of unclear testimony or a lack of credibility, your chances of winning the protest are severely handicapped.

Carefully plan your protest. Present the facts—both written and verbally—in a clear, organized manner. Unless you feel there are valid grounds for an appeal, accept the jury's decision.

The most important step in a protest, whether you win or lose, is to learn from the experience. You will probably find—as I have—that the rules you know best are the ones you've been disqualified under, at one time or another.

The Protest Room: Enter at Your Own Risk

After twelve hours of continuous racing, our two competing Maxis were never more than four boatlengths apart. The lead had already changed six times and we still had 30 miles to go. Emotions were running high. Fatigue was setting in. Calling for room, Boat M tacked away from the shore. Boat B gave little way. The boats converged and collided. Two red flags went up.

Crews need to keep a careful lookout to avoid collisions. You can just hear the shouting going on at this moment.

The next day when the boats returned, the jury spent two hours taking testimony. Boat B was disqualified while Boat M was cleared. With nearly fifty sailors from the two Maxis awaiting the outcome, there were lots of opinions. The hearing drained everyone. In hindsight, it would have been easier for both boats to give a little room regardless of which boat had the right-of-way.

As I mentioned earlier, statistics show that a boat has a fifty/fifty chance of winning or losing a protest. These are poor odds. When you lose an especially bitter protest, you try to rationalize the incident as a learning experience. But you never feel comfortable. By contrast, winning a protest is never truly satisfying. And witnesses also feel unsettled. Unfortunately, revenge some-

times becomes a factor if an incident takes place early in a regatta.

Incidents on the water are rarely clear-cut. Sailors tend to see things their way. The jury must work hard to sort through conflicting testimonies to understand the facts. As I mentioned, witnesses may twist the facts; third-party testimony is frequently driven by self-interest. To avoid this whole process, it is better to ease back when approaching a possible protest situation.

On the whole, international juries have improved over the past two decades thanks to the certification process. International judges need to pass a test to be certified. This takes considerable study and experience. Over the years I have found that justice in racing is improving.

Harsh Protest Cases

Following the unfortunate pattern of society, sailing is being overwhelmed by the horrors of litigation. If this trend continues, the courts will have a dramatic impact on participation, insurance premiums, and goodwill. Any forward-thinking sailing organization should be studying ways to strongly discourage using the courts to resolve disputes.

While litigation in sailing has been rare over the past fifty years, 1988 proved to be an important harbinger of the future. That year, New Zealander Michael Fay sued the San Diego Yacht Club over his America's Cup challenge, saying that his challenge should have been matched with a similar 120-foot monohull. Instead, San Diego answered with a catamaran. It was quite a mismatch on the water. After two years of continuous litigation through all three levels of the New York legal system (where the America's Cup Deed of Gift is held), Fay lost. Since then there have been dozens of cases filed in the United States. Many of these could easily be settled by an impartial arbitrator. But emotions often ruin any chance of an easy agreement.

Each case hurts our sport—and there never seems to be a winner. Unfortunately, no area of sailing seems to be exempt: big boats, youth sailing, inland lakes, bluewater racing, amateur sailors, and industry leaders.

Historically, sportsmen do not sue each other. As violent as football is, you never hear about players suing after questionable tackles. US SAILING is well equipped to deal with on-the-water complaints. But race organizers might do well to insist that a much stronger "waiver of liability" is signed by all participants. The alternative will soon cause skyrocketing insurance rates and certain diminished participation.

Here is a description of several cases that could have been settled outside the court system. These are the types of situations that, if allowed to continue unabated, will ruin our sport.

❖ **Mid-Atlantic Collision.** An overtaking windward boat sailing a lower course than the leeward boat struck the aft windward quarter of the leeward boat. One crew member sitting on the windward side was allegedly injured. Apparently, after some delay, the injured party has asked for a large six-figure settlement.

❖ **Small-Boat Regatta.** An American Sunfish sailor had hoped to race in an invitational regatta at an overseas event. With the entry list filled, the yacht club declined to enter this party. Instead of waiting for another year, the party sued, costing the organization considerable legal bills. In the end, the club prevailed.

❖ **Mediterranean Collision.** Two very large keelboats had a minor collision. One boat was an ultralight, which accelerated and decelerated quickly, and the other was a very heavy keelboat. The ultralight stopped after being becalmed by the larger boat's mainsail while attempting to pass to leeward, thus catching its backstay on the boom of the larger yacht. The damage was minor but the owner of the ultralight sued for $2 million for "emotional distress and damage." There were two major issues: the amount of damage, and whether the collision regulations of the International Rules of the Road take precedence over the racing rules. A U.S. court ruled Collision Regulations prevail, but that was overturned on appeal. Damages were assessed at $10,000, far lower than the $2 million requested.

❖ **Name on Trophy.** A lawsuit developed out of a Midwest long-distance race. A crew member chartered the boat and was listed as skipper. The owner went on the boat as a crew member. The boat won the event. When the yacht club went to put the charter skipper's name on the trophy, the owner of the boat sued. The yacht club offered to put both names on the trophy, but that did not satisfy the owner.

❖ **Man Overboard.** A boat practicing in East Coast waters lost a man overboard on a breezy spring day. It took considerable time to go back and help the person get out of the water. Due to hypothermia, the man overboard eventually died. The boatowner and his insurance company settled with the family of the deceased.

❖ **Little League Parents.** The most disappointing case I have heard is between Opti parents (the Optimist is a popular dinghy sailed by young racers) and the class association. Apparently, a group of overzealous Opti sailors (ages eight to fifteen) misbehaved at an event. These sailors had qualified for an international regatta, but as a result of their indiscretions, the class officials did not allow them to compete. Their parents and an interested Opti parent/attorney filed a lawsuit. It has been a complicated mess for what should have been a simple case of discipline. This case is Little League parenting at its worst. Several years later (and well out of the Opti class), one of the young sailors was thrown out of sailing for two years for getting into a fight on the water.

Is there a solution to these problems? Litigation is never easy, but common sense should prevail. Insurance companies seem to work well by removing the emotions out of incidents, particularly with automobiles. Unfortunately many insurance companies are uncertain how to deal with maritime incidents. It's up to the sailing community and the marine industry to take charge of these incidents. Arbitration and settlement should always be encouraged—and the courts should be used as a last resort.

My harshest moments in sailing have revolved around protests. It never matters whether I'm the protester or the protestee, it is always an unpleasant experience. For more enjoyable and competitive racing, avoiding "the room" is the answer.

Avoid Contact, Avoid the Protest Room

While the specifics of the right-of-way rules changed with the major revision of the racing rules in 1997 (and will continue to change subtly since the racing rules are revised every four years), the fundamental spirit of avoiding collisions remains. An over-simplified rule would be to give the leading boat, in any situation, the right-of-way.

Race committees have been a big help in managing traffic control on the course. By setting square starting lines that fit the size of the fleet and using offset marks and gates, incidents have been avoided. Race officials should try to group classes in narrow rating bands so everyone is sailing at about the same speed.

Here are some guidelines for ways you can avoid collisions and avoid the protest room:

❖ If a collision is imminent, the best policy is to give way regardless of which boat is privileged. By making an early course change, the distance lost is usually minimal.

❖ When approaching another boat, make a large, deliberate course change. Incremental course changes are difficult to detect by the approaching boat. Don't make the other boat guess your intentions.

❖ Keep a sharp lookout at all times. One crew member should be designated as the lookout. Update your observations frequently.

❖ Keep sailing at full speed because maneuvering is easier when you have some speed.

❖ Be ready to respond by keeping sheets uncleated. Remember that the most efficient maneuvers are made using a combination of the rudder, sails, and crew weight.

❖ If you do foul, be quick to accept your penalty. This sets a positive example for the rest of the fleet. The Sailing Instructions and Notice of Race, which are specific guidelines published for each regatta that cover how racing will be conducted, should also include alternative penalties.

CHAPTER 8

Trim for Speed

There are two essential ingredients for winning in a sailboat: sailing smart and sailing fast. With a speed advantage, tactical decisions are easier. If you make a mistake there is a better chance of recovering when you are sailing fast. But getting optimum speed out of a boat takes work. The rig needs to be tuned, the bottom made smooth and fair, and the sails trimmed efficiently. Taking care of these items is the responsibility of the entire crew. When everyone helps prepare the bottom there is a sense of pride that is reflected by the attitude of the crew on the water.

Gaining speed requires the entire crew to work together. While the tactician looks ahead, the sail trimmers and helmsman watch the wind and water as it reaches the boat. Over time the speed team learns what trim settings work best.

Tuning and Balance

Probably the best rig a sailboat could have is one as light as a feather: the smaller and lighter the rig, the faster the boat. Nevertheless, it's generally better to rig a boat with slightly heavier equipment than to chance a breakdown with light gear. In recent years advanced technology has improved rigs and materials. Carbon fiber, for example, is lighter and stronger than aluminum or wood. Technological advances will continue to make boats faster in the future.

The rigging should be set up to allow for maximum speed and power in the sails. Your sailmaker, boatbuilder, designer, and your own experience are all good sources for finding your boat's optimum rig. A good resource to help with tuning is your sailmaker. He can provide printed material on optimizing your rig. Better yet, ask your

Base Settings:

Headstay Pin-to-Pin Measurement:	12140mm
Rake:	Swing Arc—Use Centerline halyard pulled down to top of black band—pull forward to mark headstay.
Mark on headstay down to headstay pin:	1820mm
Cap Shroud Tension:	#35 on RT 10 Rod Loos Gauge
D1 Tension:	#10 on PT2 Wire Loos Gauge
D2 Tension:	#7 on PT2 Wire Loos Gauge
J Dimension:	3315mm
Mast Base—(Distance from forward Headstay bolt to front of mast):	3480mm
Pre-Bend:	75mm

Sail Models:

Mainsail	**Light Jib**	**Med Jib**	**Heavy Jib**
JBMC-04	LJC-04	MJC-04	HJ-04
Masthead 30g	**Masthead 40g**	**Fractional 40g**	**Masthead A-Sail 30g**
MHL-04	MHH-04	FS-04	MHA-04

Quick Adjustments (full turns from base settings)

True Wind Speed:	**Sail Selection**	**Headstay:**	**Cap Shrouds:**	**D1s:**	**D2s:**
Really light (0-5k)	LJ-04/MHL-04/MHA-04	-10	-2	-2	Base
Light (5-9k)	LJ-04/MHL-04	- 7	-1	-1	Base
Medium (10-15k)	**MJ-04/MHL-04**	**Base**	**Base**	**Base**	**Base**
Heavy (16-20k)	MJ-04/MHH-04	+ 7	+1	+2	Base
Really Heavy (21k+)	HJ-04/MHH-04	+15	+2	+3	+2

Tuning guides for individual classes are often found on sailmakers' websites. As an example, here is a Mumm 30 tuning guide. This tuning guide provides base tension settings for the headstay and shrouds as well as their corresponding settings as wind speed increases. It also suggests various sail combinations for different wind speeds. It is important to note that tuning techniques change frequently as competitors learn how to sail faster. (North Sails)

sailmaker or the champion in your class to come for a sail in order to provide guidance on your tuning. Most classes do not allow you to tune a rig during a race, but you are able to make adjustments with the sails, sheets, and backstay. Boats of all sizes require different setups depending on the wind strength. Learn what works best for your boat and make adjustments *before* each race.

The Mast

A great deal of study has gone into finding the best mast shape. The less windage on the mast, the faster the boat. Boats sail best when their masts are straight athwartships, not leaning over to one side. Set your mast up so it's as straight as possible. To check its straightness, hang a weight on a light string from the masthead and observe how the string rests. Ideally, it should be right next to the mast.

In addition to keeping the mast in the middle of the boat (side to side), you want to sail with the proper rake. Rake is how far you tilt the mast forward or aft. To start, haul a tape measure on the halyard and measure the distance from the top of the mast to the stern. Again, talk with your sailmaker or the champion in your fleet to get a handle on how much rake you should have.

Sight up the mast as you adjust the shrouds. A tension meter attached to the shrouds guides you in putting equal tension on both shrouds. Large boats often use a hydraulic mast lift that allows precise rig tun-

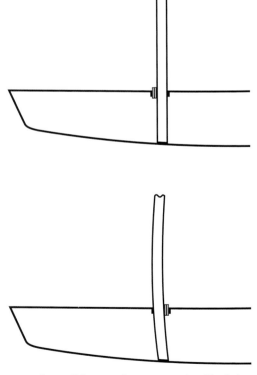

Blocks in front of the mast keep it straight. Blocks behind the mast help induce bend.

ing. The mast lift also tensions the rig without the need to go sailing.

Spreaders control mast side bend. It's important for the spreaders to be tightly secured to the mast. Spreaders should be a streamlined, airfoil shape (much like an airplane wing) to minimize the force of the wind. Spreaders and mast fittings should also be faired in, so that the wind flows around them easily. Spreaders should be fitted to hold the shrouds in the same location they'd be without spreaders. Pushing spreaders forward forces the top of the mast forward; moving the spreaders aft forces the middle of the mast forward and the top of the mast aft.

There should be absolutely no play between the mast and the mast partner at the deck. Control mast bend by adding or subtracting blocks at the mast where it enters the deck. By putting blocks in front of the mast you restrict bend. By putting blocks behind the mast you increase bend. Additionally, halyards should be kept tight so they don't flap in the breeze. Flapping halyards disturb wind flow and are distracting to the sailors on the boat.

Balance

There are many factors that go into balancing a boat so it sails efficiently. Your goal is to get the center of effort directly over the center of resistance. You can feel this by the pressure on the helm. If your boat wants to round into the wind, there is too much windward helm. My measure of a balanced boat is if I let go of the wheel or tiller, the boat will sail straight or slowly turn into the wind. A perfectly balanced boat will sail along with no course change. If a boat is heeling too far, it creates windward helm. If it is too flat, it might have leeward helm. Experiment with your angle of heel so the helm has a good feel in your hand.

A boat should sail on the angle of heel that allows it to move fastest through the water. This is called *sailing on its lines*. In a Laser, the optimum angle of heel is between 0 and 10 degrees, depending on the wave conditions. On an offshore yacht, the optimum angle of heel may be 25 to 30 degrees, because the boat has a high freeboard and creates a longer waterline when it heels over. You can check your angle of heel with an inclinometer.

Your objective is to sail with a long waterline, keeping the water flowing evenly off the stern. To accomplish this, the crew's weight should be distributed so it's in the widest part of the boat, normally as close to the center as possible. If the crew's weight is too far aft, the stern will dip and form a vacuum underneath the hull, which produces centerboard cavitation. This is where air gets trapped under the boat and makes the centerboard (or keel) inefficient. It's important to keep uniform water pressure on the centerboard or keel, since this is the force that counteracts the sideways force of the wind in the sails and allows the wind's forward force (in combination with the keel's lateral resistance) to push the

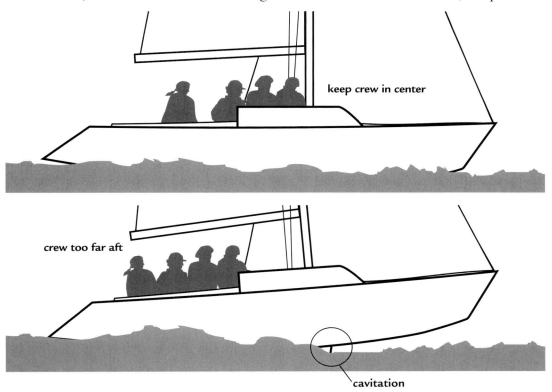

Avoid centerboard cavitation—which occurs when the stern dips, forming a vacuum under the hull—by making sure the crew's weight is centered amidships and not too far aft.

Steps to Reduce or Increase Weather Helm

To reduce weather helm:

1. Flatten the main (and jib) by tensioning the backstay and outhaul.

2. Move crew weight outboard and forward.

3. Flatten the boat by pinching more and easing the traveler to leeward.

4. Raise the centerboard a bit. If you can, move your board back in the centerboard trunk (on a dinghy).

5. Move the mast forward (on a dinghy).

6. Reef the main.

You can increase pressure on the helm in the following ways:

1. Heel the boat by moving crew weight to leeward.

2. Move crew weight aft.

3. Make the main and jib more powerful by easing the backstay and outhaul.

4. Pull the traveler to windward.

5. Add mast rake, or move the mast back to move the sail plan aft.

This well-balanced boat is sailing to windward with 10-degree heel.

boat. Ideally, a boat should sail both at the optimal angle of heel (on its lines) and balanced fore and aft by the crew's weight. A heeled boat also extends the length of the waterline (longer is faster). Heeling also helps the sails keep their shape.

Windward helm, also known as weather helm, is the product of all the factors that go into balancing (or in this case, slightly unbalancing) a boat: from rigging, to crew-weight distribution (side-to-side and fore-and-aft), to sail trim. Most boats sail best with 3 to 5 degrees of helm. A windward helm forces the boat up into the wind. When I coach sailors, I find that one of the major reasons why they are not pointing is that they simply are not steering the boat up into the wind. Windward helm will help alleviate this problem.

Windward helm can be increased by shifting crew weight aft, heeling the boat to leeward, raking the mast aft (so that you have more power in your sails aft of the centerline), or simply trimming the sails tighter. Likewise, shifting crew weight forward, heeling the boat to windward, easing the sails, or moving the mast forward creates leeward helm, or at least reduces windward helm.

Sail Trim

After the proper boat preparation, sail trim is the most important factor in achieving superior boatspeed. Sails have to be constantly reshaped to conform to ever-changing wind and wave patterns. Cleating sheets is a mistake because of these continuous changes. Keep track of 1-knot wind variances, the smallest waves, the boat's pitching moment, and the temperature of both air and water. Changing gears and adjusting your sails is an art form to be perfected

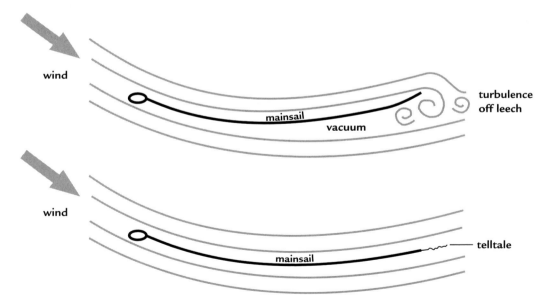

The wind bends around the sail, creating a vacuum on the leeward side. There is turbulence off the leech of the sail at top, which is over-trimmed and thus stalled. Telltales help indicate whether sails are trimmed correctly, as the sail at bottom is.

throughout a race. This is the secret of sailing a boat fast.

No matter what sail you may be flying—mainsail, genoa, spinnaker, or staysail—they all work on the same principle: wind bends around the sail, causing a vacuum on the forward leeward side. The boat moves forward to fill this vacuum. The energy transfer of the wind around a sail generates a sail's power. If the wind overbends around the sail, there will be too large a vacuum and backwind will result. This forces a boat to "stall out" (see illustration previous page). On the other hand, if too much wind is caught by the sail, the boat will heel beyond its designed lines and slip sideways. Telltales attached to the sails are an effective way to monitor how the air is moving. The best telltales are pieces of yarn attached to the sail. Telltales should be about one foot long and placed at least six inches behind the luff and also along the leech. Each sail should have at least three telltales

spread evenly from the top to the bottom.

Your aim is to generate as much power in the sails as possible while keeping the boat sailing on its lines. When it comes to draft (the depth of curvature in a sail), it is just as important to have the proper *amount* of draft, as it is to *position* the maximum draft correctly. The trick is to use your available sail area while creating the most powerful (i.e., the fastest) shape.

The Art of the Trimmer

Trimming sails is a challenging crew position that requires knowledge, experience, boat-handling prowess, and the ability to work with the rest of the crew. The goal is to make your yacht perform at peak efficiency and use that speed to out-sail your competition. A trimmer must be able to recognize changing conditions in a short time frame and adjust sail trim efficiently according to weather, sea state, and tactical position on the racecourse. The trimmer

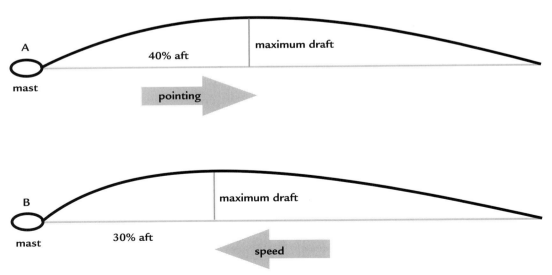

To maximize pointing, move the draft aft (A). To maximize speed, move the draft forward (B).

Successful Trimming: A Checklist

Championship crews are set up for victory before they even leave the dock. Proper preparation is key; here is a trimmer's checklist for pre-regatta preparation:

1. Check for any problems with the blocks, sheets, winch handles, or hydraulic handles. Include in your inventory: duct tape, plastic colored tape, colored markers, lube, wool/rubber bands for packing spinnakers, spare winch and deck gear parts, sail repair kit, water, energy bars, lunch (when appropriate), and gloves.

2. Insert the rule book, Sailing Instructions with amendments, and Notice of Race in a waterproof folder. Read these carefully. Tacticians are known to forget important information during the heat of battle. You can be a valuable backup source of information when the heat is on.

3. Check your working area on board to make sure all inventory is aboard; sails are dry and packed; extra weight is off boat (I like to assign a "weight czar" to keep extra gear off); hydraulics are working properly (no leaks; check fluid level in reservoir); and leads, sheets, and halyards are all marked for proper settings for each sail. Spray silicone on shackles for proper closure (replace locking shackles if they are worn); work kinks out of halyards, sheets, and runners; check winches for good working order; tie knots in ends of halyards so they won't slip up the mast; store sails down below; sew telltales on sails; and check that pre-feeders and jib luff tapes are all in good order. All sail bags need to be marked prominently, and the right sail needs to be in the right bag.

4. Keep the target boatspeed on a card. This information should be updated and posted so the crew understands when each sail should be set. Review the possible sail selection and wind-strength crossovers (the wind speed or angle that determines when to change sail) with the tactician.

5. Leave the dock with a good understanding of the forecasted weather and know your available sail inventory.

6. Place the battens in the jib and main with the correct tension for the forecasted weather. Tape batten ends so they don't rip the spinnaker or foul the halyards. Don't allow battens to stick out past the leech.

To avoid problems, ask everyone to check their own area of the boat before each race to make sure nothing is loose or worn. A laminated checklist, divided by position and posted on the boat, helps make sure nothing is missed.

who can recognize the fastest options, implement them quickly, and commit the fewest mistakes has an edge. The sections below refer to trimmers of all sails, not just the trimmer of the headsail.

Great trimmers set specific goals, whether that goal is to improve sailing skill, have more fun at sailing, win the club championship, or capture an Olympic medal. Trimming sails on a dinghy with one crew or on a Maxi boat with twenty-four crew is equally rewarding. Defining the mission, setting parameters, prepping your trimming area, staying focused, executing, and reviewing your fastest trim will make you successful.

BUILD A STRONG SPEED TEAM

The helmsman, main trimmer, and headsail trimmers make up the core speed group. These crew members are responsible for keeping the boat operating efficiently and on target boatspeed—whether the boat is sailing in a straight line or accelerating to full speed after a maneuver. On larger yachts, separate traveler and backstay operators are included as part of the speed team.

The goal is to keep the speed loop as short as possible. The *speed loop* is the time it takes to achieve target speed and optimum wind angle with the sails sheeted in all the way after a tack, jibe, a set of waves, or sailing through disturbed wind. Here are two examples of a speed loop. In both examples our boat starts out sailing upwind at 8.5 knots at a 45-degree true wind angle (TWA) in 12 knots of breeze and choppy seas.

Example One: Dave is driving above target speed with Mike trimming the main and Jenny trimming the genoa. Dave has been looking back to see where his competitors are heading and misses an approaching steep wave. The bow hits the wave in a light-wind spot. Ralph shouts "Wave!" from the weather rail. In 3 seconds the boatspeed is down to 8.2 knots because main trimmer Mike has been concentrating on pumping the outhaul. Simultaneously, Jenny has trouble releasing the genoa out of the self-tailer. Finally, the bow gets pointed down 4 degrees; to build speed, the jib goes out. Mike returns to the main and eases the traveler. In 15 seconds, the boatspeed drops to 8.1 knots and is 50 degrees off the wind. The speed is still dropping. Mike eases the mainsheet and the speed starts to improve. The call is made, "8.2 . . . 8.5 . . . 8.7 . . ." Dave starts steering the bow back up. Jenny trims the jib in, but it backwinds the main. To compensate, Mike trims the main in. Boatspeed is now 8.8 (0.3 knot over target). The helm has to be corrected to get on course. Finally, 45 seconds into the evolution, Dave is back on target speed at 8.5 knots and 45 degrees. This is the 45-second speed loop.

Example Two: Dave is driving on target speed. Jenny hails "Good speed and angle." Ralph shouts from the rail, "Wave in five seconds with a light spot." Jenny calls, "Press for speed." Mike drops the traveler an inch and eases the mainsheet a half inch. Jenny eases the genoa sheet a half inch. Helmsman Dave puts the bow down 2 degrees to build speed. Mike eases the backstay a half inch. The boat hits the wave at 8.6 knots at a 47-degree TWA. The speed drops to 8.35 knots 15 seconds into the encounter but then starts to build. Dave points the bow back up to a 45-degree TWA as the traveler comes up and Jenny trims the genoa. Boatspeed climbs; the mainsheet is trimmed. The boatspeed is now 8.4. Mike pulls the backstay back on. The boat is quickly sailing 8.5 knots at 45 degrees. Jenny calls, "Back on target" 25 seconds into the evolution. This is the 25-second speed loop.

By staying focused, communicating in a timely fashion, and preparing the boat for what lies ahead (whether it's a wave or a light-wind spot), you can reduce the number of degrees you need to bear away or the amount of time you are off target speed. The goal is to shorten the speed loop. Crews with the shortest speed loops will prevail.

Alinghi *setting her spinnaker. Every crew member has an assigned job and is in sync during this maneuver.*

THE IMPORTANCE OF COMMUNICATION

The speed-loop examples demonstrate how good communication can help you sail around the racecourse as quickly as possible. Reconfirm your target speed aloud frequently, so the whole crew stays alert. And remember, conditions are constantly changing.

Being a trimmer puts you in the center of the action—and that makes you one of the best people to pass commands from the tactician to the team on the bow. (The pitman is also a good person to pass commands up to the bow, since he or she is also centrally located.) Here are some tips for good onboard communication.

❖ Turn your head toward the person you're talking to.

❖ Always verbally confirm the new sail.

❖ Avoid tripping the spinnaker pole during a jibe without the "trip" call from the tactician.

❖ Don't hoist the spinnaker at the weather mark without the tactician's call. This is particularly dangerous with a boat to leeward.

❖ "No" and "Go" are words that sound too similar. Try "Stop" or "Hold."

❖ Give direction rather than your status. Instead of saying "You're low," tell the helmsman "Head up."

❖ Be concise. Instead of saying, "Looking up the course, I think in about eight or so seconds there will be a puff of wind." Just say, "Puff in eight seconds."

❖ Bowman needs to call "clear" before a tack or jibe after a mark rounding. The bowman is in the best position to see that the jib sheet is clear of all obstacles in front of the mast.

SAIL SELECTION AND CROSSOVERS

One of the primary responsibilities of the trimmers is a good understanding of the sail inventory, wind ranges, and angles for each sail. This includes crossover. A *crossover* is a point in wind speed or angle that determines when to change sails. A chart based on experience is a helpful aid. The best sail inventory has some overlap for each wind range. The trimmers and tactician should keep a laminated wind range chart on board. Adjust the numbers on the card as you learn when to use specific sails.

As shown in the accompanying table, the crossover between the medium/heavy #1 and the #2 is 14 knots. Depending on the wind trend (whether it's building or dropping), you can use the appropriate sail. In this case there is an overlap of 1 knot of wind speed.

Select the correct sail before the windward leg, and before the start of the downwind leg. This is a test of experience in evaluating the wind conditions. The present conditions are obvious. But figuring out what the wind strength is going to be ten minutes later takes a good eye, concentration, lots of experience, and sometimes even luck.

Study the flexibility of your sail inventory. Consider tactical options. Will you be tacking or sailing in a straight line? If in doubt, place two genoas on deck until you are ready for the final call. Prep the trimmers so they will adjust the leads.

Wind Range/Sail Selection Chart

TRUE WIND SPEED (TWS) (knots)	UPWIND	LEAD	HALYARD SETTING	NOTES	DOWNWIND	NOTES
0–9	Light #1 Headsail	10–12	4–5.5	Firm halyard tension spinnaker	0.4 oz. VMG	Trim pole down
8.5–15	Med/Hvy #1	9–10	4–6	Better low spinnaker end	0.6 oz. AP	Good at top of range
14–18	#2	4–6	7–9	Outbd track @ 17.5 kts	0.6 oz. Runner	Starting to show age
17–25	#3	3	6–7	Leads @ 10 setting	0.75 oz. Runner	Likes pole up
24+	#4	2	10	Leads all the way aft	1.5 oz.	Likes to be led at primary on rail

Mainsail Trim

"My mainsail won't catch the wind," the voice on the phone said to the late Tom Blackaller. The irritated customer of this famous sailmaker was clearly upset with her new purchase. Blackaller was confused by her comment, so he offered his only remedy, "Ma'am, let's take your boat sailing this afternoon and let me see if I can make your mainsail 'catch the wind.' "

After leaving the dock, Blackaller asked the woman to set sail. The mainsail and a large, very full #1 genoa jib were hoisted. In the stiff San Francisco Bay breeze, the mainsail was completely backwinded. Blackaller—a silver-haired, sweet-talking, former Star class world champion—said, "Okay, let's take the jib down." When the jib was down, the main popped into perfect trim. Never one to miss an opportunity, Blackaller sold the woman a new jib on the spot. It was a good lesson. Too much back-wind destroys the shape of the main. Needless to say, the woman was impressed.

The mainsail is the most versatile piece of equipment on a sailboat. It provides speed on all points of sail, can be used in all wind conditions, assists with maneuvering, helps with acceleration or slowing down, easily changes shape or size, provides shade, steadies the boat in a rolling seaway, gives a boat identification, acts as a wind vane, helps you read the wind, and—best of all—it's easy to see and use.

A racing sailboat uses numerous controls to create any desired shape to the main. The trim team fine-tunes the shape with the finesse of a concert conductor. The mainsail works similarly to an airplane wing. Your goal is to achieve maximum power and minimum stall. Stall occurs when the sail is over-trimmed and there is turbulence coming off the back of the sail. It's similar to putting the flaps down on an airplane wing: it slows the plane down and forces you to fly lower. The leech telltales on the battens help you read if the wind is flowing directly off the sail. If the telltales are flowing forward there is usually turbulence, indicating that the sail is trimmed too tightly.

MAINSAIL TRIM TECHNIQUE

Be sure that your lines run smoothly through the blocks. A traveler should be easily adjustable. All race boats should be equipped with a boom vang. Use a cleat as a backup for self-tailing winches.

While sail area is important, the priority is the position and amount of draft. Most mainsails work best with the draft 40 percent of the way aft. If you need more speed,

move the draft forward. If you want to sail closer to the wind, move the draft aft (see illustration on page 166). Any tensioning on a sail moves the draft in that direction. Although you may be concerned about wrinkles and backwind, proper sail shape in relation to draft is the priority. To begin trimming, set the sail for maximum power (fullness) in light wind. If it's breezy, start with a flat sail. After the sail is set and these adjustments are made, note the angle of heel. In light wind your sail should help heel the boat to provide power and speed.

The helmsman should first think about going fast before sailing close to the wind. If the wind increases and the boat heels too much, reduce the power in your mainsail. Too much heel causes leeway.

Even with the mainsail well eased, the boat on the right is overpowered approaching the starting line. Easing the boom vang would help relieve the pressure.

To reduce pressure on the main, twist the upper leech. This is achieved by one or a combination of adjustments, including easing the mainsheet, dropping the traveler, tightening the backstay, bending the mast, easing off the boom vang, or flattening the sail by tightening the downhaul and outhaul. Many sailors tend to over-trim their sails. To check trim, ease the sail out until it begins to luff, then trim in just until it stops luffing. This is the optimum trim setting. If you need to sail a course closer to the wind, move the draft aft by pulling the traveler to windward, trimming the main in (which tightens the leech), and straightening the mast by easing the running backstay.

The mainsail has a curved leading edge (luff) that, in combination with a straight mast, gives the mainsail its curvature. As you bend the mast to conform to the shape

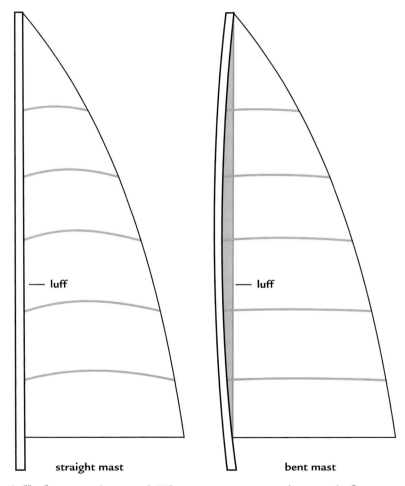

The leading edge (luff) of a mainsail is curved. When it is put on a straight mast, draft or curvature is created in the sail. To remove draft or flatten the sail, the mast is bent.

of the leading edge, the mainsail will flatten. The two mast-bend controls are the backstay and the mainsheet. It's important to clearly mark the maximum amount of tension on the backstay. You might also use a reference mark on the mainsheet. Keep a marker handy. The sail is best read from behind. Your goal is to avoid a hooked leech, which creates stall.

If your boat becomes overpowered because of too much wind, reefing the mainsail is a good solution. Modern boats tend to favor a large mainsail / small jib setup. But reefs are very effective: you reduce sail area at the top of the mast where you have the most pressure from the wind,

causing you to heel. It's often easier to take a reef in your main than change jibs, particularly if you are sailing in a straight line and heading directly for the next mark.

A MAIN TRIMMER'S REFERENCES
There are many references to help with sail trim. While many people watch the luff, it's the leech that is the most critical. When I look up at the leech I want to see an even flow on the sail. As mentioned the telltales are my best indicator.

The next reference is pressure on the helm. If the boat tends to round into the wind (windward helm), the draft is too far aft or the sails are over-trimmed. In this case,

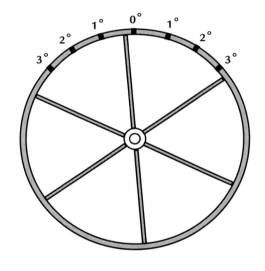

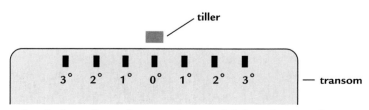

Use degree indicators on the wheel or tiller to determine how much helm is being used.

first ease your sails a small amount if you are slow. If you feel leeward helm (the boat steers away from the wind), trim the sails. I like to sail to windward with 3 to 5 degrees of windward helm. You can judge how much helm you have by putting 1-degree marks on your wheel or on the stern where the tiller pokes through the deck (see illustration opposite). Use a large protractor on top of the rudder to determine 1-degree increments.

Be aware that there is a difference between the true wind direction and the apparent wind direction. The two can vary by as much as 20 degrees. I find it helpful to use a piece of yarn or a piece of a cassette tape (a telltale) streaming from the shrouds. This gives me an accurate reading of the apparent wind direction close to the sail. You can pick up the true wind direction from the angle of the waves on the water.

The luff of the mainsail should be pointing directly at the apparent wind. Occasionally, the apparent wind direction at the masthead will be different from the direction much lower. This is called wind shear. Trim your sails according to the wind shear. If the wind up top is farther forward, sail with a tight upper leech. Always watch the masthead because wind changes at the top of the mast first.

Additional references are other boats or the speedometer. When I am trimming, I adjust the main until the aft end of the top batten is parallel to the boom. (Telltales should be sewn at the end of each batten.) If the batten hooks to windward, your sail is over-trimmed. If the sail is stalled, the telltale will fly forward. Ease the sail in this case. Your goal is to keep all the telltales flowing aft evenly.

Jib and Genoa Trimming

Jibs and genoas are trimmed like a mainsail: the maximum amount of draft should be about 40 percent of the way aft. The bottom part of the leech should hook slightly to windward of the top of the sail. The jib should be trimmed until you get backwind in the main, at which point the jib lead should be moved outboard or aft. A boat should have an adjustable lead on a track or different positions for the block that the jib sheet runs through.

The jib works in conjunction with the main and must be constantly tended by the

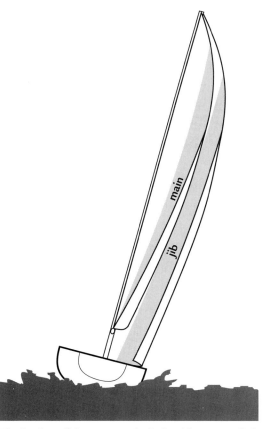

The leeches of the main and jib should run parallel.

sail trimmer. The leech of the jib should form a parallel line with the leech of the mainsail. Trim the leech of the jib parallel to the main by watching the slot between the mainsail and the jib.

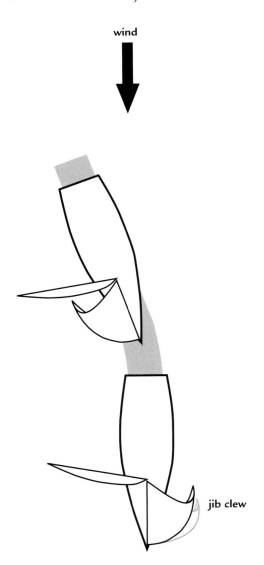

wind

jib clew

When sailing directly downwind you can "wing" your jib to windward. With the main to leeward the boat will accelerate. This is known as sailing "wing-and-wing."

Downwind, when the apparent wind is forward of 150 degrees, the jib works best trimmed on the leeward side of the boat. However, once the wind is aft of about 160 degrees, the jib is more effective trimmed to windward. This is known as sailing wing-and-wing. To trim a jib to windward, hold the clew of the sail as far as possible away from the boat. If the jib has a tendency to luff, ease the sail out and let the clew fly forward. This helps the sail fill sooner. It takes some experimenting to place the clew in the most efficient spot.

All boats have some jibstay sag. To determine how much jibstay sag you have, attach a halyard to the bow at the tack of the jib. Place a telltale in the middle of this halyard. Tighten the halyard. Use the telltale to note the distance between the halyard and the luff of the jibstay. This distance indicates how much sag you are sailing with.

The only reliable way to minimize jibstay sag is to ask your sailmaker to adjust your luff round on the jib. The idea here is to add fullness to the sail in light wind. This is a critical adjustment. Sailmakers spend a lot of time experimenting with the correct shape of the leading edge of the jib. In light wind it's okay to let the jibstay sag. As the wind builds tighten the jibstay with the halyards, backstay, and mainsheet.

In shifty winds, trimming the jib in coordination with the helmsman can be challenging. On most boats there's a constant battle between the trimmer and helmsman, so once these two crew members work together your boat has an edge over the rest of the fleet.

The trimmer has to watch what the wind is doing. If the wind fairs and the boat

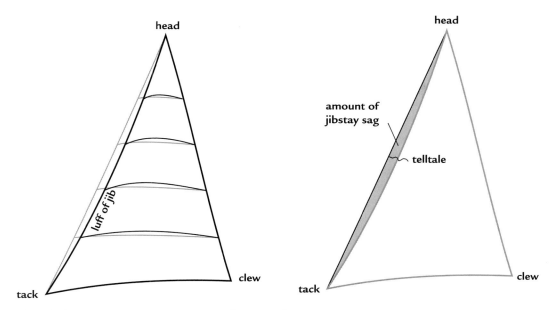

When the headstay is tightened the jib will flatten (left). To measure jibstay sag, take a tight halyard to the jib's tack. Attach a telltale to the halyard to determine jibstay sag (right).

is lifted, the jib needs adjusting or it will be over-trimmed, forcing the boat away from the wind. The trimmer should first ease out the jib, so that the boat increases speed. The helmsman shouldn't have to use much rudder to bring the boat up. When the boat starts to accelerate, the rudder should then be turned to head up. Now the trimmer should trim the jib in slowly. If the wind heads the boat, the trimmer should trim in his jib to force the bow away from the wind. It is helpful for the trimmer to verbalize his/her actions in a mild way. In time it will become second nature.

SELECTING THE LEAD AND HALYARD TENSION

These critical adjustments to the jib and genoa affect each other. The jib halyard tension controls the amount of depth, draft position, and distance from the spreaders (i.e., a tight halyard tightens the leech). Lead position determines leech and foot shape, luff tension, sail depth, and the distance off the spreaders. The word you want to keep in your head when thinking about the lead and halyard adjustments is *balance*.

Your goal is to have the leading edge (luff) of the sail breaking evenly from the head to the tack. The best indicators are the telltales. These should be flowing aft horizontally. Use five sets of telltales spread along the luff of the sail (on dinghies three or four sets of telltales are adequate). If your sail is breaking evenly, the draft of the sail will be about 40 percent of the way aft. The leech will have an even twist that matches the mainsail leech. This combination will achieve balance.

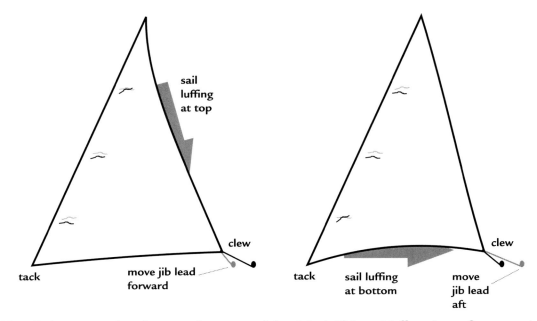

Use telltales on your jib to determine the position of the jib lead. If the sail luffs at the top first, move the lead forward. If the sail luffs at the bottom first, move the lead aft.

If your lead is too far aft, your sail will luff first at the top set of telltales. This will also make the foot of the sail too flat and twist the leech off at the top, which depowers the sail. If your lead is too far forward, the sail will first break at the bottom, close the leech, and create a foot that is too full and unbalanced with the rest of the sail.

Halyard tension can have a big effect on the designed depth of a sail. The halyard makes a sail versatile in a wide wind range. As you pull more halyard on, the draft of the sail moves forward, flattens the shape of the sail, brings the belly of the sail closer to the spreaders, and tightens the leech of the sail. As you ease the halyard off, the reverse is true. The draft moves aft in the sail, makes the sail deeper, and allows the leech of the sail to twist off. You will also notice

the body of the sail getting farther away from the spreaders.

As an example: you are sailing up a windward leg and the wind is increasing from 12 to 15 knots. Your initial setup looked good before the start, but now it looks vastly different. The sail looks deep. There are wrinkles appearing along the luff. The leech is twisting off even when you are trimming the sail in. And the whole sail is farther from the spreaders. Your helmsman is having trouble building speed. Your tactician is complaining that the boat is not holding pace with the rest of the class. As the wind velocity increases you need more halyard tension. Note that the halyard makes a 180-degree turn over the sheave at the top of the mast, which doubles the load. Use caution when you put extra pressure

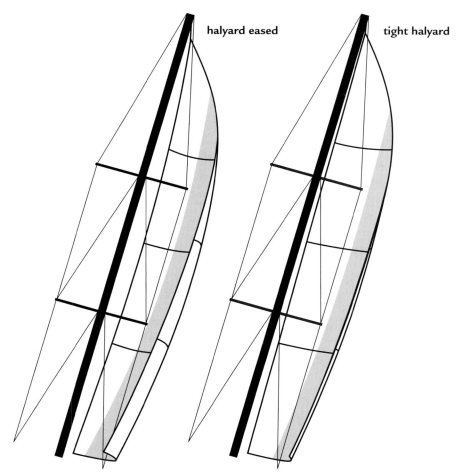

halyard eased   **tight halyard**

Halyard eased, full sail; tighten halyard, sail flattens.

on the halyard under load, for it can break. To avoid this, your options are to hoist the halyard during the next tack, or luff up 20 degrees at the same time the trimmer eases the sheet. Both options relieve the pressure on the sail. You will lose little boatspeed if you execute this correctly.

Now the wind increases to 17 knots and you are at the top of the wind range for your heavy #1 genoa. You have 1 mile left on a 3-mile beat. A jib change would cost too much distance. One of the rules of sail-ing upwind is that the main is king. The leech of the main must always be full of pressure. If the leech of the main is not full, your boat slips to leeward. Backwind in the front of the main caused by too large a jib is acceptable at the top end of the range for a sail; but if the leech is waving, distance is lost. The leech of the main should be used as a lifting foil. If you are overpowered and the boat is heeling too much, open the slot between the genoa and the main by moving the jib lead aft to twist open the leech of the

Wind Shear and Gradient

A trimmer should be aware of abnormalities when setting up the main and jib. The combination of weather patterns together with water and air temperature creates two phenomena: wind shear and wind gradient. *Wind shear* is the difference in direction at varying heights above the water; *wind gradient* is the difference in wind strength at varying heights above the water. These conditions are most commonly encountered on boats with tall masts, but they can also be experienced on any size boat. To make the best of the situation, a trimmer works with sail twist and lead position.

If wind direction is reading either farther right or left at the masthead compared to what is indicated on the lower telltales, your sails will require a different setting on each tack. You might find your jib leads will be in different positions on each tack. Use the leads to make the telltales flow evenly at the top and bottom of the sail. Remember that the wind changes at the top of the mast first. This helps forecast the direction of the new wind. Also note there is usually more wind aloft.

jib. If you can't move the lead any farther aft, try easing the sheet. Find a balance between moving the lead aft and easing the jibsheet. If your boat has outboard tracks, try sheeting farther out to open the slot. Experiment with the lead position to see which way seems better compared with another boat. In extreme conditions, luffing the jib a few feet is acceptable to keep the boat sailing on its lines.

Before the start, sail upwind to test where your jib leads and halyard should be set. Racing off the starting line with the proper halyard tension and lead position is critical; with proper settings, you can hold your pace with the rest of the fleet.

HEADSTAY TENSION

Another important control for the genoa is headstay tension. You adjust the sag in the headstay with the running backstay on a fractional-rig boat; on a masthead boat, you use your permanent backstay. The effect is the same. By easing the backstay you are making the sail deeper and adding power. This action closes the slot between the headsail and the mainsail. The reason is the luff of the headsail falls to leeward and rotates aft. This also reduces the twist in the leech of the headsail, which also closes the slot. When sailing into a light-wind spot, ease the backstay to add fullness and therefore maintain your speed. The reverse is applicable when sailing into an increase in wind speed. By adding tension to the headstay, you flatten the headsail and rotate it to windward. This creates more twist in the leech and opens the slot between the headsail and mainsail. Flattening the headsail decreases the angle of attack (entry angle) of the headsail direction. This allows you to point higher. But you sail slower. It's a tricky balance to get right. Work at it.

JIB REACHING

Most of the same rules regarding luff balance and lead position apply to jib reaching. Since your wind angle will be much wider when reaching than when beating, the entry angle of the luff of the headsail will be much wider. Move your lead forward and outboard. This allows the slot between the jib and main to open. The mainsail trimmer

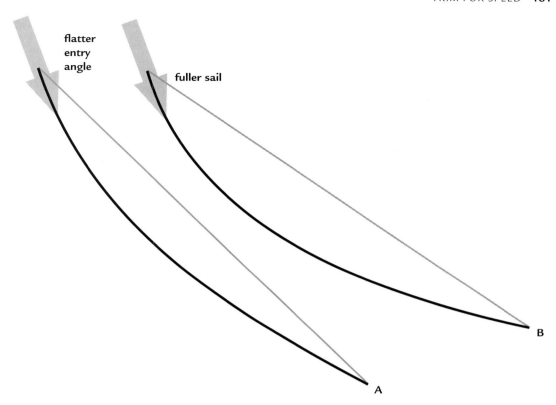

A flatter headsail allows higher pointing but slower speed. A fuller headsail allows more speed but lowers pointing ability.

should drop the traveler to leeward to improve the entry angle of the mainsail. Create balance between the jib and main. Your telltales are your guide to making sure you have optimal flow.

Sometimes when the true wind angle is not quite wide enough to take your jib lead entirely to the most outboard position, try two sheets on the clew of the headsail. Split the difference between the inboard track and the outboard track. Lead the tail of one sheet to the weather-side winch to keep the crew weight to windward. The trimmer can usually see the telltales from there as well.

If your class rules allow, consider a reaching sail. This is called a *jib top reacher* (JT) (see illustration next page). This is a deeper sail with a high clew. The foot of the sail is high so the water is not trapped when the boat heels. Heavy pressure from water spilling into the foot of a sail can cause it to rip. The JT clew is higher, so your lead will trim much farther aft. The JT might require a second line to pull the sheet down.

Another sail for reaching is the jib top's tough brother, the *blast reacher*. It is smaller in area, flatter in shape, and made of heavier material. This sail keeps the boat from heeling over in heavy winds.

Spinnakers and Downwind Sails

Trimming a spinnaker is much like trimming a genoa or the mainsail. Once again, the maximum amount of draft should be near the middle, or about 40 percent of the way aft. Haul the spinnaker halyard all the way to the head of the mast. If you are having difficulty flying the spinnaker, you may want to ease the spinnaker, halyard off a few inches to move the head away from

Rig up a jib top sheet adjuster to trim a jib top reacher. This gives more flexibility on the course. If the top of the reaching sail starts luffing, the sheet adjuster is pulled down to tighten the jib's leech. If the bottom of the jib luffs first, the sheet adjuster is eased up.

the mast. Be sure that your spinnaker hal-yard is strong enough. A weak halyard will stretch when a puff hits, absorbing energy that should be going into the sail.

To check whether the draft is in the middle of the spinnaker, see if both clews of the sail are parallel to the water. If one clew is higher than the other, pole height needs adjusting. Lower your pole to move draft forward in the sail for more power; raise the pole to move draft aft to flatten the spinnaker for less power. The center seam should be perpendicular to the horizon. If the center seam meets the water at an angle, your pole needs adjusting.

Have your spinnaker pole extending from the mast at a right angle. The farther the pole end is away from the mast, the eas-ier it is to fly the spinnaker. If the pole is cocked up at an angle, the spinnaker has moved closer to the boat and is not as effi-cient. The trick to good spinnaker trim is to get the spinnaker away from the boat as far as possible so that the air flows freely around the sail, which creates more power. An over-trimmed spinnaker is slow. The trimmer must constantly ease the sail to keep it open.

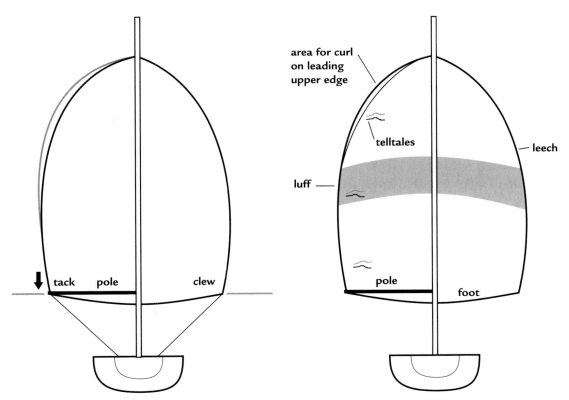

Keep the clews of the spinnaker perpendicular to the centerline of the boat. If the tack is too high, lower the pole until the clews are even (left). Keep a small curl on the leading upper edge of the spinnaker. Use tell-tales for reference. Use the pole to keep equal tension on the luff, leech, and foot. Place telltales on the luff of the spinnaker at equal intervals 6 to 12 inches from the leading edge (right).

It is important for a spinnaker trimmer to watch all parts of the sail to see that it's trimmed correctly. The luff, the leech, and the foot should all have about equal tension. The sail should curl about in the middle to the upper part of the luff. Telltales on the luff of a spinnaker are useful and should be placed at intervals from the top to the bottom. Telltales on the spinnaker work the same as telltales on the jib. Three is probably the best number, about 6 to 12 inches aft of the leading edge of the sail.

The spinnaker trimmer must be in good position to see the sail. Normally, this is well forward on the windward side of the boat. On a trapeze dinghy, the crew can extend from the wire while the skipper sits to leeward to balance the boat.

The spinnaker must be played constantly to keep the maximum amount of draft in the sail. The air bends more slowly around the wide spinnaker, compared with a main or jib, so this sail can be flown with more draft. I like to keep about 6 inches of curl in my sail.

Staysails

Staysails are fun to work with. They can be set in conjunction with a spinnaker or jib. In winds over 11 knots (when whitecaps are forming) staysails are effective. If the boat becomes overpowered in too much wind, it's time to take the staysail down.

Many staysails are wrapped around a roller furler. Simply haul the sail up and then unwind it. The most effective staysail

The trimmer and grinder work with intense focus to maximize speed.

Notice the double slot effect of the spinnaker, staysail, and mainsail combination as this boat surfs downwind.

tends to be tall on the hoist and short along the foot. The added sail area and accelerated wind flow between the main and the jib or spinnaker give a boat more speed.

There are several ways to determine if the staysail is helping performance. The best reference is other boats. Take bearings to see if you are gaining. If the jib or spinnaker seems to be moving in toward the side of the boat when the staysail is set, there probably is not enough wind to fly it effectively. If the staysail makes the spinnaker collapse or makes it difficult to trim, take the staysail down.

Note your speed before and after setting the staysail. Also monitor your course. Ideally, your boat is faster while sailing on the same heading. If you must sail a higher course to keep the sails full and this new course is taking you away from the next mark, it might be better to take the staysail down.

Setting up a staysail is similar to a jib. When using the staysail with the jib, called a double-headstay rig, the halyard tension and leech curvature should match the jib. The telltales on the luff and the leech of the staysail should flow aft evenly. Like the jib, move the sheet lead forward if the top of the sail luffs first. Keep the halyard fairly tight. If the luff sags to leeward, it can adversely effect the spinnaker or jib.

The fore-and-aft position of the tack is an important adjustment on the foredeck. As a rule, staysails work best when the tack is well aft to keep it away from the jib or spinnaker. If the staysail is creating backwind on the main, it has been set too far aft.

The staysail sheet should be trimmed as far outboard as possible. If the sail luffs, the lead is too far out.

Frequently sailors will use a jib as a staysail with a spinnaker. But I find the jib is set so far forward that the spinnaker is less effective. There is a narrow range when a jib and spinnaker can work simultaneously. Short-footed staysails or jibs work best with spinnakers. Large overlapping genoas should rarely be used as a staysail in combination with a spinnaker, because the extra sail area makes the spinnaker collapse.

Sometimes you see a genoa hoisted halfway up to act as a staysail. This technique is popular on the final approach of a leeward mark, but I don't recommend it. The shape is all wrong and the technique rarely works. It also becomes a distraction.

I find it better to hoist the jib right up to the top. Forget about using it as a staysail. Favor the spinnaker over the jib. Letting the jib luff will allow the spinnaker to stay filled with wind.

One experiment to test in a practice session is whether a short-footed jib like a #3 set with a staysail is faster than flying a #1 with no staysail. On a close reach in winds over 12 knots, the two-sail setup might work. Give it a try.

Plan in advance when and how to set a staysail. This will help minimize the crew spending time on the foredeck.

Be careful not to over-trim the staysail. If the staysail is too tight, the mainsail will be over-trimmed too. This will slow you down. A good way to make sure you are not over-trimmed is to keep the top of the staysail trimmed so the top set of telltales is stalling slightly, i.e., pointing straight up or streaming forward.

When a staysail is set properly you can gain valuable distance in a short period of time. As you learn the fastest combinations for different wind angles and wind speeds, make a note of this information on your sail selection chart.

Asymmetrical Spinnakers

With the invention of asymmetrical spinnakers, sailing downwind is more exciting for both small boats and large yachts. Asymmetrical comes from the Greek word *asymmetria*, which means lack of proportion. In practical terms, the luff is longer than the leech. The shape of the sail is not the same when you divide the sail in half. Symmetrical, on the other hand, means that if you divide the sail down the middle, one half of the sail is identical to the other.

These innovative spinnaker shapes give boats more speed, especially in light winds. Jibing must be done with care. There is really no mystery to trimming an asymmetrical (an A sail) as opposed to a symmetrical spinnaker. The pole height should be adjusted so the luff is balanced all the way up. The pole should be trimmed aft just enough to keep the sail efficient. As a rule, the pole should be perpendicular to the apparent wind angle. When a sprit is used for the spinnaker pole it isn't possible to trim it aft. These boats tend to sail more on a reach. Again use the telltales on the luff of the sail as your guide when trimming.

The benefits of an asymmetrical sail over a symmetrical spinnaker depend on

Big asymmetrical sails help small dinghies sail fast. The trimmer has to feel the trim through his hands, since much of the asymmetrical spinnaker is hidden behind the mainsail.

the wind strength. In summary, the benefits of an asymmetrical sail are:

❖ The luff is longer than the leech, which provides a longer driving force.

❖ An asymmetrical sail has more twist in the leech, which opens up the slot between the mainsail. This allows you to ease the mainsail farther while causing less backwind on the asymmetrical leech.

These examples further illustrate when an asymmetrical sail is beneficial:

❖ A symmetrical spinnaker on a boat sailing at apparent wind angles of around 90 degrees will have the pole close to the headstay, which forces the leech to curve back into the mainsail. The backwind makes the mainsail trimmer over-trim the main and this slows the boat down. The tighter the apparent wind angle, the faster the asymmetrical sail will be over a symmetrical sail.

❖ An ultralight Santa Cruz 70 sailing in 8 knots of true wind with asymmetrical sails will be eight seconds a mile faster than with a symmetrical sail. As the wind strength builds, or the apparent wind angle gets wider, the asymmetrical sail gets less advantageous. In 14 knots of true wind speed, an asymmetrical sail on the same Santa Cruz 70 might only be two seconds per mile faster in a straight

The crew of Oracle *is dwarfed by the asymmetrical spinnaker. Notice how narrow this America's Cup yacht is.*

line. In 16 knots the symmetrical sail will be faster. This is the crossover point between sails.

Some production boats now favor a bowsprit. The sprit can't be squared, so adjusting the tack-line setting becomes important. In order to rotate the asymmetrical sail around and get it out away from the mainsail, ease the tack line up a foot or two, depending on the size of the boat and the shape of the sail. When you are going fast, mark the position of the tack line so you can repeat your setting. If you over-ease the sail and it becomes unstable and hard to trim, try easing the halyard a foot or two along with the tack line. Test which adjustment is faster.

ASYMMETRICAL VS. SYMMETRICAL CROSSOVERS

If you have both asymmetrical and symmetrical sails in your inventory, make sure you understand which is faster in different conditions by creating a crossover chart. Designers of asymmetrical sails have raised the upper wind limit. On lighter boats and dinghies, the sail-area-to-displacement ratio is very high and you operate in narrow wind angles. Boats like the Melges 24 never need a symmetrical sail. Conversely, on large displacement boats asymmetrical sails don't always increase your speed, so sailing with symmetrical sails is very effective. The question is what sail (A or S) gives the boat the best VMG? Experimentation and recording the results will give you the optimum crossover point.

Similar to symmetrical sails, you use lighter material sails for light winds and heavier material sails for stronger winds. In winds under 9 knots, carry a smaller asymmetrical sail ("A1" in table next page) because the wind velocity might not support a full-size symmetrical sail. In the accompanying crossover table for a 40-footer, notice that some of the wind speeds overlap. Test which sails work best in different conditions. Keep track and periodically update your crossover chart.

JIBING THE ASYMMETRICAL SAIL

In many cases, and all things being equal, a good asymmetrical sail will be faster in a straight line than a symmetrical sail. The challenge arrives when you must jibe. Jibing with the pole near the headstay in medium winds is relatively easy if you are operating off a bowsprit. It's a matter of timing. The trimmers ease and take up on the new side as determined by the rate of turn by the helmsman. On many boats you jibe "inside," which means the sheets are inside the luff of the asymmetrical sail. Turn the asymmetrical sail inside out with the clew moving inside the tack.

When the wind is light, the acceleration of an asymmetrical sail after a maneuver is superior to a symmetrical sail. The exposed luff area and twist open the slot and allow the main to attach flow sooner. On larger boats in higher wind speeds, it is better to jibe "outside," which means the sheets are outside of the luff. When turning, trim the clew around the luff of the sail. Jibe inside in stronger wind strengths when you have a great deal of sail area to pull around the ends. Test each jibing method in a number of wind strengths to learn which way is faster. If you are jibing outside, it's important to tighten the luff early during the maneuver. This helps in two ways:

Sail Crossover Table for a 40-Foot Sailboat

WIND SPEED (knots)	TRUE WIND ANGLE (degrees)	APPARENT WIND ANGLE (degrees)	SAIL	MATERIAL	NOTES
0–9	115–135	55–90	A1	0.5 oz.	Pole low, small
8.5–14	120–145	80–110	A2	0.6 oz.	Good all around
11–18	130–158	85–145	S2	0.6 oz.	When puffy
16–23	155–175	135–160	S3	0.75 oz.	Keep bow up
22–30	160–175	150–160	S4	1.5 oz.	Lead forward
28+	175	165	S5	2.2 oz.	250 sq. ft. smaller

1. The firm luff makes it easier for the sail to physically get around to the new side.

2. The tight luff will help the sail fill sooner because it won't be sagging to leeward.

In heavy winds, switching the pole is the hardest part of jibing an asymmetrical spinnaker. The helmsman is the key person in this maneuver. Expose the asymmetrical sail to the wind immediately after the jibe, but don't head up onto a reach until the pole is set and the trimmers are prepared.

Remember your sail selection crossovers. Keep the sail balanced with the pole height and fore-and-aft position. Work on the timing of the jibe between the trimmers easing and taking up in coordination with the rate of turn of the helmsman. As soon as

---

Sail Trim Tips

❖ Keep the wind flowing off the leech of the sail.

❖ Top batten should be parallel to the boom.

❖ On jib, if top telltale stalls, move the lead forward. If bottom telltale stalls, first move lead aft.

❖ If the boat is overpowered, flatten the sails. If overpowered, twist off upper leech to spill out wind. If still overpowered, reduce sail area.

❖ Steer to the telltales or sails, not to the compass.

❖ Hold the rudder still and on centerline for long periods of time without changing course. Adjust the sails instead.

❖ The mainsail trimmer should constantly test the trim relative to the angle of heel. If heeled too far over, the boat will sail slowly.

Experiment Like the Pros

There is a lot to be learned while observing regattas. At a match-race championship on Long Island Sound, I marveled at how Dutchman Roy Heiner won race after race by passing J/105s downwind. His secret was winging the asymmetrical spinnaker to windward and simultaneously easing the halyard off about 6 feet. All the other competitors tried winging too, but they kept the halyards hauled up to the top of the mast. It was interesting that no one else figured out Heiner's clever trick. He went on to win the championship. The lesson here is to experiment with halyard tension. Heiner clearly found the magic formula.

the asymmetrical sail fills, give the sheet a big ease. This prevents over-heeling and too much pressure on the sail. Communication between the trimmers and helmsman is key.

When sailing in a straight line, it's better to sail 1 or 2 degrees too high than low. This will keep your speed up. Test bearing off in the puffs. Alternatively, trimmers should say when the pressure in the spinnaker feels soft. In this case, head higher to regain speed.

CHAPTER 9

Steering Fast

The essence of sailing is steering. There is no greater reward on the water. Your senses and physical actions combine with every movement of the boat: it's as if your mind and boat are one.

Good steering is a blend of mechanical skill and intuition. The best helmsmen have certain traits in common. Intense focus and heightened senses are two hallmarks that all championship helmsmen share. They also demand clear visibility, accept input on performance, understand changing tactical options, use correct posture, and have the ability to "will" their boat to sail faster.

For many sailors, effective helming comes naturally; others must practice continually. The great pianist Vladimir Horowitz said he could tell if he missed just one day of practice, and his audiences could tell if he missed two days. Even for a virtuoso, practice makes a big difference. Top sailors are no different, and there is no substitute for solid practice time. Luckily, as a sailor you learn to steer every time you take the helm. Use every available moment, even when you're making a short passage to or from the racecourse, to improve your steering skills.

Correct Posture

On a boat with a wheel, always stand facing forward with both hands on the wheel. Standing gives you more visibility and allows for better concentration. Sitting limits your visibility and forces you to keep your head turned forward, which can create soreness and eventually fatigue. When you are standing, only your feet and hands are touching something and therefore your whole body acts as a sensor.

When holding the wheel, spread your hands shoulder-width apart. With a tiller, keep your arms and legs parallel. The hiking stick or tiller should be an extension of your arm. A firm grip puts you in control.

Always steer from the windward side. You have better visibility and can feel the elements better. The only exception is in light wind under 5 knots, when it might be helpful to sit to leeward to help heel the boat.

On a boat with an easy-moving, big wheel, lean against the wheel with your legs to create friction. This steadies steering motion. Experiment until you find the best

Buddy Melges, one of America's best helmsmen, uses all his senses to steer.

steering position—and one that is comfortable for you.

If you're using a hiking strap, be sure your weight is evenly distributed between both legs. Adjust the straps so that the inside edge of the deck touches the middle of your calves; the gunwale should touch the middle of your thighs when your knees are bent at an angle.

Stretch out before and after steering to relax your muscles. When you're at the helm, make yourself comfortable. Attach pads to the rails, just as Finn sailors do. Pad your hiking straps with the black neoprene tubing used for insulating air-conditioning pipes. Hiking pants reduce the pressure against the backs of your thighs. (These are tight-fitting shorts with battens stitched into the backs of the legs to keep the boat's gunwale from digging into your legs and restricting blood circulation.) As I've gotten older, I've found hiking pants extremely valuable while racing an Etchells.

Spread your weight evenly to reduce fatigue caused by the restriction of blood circulation. If you do start to lose circulation in some part of your body, it's time to change your position. Sometimes standing up for a few seconds will get the blood moving again.

When you're at the helm, focus on steering the boat. Never steer holding a coffee cup, eating a sandwich, or looking at a chart. And make sure you are wearing the right clothing for the conditions. Being cold, hot, or wet makes you fatigued. Gloves are helpful; sunglasses and a hat are essential.

When you are helming at night, everything feels bigger and faster. If you're wearing a hat or a hood at night, take it off so you can feel the wind better. During the height of the infamous 1979 Fastnet Race storm, our skipper Ted Turner told me to take my hat off so I could sense the wind. It worked.

Getting in the Groove

There are many references to help you steer better. Use them all. My favorite reference is angle of heel. Line the horizon up with the bow so it's easy to detect any changes in your heel angle. Heel angle lets you know if you are sailing in more or less wind. When you are going fast compared to other boats, note your heel angle and strive to maintain it.

The optimal sailing angle to windward depends on wind strength and sea condi-

tions. In smooth water, for example, it usually pays to sail higher than you would when sailing through chop.

The average sailor steers a boat too fine; that is, too high and too slow. This often happens when a sailor gets nervous. When you feel anxious, the best strategy is to put the bow down and foot for speed.

There is a thin line between being in the groove or out of whack. To sail at peak efficiency (or in the groove), set your sails at their fastest shape for the wind conditions and your point of sail. Then observe your performance against other competitors. Next, balance the helm by adjusting your sails and crew weight. Ideally, you will feel a slight pull to windward. Once the boat feels right, start experimenting. Small ad-

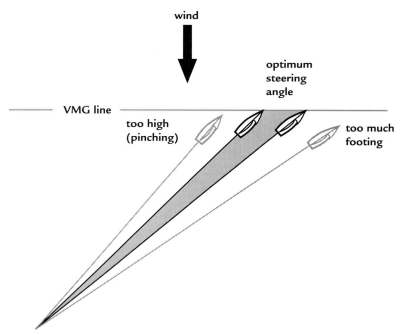

Every boat has an optimum sailing angle off the wind. This can vary as much as 5°. If you sail too high, or pinch, you lose velocity made good (VMG). If you foot away too much, you lose VMG again. The goal is to sail in the shaded zone.

justments make a big difference in performance. Make only one change at a time so you learn what works. The competition racing alongside is your best reference.

A tactician sets the pace. If the tactician calls for more speed, bear off a few degrees and ease your sails. (Remember that sailboats only increase speed when bearing off if you ease out your sails.)

Before any movement of the helm, announce your intentions to the trimmers. Continuous communication insures that no one is caught off guard. I find it helps to change crew responsibilities within your boat periodically so you understand the problems of the other crew.

The length of time one is efficient at the helm varies dramatically. On a heavy wind reach, thirty minutes is plenty. When you are sailing to windward in a moderate breeze and smooth water, two hours is no problem.

When you take the helm from another helmsman, it takes a few minutes to get into a fast groove. To minimize this time, first observe the helmsman you are replacing. Note the boatspeed, heel angle, and wind angle, and ask about any special problems. Talk about performance.

Windwaves (ripples on water) and windshifts cycle through their oscillations every few minutes. Make a mental note of each change as it happens when you first take the helm. It should take you one cycle to understand the pattern and get into a smooth rhythm.

Once the boat feels good, try to top your performance. Use the references that are most helpful. Of the many helmsmen I have raced with over the years, two stand out. Dennis Conner has a beautiful way of exceeding his targets for long periods of time. If the fastest course is at, say, 21 degrees apparent wind at 8.1 knots, Dennis will achieve 19 degrees at 8.2 for six boatlengths. Once his numbers start to fall, he quickly adjusts and starts over again.

Buddy Melges is the most natural sailor in America. He doesn't need instruments. At one regatta where the boats were provided, a heated argument broke out at the skipper's meeting over the use of speedos (boatspeed indicators). Apparently some of the boats didn't have one. Melges stole the show when he asked, "What's a speedo?" The regatta organizers eliminated their use.

Both Conner and Melges excel during turns. Maneuvering smoothly is essential for all helmsmen. I have spent a lifetime practicing tacks and jibes. No matter what size boat I'm sailing, the same routine works.

Before any maneuver first accelerate to full speed. Wait for a puff, which will help you accelerate following the turn. Remember to let the puff build speed before turning. Use your sails and crew weight in combination with your rudder. Remember a rudder acts like a brake. The initial turn should start slowly. The faster you turn, the more you slow down.

Think of a tack (or jibe) in three parts. The first third is slow and deliberate. Just as the sails luff, increase the rate of speed of the turn (the second third). The final third is even faster, until you are on your new acceleration course (see illustrations next page). At this point be patient. Most boats take two to four boatlengths to accelerate to full speed.

The most common error I see helmsmen making is spinning too fast on a tack or

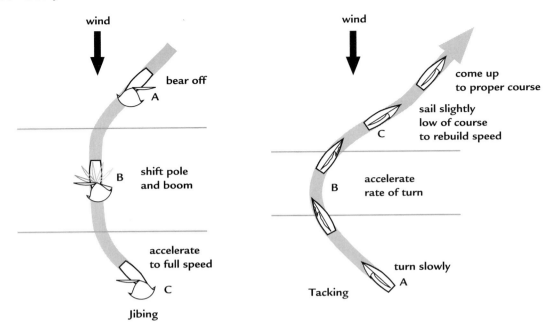

Think of your jibe (left) or tack (right) in three phases. The first phase is slow and deliberate (A). Increase your rate of turning speed in the second phase (B). Accelerate in the third phase (C).

jibe. You should not turn any faster than the sails can be shifted from one side to the other. If your path through the water has a question mark shape coming off the stern, you have turned too quickly.

America's Cup champion Russell Coutts is a master at turning a boat. He always starts slowly and then accelerates the turn after passing through the wind. His arc through the water looks both purposeful and graceful. Few top sailors turn as slowly as Coutts.

The helmsman should have a reference before every turn. Use the course of other boats, a compass, the sails, an object on land, the wind, telltales, or an anchored object in the water as a reference to steer for at the end of a tack or jibe.

Instruments are a good reference when accelerating. Use a crew member to call out speed so the helmsman can watch the water, the sails, and the angle of heel. Don't scream this information so the competition hears it.

Considerable distance can be lost during a maneuver. The helmsman is in the best position to see or sense any problems. For example, if the jib is slow to be trimmed, the mainsail should be eased so the boat doesn't round into the wind. The trimmers and helmsmen must be alert to each other's actions.

The amount of helm being used is an excellent reference for the trimmers. Mark off 1-degree increments on the wheel (see illustration on page 174). If there is too much windward helm, then depower the sails. On a puffy day, the main trimmer is really driving the boat and must stay alert.

During this critical period of time (while maneuvering) keep the crew off the bow. Stay low, focused, and quiet. Once the boat is up to full speed the crew can then resume their sail-setting activities.

One trick is to move crew members down below when you don't have any helm in light air. During a Liberty Cup in New York Harbor, we found that sailing in light wind and chop was tough. In those conditions I put four of my six-man crew be-low, on the leeward side of the keel. It was really fast. On a Maxi boat I've had twenty people down below sitting on the keel. When you do this, make sure to rotate crews and give them a pep talk, because they won't be able to see any of the action on the course.

Crew can also help the helmsman by minimizing distractions on board, such as unnecessary chatter, standing in the way, or flicking cigarette ashes.

Steering References

There are many references to use when steering. It's possible to keep each of the following elements in mind simultaneously. In many ways it's like driving a car—you want to be attuned to everything going on around you.

Angle of heel compared to horizon—this tells you the force from the wind in the sails.

Trim of sails—over-trimmed or under-trimmed sails indicate that you are off course or the sails need adjustment.

Performance compared to other boats—the most reliable reference is watching other boats.

Windwaves (ripples)—the dark patches on the water tell you how strong the wind is.

Masthead fly—look at the masthead fly frequently. The wind changes at the top of the mast before it changes on deck.

Instruments—there are always a few seconds' lag time with instruments, but they are a steady indicator of performance. Here are the most beneficial instruments:

Boatspeed—your goal is to keep steady boatspeed. The best helmsmen experiment with sail adjustment and the course to generate extra speed.

Wind direction—if you monitor your speed, sail trim, and compass course, you can easily detect changes in the wind direction.

Apparent wind angle—this is a good reference to use. If the wind shifts and the apparent wind angle remains the same, you'll be sailing on a new course.

True wind speed—most instruments calculate true wind speed. This helps you keep track of what the wind is doing.

Turns of the wheel (helm)—this indicates how much pressure is created by the sails. When you are going fast according to the instruments or compared to other boats, note how much helm you have and work to maintain it.

Flags, land references—use every source available to read the wind.

Amount of helm—most boats sail best with 3 to 5 degrees of helm.

Telltales on shrouds—help you read apparent wind angle.

Compass—a steady reference to keep track of your course.

At night, use instruments, waves, stars, moon, clouds, stern lights, angle of heel, points on land, and the horizon.

The Ultimate: Steering *Endeavour*

"Would you like to take the helm?" are magic words on any boat. But aboard the beautifully restored J-class *Endeavour*, the question was particularly sweet. At that moment, the 130-foot sloop was head-to-wind and motionless. The jib was backed by one of the eight professional crew. The bow began to slowly swing against the shore. At first everything happened in slow motion. The sails filled. On the water the wind looked to be about 6 knots. At the masthead, 165 feet up, the wind instrument indicated 16 knots. The boat heeled and started moving. At the helm, the sound of the water started as a trickle and built to a waterfall. Through my hands on the wheel and feet on the deck, a surge of awesome power gripped me as *Endeavour* accelerated. The boat came alive.

Soon we were sailing to windward at 10 knots. The pressure on the helm felt both light and direct. The boat responded nicely to subtle adjustments to the wheel, although such a heavy boat turns slowly, so maneuvers must be planned well in advance. The two-boatlength circle in a race would begin almost the length of a football field away from the mark.

What a privilege it was to be sailing on this powerful, yet elegant yacht—the 1934 America's Cup challenger, which won two races, then lost four in a row. Since her restoration by Elizabeth Meyer (between 1984 and 1989), 3,000 sailors have had the same opportunity. During the ten years Meyer owned *Endeavour*, it sailed over 100,000 miles. Now, under charter to Meyer, we sailed for a week along the Maine coast. Even in the most remote areas, spectators on all kinds of craft appeared out of nowhere to watch *Endeavour* sail past.

The boat makes a singular statement underway, bringing you back to a grand era of sailing. Even though we were daysailing by ourselves, we imagined another J-boat alongside and therefore maximized our speed all the time.

The J-boats of the 1930s had a reputation for being difficult to sail. They frequently broke down because the loads on the rig, sails, and equipment were so great.

Today, *Endeavour* is a highly engineered machine. Modern technology is a big asset to the steel-hulled vessel. All the winches and other deck hardware have been beefed up, and the deck has been reinforced. The mast is aluminum, and the Spectra sails are laced with carbon fiber, reinforced at the corners with titanium. Not only is the strength needed, but stainless fittings rust when they come into contact with carbon fiber. Even the cringles are titanium.

The sails are immense. The staysail is larger than a Volvo Ocean 60's main. In 1989 *Endeavour* had a main made out of Dacron; it weighed 1,800 pounds. The current one weighs in at 1,150. The sail inventory is ready for racing, including gennikers of 7,000 and 9,000 square feet.

A small (1-foot) trim on the mainsail makes a big difference in performance. J-boats are mainsail-driven boats, and the leech is like the wing of a large aircraft. While steering on the wind I experimented with finding the fastest groove. I could achieve the optimum VMG through a wide range of wind. The biggest challenge was trimming the sails for wind shear; wind strength could be 10 knots greater aloft and shifted by 30 degrees. Like all bigger boats, *Endeavour* has a full instrument package, but I preferred steering using the telltales and the angle of heel as my references. The boat is massive, but over the course of the week I became more comfortable with her size.

Endeavour easily sails at 10.5 knots to windward with a tacking angle of 80 degrees. It's important to foot the boat and not pinch. She makes considerable leeway if you point too high. On a reach, *Endeavour* sails at a steady 12.5 knots. It made me wonder how this class might perform if the

"Would you like to take the wheel?" are magic words for any sailor. Gary Jobson at the wheel of Endeavour.

The J-boat Endeavour *sailing to windward with a double-headsail rig.*

boats had bulb keels with winglets like the current America's Cup class.

I sat in different spots on the boat to understand how *Endeavour* felt. On the bow, the boat travels so fast that the water flowing past looks like an optical illusion. The foredeck is wet as the spray comes aboard at high speed. Sitting at the leeward shrouds the angle of heel is pronounced. The water rushes past loudly, and you feel at one with the boat. Boats always feel good in the mid-deck area. The sensation changes on the stern. It's tranquil. The wind seems softer, the water quiet, and the actions on deck are far removed. Down below the motion is gentle, quite a contrast to today's light racers, pounding hard in waves. *Endeavour* features a deckhouse. The visibility through the rectangular windows keeps you involved and yet it is quiet and warm.

Meyer was a visionary to bring a rusty hulk of the past back to life, something we really appreciated as we raced the ghosts of other Js. We never crossed a finish line, but our time aboard made us appreciate the past (with some help from modern technology). *Endeavour* is the epitome of elegance under sail.

If you feel tired, pass the helm to another crew member. Rotating the wheel can help build crew loyalty. The best way to bring new people into the sport is to give them the helm. Young sailors learn this at an early age. When they take the helm, they are suddenly in charge of their own destiny.

To steer and coexist as one with a boat under sail is one of the highlights of life. You should savor every moment.

Steering Like the Pros

A helmsman's ability to steer a grand-prix boat at top speed is enhanced by numbers. With the help of a velocity prediction program (see pages 140–41) and recorded performance data, a crew can develop specific sailing numbers for every wind speed and true wind angle. Top crews develop a graph with the best sail combination for every wind condition. While the boat might feel good when you're sailing outside these numbers, you're actually losing VMG (velocity made good).

For every maneuver there's a procedure to follow and each crew member is assigned a specific task. Regardless of the wind strength, the foredeck crew is always poised. Knowing that the person next to you will perform flawlessly builds confidence.

Steering a grand-prix yacht is pure pleasure not only because it is a powerful, stable, and high-speed boat, but also because the sail trimmers make you a hero. If you bear off 2 degrees, the sails automatically go out. But responsibility goes along with the opportunity. If a helmsman is struggling, the trimmers will at first coach him to sail a better course. But if there's no improvement after ten minutes, they'll suggest a rotation. Everyone knows the boat's potential, and the numbers are the scorecard. There's little tolerance for under-performance.

The whole crew helps the helmsman too. Weight on the rail, even on a Maxi, is crucial, as is fore-and-aft trim. If conditions warrant, the crew should constantly shift— just as you would on a dinghy. The rudder of a Maxi is big and powerful and slows the boat down when you turn it—so during maneuvers use sails and crew weight together, even roll tack (see page 204) in light air.

With all the instrumentation available, I find the true wind angle and angle of heel to be the best references. I play a game at the wheel, splitting my time between watching the numbers and relying on intuitive feel. As time goes by, I have come to believe in the numbers. Heeling too much is the enemy of speed. If we heel too much, the helmsman heads up a few degrees, straightens the boat, and the speed accelerates.

CHAPTER 10

Maneuvering for Advantage

The principles for maneuvering included in this chapter apply to boats of all sizes. The key is learning how to maneuver your boat so that it behaves precisely as you wish. You will have moments on the racecourse where you'll need to accelerate for more speed. You'll have other moments where you'll need to decelerate to avoid a collision, or set up for a better position. Learning the characteristics of any boat can be easily done if you follow the basic principles outlined below and spend time practicing.

As the helmsman, there are three key factors that help you turn: the rudder, the sails, and the position of the crew. Keep your mind outside the boat so you can concentrate on your turn; let your crew concentrate on handling the sails and moving their weight. Coordinating these three elements will make your maneuvers success-

ful. But this type of coordination does not come easily. Again, practice is key.

If you are sailing a new boat for the first time, spend time maneuvering next to a buoy or another boat to get the feel of the boat's sailing characteristics. Start by making very tight turns. Then make wider turns to see how far your momentum will carry your boat. Sit next to a buoy at a dead stop with a stopwatch and note how long it takes to accelerate to full speed. Once you've mastered acceleration, pass the buoy at full speed and see how long it takes you to bring the boat to a dead stop.

Before any maneuver—be it a jibe, a tack, bearing off, or heading up—make sure your boat is sailing at full speed before making a turn.

Probably the biggest mistake most sailors make when maneuvering is turning the boat too quickly. The faster you turn a boat, the faster it loses speed. To maintain momentum, move the rudder slowly. Try to steer like Russell Coutts and start each turn slowly.

If you were to get off your boat for a day and watch the rest of your fleet race, you'll notice that most boats turn very quickly. Practice a tacking duel with another boat that goes the same speed as your boat. Keep one boat tacking at the same turning rate while the other varies its turning rate; see which tacking technique works best.

Racing sailors spend their lives trying to make boats go faster; but at times, it pays to make your boat sail slower. Using violent action on the helm alone is the wrong way to decelerate. Use your sails and your crew weight instead. When you luff your sails, make sure that both sails luff simultaneously. If you luff the jib and keep the main trimmed in, the boat alters course toward the wind. If you keep the jib trimmed and the main goes out, the boat bears away. Both these actions require an opposite reaction by the rudder. As a general rule I never back a jib when turning unless I find that I'm in trouble. When you back the jib, the boat slows down dramatically.

If you need to slow down for better position—for example, at a leeward mark—it's often better to sail extra distance than slow your boatspeed, for it's difficult to accelerate again. If you find youself trapped outside an overlapped boat at the leeward mark, you can improve your position by making a large alteration of course to leeward and letting the inside boat round first. Then make a smooth turn by rounding on the inside. You will sail extra distance, but you won't lose any speed or find yourself trapped outside of an overlapped boat.

While most sailors think about the sails and the rudder for maneuvering, the position of your crew weight and angle of heel will also make a big difference. I always try to keep the boat at an angle of heel that keeps a little pressure on my rudder in the direction I want to head. So if I want to luff toward the wind, a leeward heel helps me. If I want to bear off, a windward heel helps. If I'm anticipating a quick luff, moving my crew weight aft helps me turn into the wind. If I need to bear off suddenly, moving my crew weight forward can be helpful by getting the stern out of the water.

When making any maneuver, keep the actions of your crew, sail trim, and steering coordinated. The helmsman should announce his intentions before he makes a maneuver. The conversation should go like this. "In two boatlengths, I'm going to bear off twenty degrees," says the helmsman. As he starts to turn the rudder he says, "I'm bearing off now, ease the sails four feet." By putting your commands into minutes and seconds, feet and inches, boatlengths or degrees, the crew will have a better understanding of when and how much you will be turning. This takes the mystery out of your sailing and makes for better teamwork. Avoid saying, "Ease the jib a little." How much is a little?

The toughest thing to do in sailing is to maneuver a boat that is at a dead stop. Boats with big mainsails and small jibs are often difficult to get out of irons. You must therefore use the forward sail to rotate the boat and get it on course to accelerate. Using crew weight to roll the boat in one direction can also help turn a boat when you have no forward motion.

Understanding how your boat maneuvers will give you a big edge on the racecourse. By practicing maneuvers before a race, you will also get your crew tuned up. Take chances during these practice sessions; experiment and see what you can do with the boat while you are maneuvering near a buoy. After an hour of practice you'll have the confidence to maneuver in a big crowd of boats.

Tacking

Generally it takes from one to three boatlengths to tack in winds stronger than 5 knots, and as much as five to seven boatlengths in winds less than 5 knots. This is true for all boats. For this reason, you should only tack when you are up to full speed (or at least going as fast as your competition). Never tack if you are going slower than the competition. Your aim is to maintain your speed and assume a new course as quickly as possible.

By using your weight, heel the boat slightly to leeward before tacking. As the boat heads into the wind, heel it hard to windward and "roll" the boat through the tack. To maintain your speed, use as little helm as you can. As you head into the wind, trim your sails in and keep them full. In a sloop, you should trim both the main and the jib at the same time. This move is called *roll tacking*. Years ago, it was a maneuver used only in dinghies. Today, it works for almost all boats. It's easy and fun—and it will help you get your boat up to full speed quickly.

The crew of this small keelboat helps heel the boat to windward during a roll tack.

Whenever you tack a lot, put more power into your sails so that you increase speed sooner. It may help to head down slightly after a tack, close-reaching to accelerate. As your speed increases, head up to your normal course while playing your sails for maximum speed.

Jibing

The time to jibe is when you are moving fast. It's easier to keep wind in your sails at that pace, and you will lose the least distance. In a dinghy, the best time to jibe is when you are surfing down a wave with maximum speed; you have less power in the sails (the apparent wind is less) and your boat is therefore more stable. Always keep the boat flat. The centerboard should be down about one-third of the way for control. Too much centerboard will cause the boat to capsize.

On larger boats, use all your crew during a jibe. Station everyone at different parts of the boat to handle the sails. Use marks to indicate how much to ease or trim your spinnaker sheets and guys. Marks can also tell you how far to dip your spinnaker pole when passing it underneath the forestay. Trimmers should keep a marking pen nearby to write on the sheets.

When jibing the spinnaker, keep the sail away from the boat as far as you can. Before swinging the pole over, trim it aft so it is nearly perpendicular to the mast. In this manner you will be able to change course quickly on the new jibe and the spinnaker will not collapse, since it is already on the new leeward side of the boat. As the pole comes aft on the new side, the spinnaker will follow automatically.

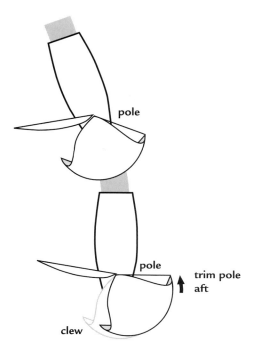

Before shifting a pole on a jibe, trim the pole aft so it is perpendicular to the mast. Keep the clews of the spinnaker on opposite sides of the headstay during a jibing maneuver. If the boat is turned quickly, shift the pole early. If the boat is turned slowly, wait to shift the pole until the boat is downwind.

Try not to jibe the main over until the wind is just passing straight aft of the boat. Jibing the main too early will collapse the spinnaker. You would do this differently if you were using a jibe to do a circling maneuver at the start. On any boat, throwing the mainsail over early (pre-jibing) will cause the boat to jibe sooner and round the boat into the wind. This technique helps you make a faster circle.

Many sailors lose as much as two boatlengths when jibing, especially in light air, because they make too great a change of course. In winds of 5 to 10 knots, you need to change course only about 60 degrees to jibe. In heavier winds you need to change course only 40 degrees.

Roll jibing will help prevent too great a course change. It works well in dinghies, particularly in light air. First heel the boat to leeward, then heel it hard to windward so that the main changes sides quickly. By doing this, you will not have to make a great alteration of course. College sailors are masters of this technique.

Another common error helmsmen make in jibing is forgetting to change hands holding the sheet and the tiller, which can put them off balance. To avoid this, it may help to switch hands before you jibe.

Catch a Wave or a Tow

When sailing downwind, you can gain valuable distance by making your boat plane, surf, surge, or catch a tow from another boat. These techniques work well on all sailboats. A boat *planes* when it breaks the friction with the water and rides on top of the water. You are now sailing faster than

The Laser in front looks like it is flying as it takes advantage of small waves to surf downwind. The boat behind is heeling too much to gain as much speed.

hull speed. It *surfs* when a wave propels the boat past the point of friction. To bring a boat up out of the water, you must accelerate for extra speed.

For a boat to plane, it must first be in balance so there is absolutely no pressure on the rudder. Have your sails trimmed and keep the boat flat. A light-displacement sailboat will not plane if it is heeling excessively. As a puff hits, hike the boat down flat, bear off slightly, move your weight aft to get the bow to ride up over the water, and accelerate by trimming your sails rapidly. Adjust your boom vang so the boat is still under control but the top batten of the mainsail is parallel to the boom. Ease your outhaul and cunningham. Trim both the guy and the sheet of the spinnaker at the same time to increase sail area. These adjustments help give you the momentum to start planing or surfing. The centerboard should be pulled up at least halfway to reduce lateral resistance.

For surfing, the course of your boat should be perpendicular to the waves passing under your hull. Since waves crisscross each other on diagonals, watch ahead for waves 45 degrees on either side of your bow. Aim your bow into the deepest trough and toward the highest peak. As the wave passes under you, give the boat extra acceleration by trimming the sails or heeling the boat to windward. This "rocking" creates wind in your sails; but more important, it breaks the friction underneath the hull so the boat will start surfing with the wave and begin planing. These actions can only be used to initiate surfing, not maintain it. Moving your weight forward will help accelerate the boat down the wave. Once you start surfing or planing, return your weight to an aft position, and keep the boat flat and level.

Once you catch a wave, bear off so you don't plow into the wave ahead. Stay with the wave you are on, just as a surfer would by cutting across it on a diagonal. This way you make valuable distance to leeward and stay with your puff and wave for a prolonged time. Keep watching the waves and practice steering from one wave to the next as long as you can. With practice you will be able to sail 50 percent faster than the fleet every time you catch a wave, even though you may be sailing by the lee by as much as 20 degrees.

It's difficult to get larger boats to plane or surf, but you can get tremendous surges that may lead to surfing. The problem is that when a boat gets going so fast the apparent wind drops, making it difficult to maintain the ride.

Catching a tow works best when the apparent wind is between 70 and 120 degrees and the backwind of a lead boat is not sufficient to hurt the boat behind it. On this point of sail, keelboats are moving their fastest and making the biggest waves. The towing technique allows your boat to sail in the dead water of the boat ahead while avoiding blanketed air. You can catch a tow off a boat that is 2 to 4 feet longer than your boat. A larger boat creates a big wave behind it and a smaller boat can use that wave to its advantage.

To catch a tow, position your boat so it's within one boatlength astern of a boat ahead of you. This is done by heading up and going right for the stern of another boat as it passes you. That boat would normally

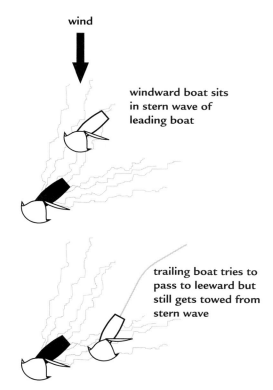

wind

windward boat sits in stern wave of leading boat

trailing boat tries to pass to leeward but still gets towed from stern wave

It's possible to catch a tow from a larger boat by heading up and going right for the stern of a boat as it passes you.

pass you to windward, but passing you to leeward is preferable for your purposes. You may be able to influence the passing boat's route: intimidating a larger boat with a potential luff may force them to pass to leeward. Once you are in position behind the bigger boat, your boat will be towed along at the speed of the boat ahead. The defense against a tow is to bear off sharply or to luff up hard, so the boat behind has to get off your wave to avoid hitting your stern. The idea is to break the pattern of your wave so the trailing boat can't stay in the trough.

Sailing by the Lee

Contrary to traditional racing tactics, sailing by the lee can occasionally be advantageous in certain wind conditions. You are sailing by the lee when you are sailing downwind and the wind is hitting your sails over the boat's leeward quarter. There are many tactical situations where this point of sail can be useful. You can avoid a time- and distance-consuming jibe, or gain some distance to leeward.

But sailing by the lee should be done with considerable caution, as this position can result in an accidental jibe. Sailing by the lee works best in light to moderate air. A boat can become unstable sailing by the lee in heavier winds and for sustained periods of time.

When sailing by the lee, beware when your boat begins to slow down. Head up quickly to keep the boat under control. A skipper can easily be lulled into sailing by the lee and end up capsizing to windward.

Watch the angle of your masthead fly and avoid sailing more than 20 degrees by the lee. If the boat feels out of control and you are losing steerage, simply head up. You will normally be on a 10-degree windward heel on this point of sail. If you are flying a spinnaker, you can increase the boat's stability by over-trimming the sail; place equal tension on both the sheet and guy so the clews stay on opposite sides of the headstay. Placing both clews on the same side of the boat will induce rolling and instability.

After jibing and continuing to sail by

Sailing by the lee for a short period of time can be effective, but this boat looks like it is about to go out of control. The remedy is to sail a higher course to get the boat back under control.

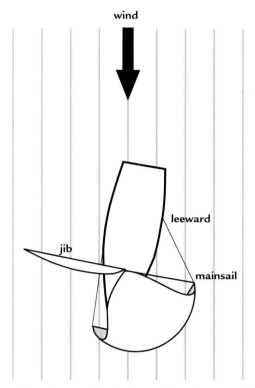

wind

leeward

jib

mainsail

Sailing downwind with the wind on the same side of the boat as the main (the leeward side) is known as sailing by the lee.

the lee, trim the spinnaker so it's in clear wind and not blanketed behind the mainsail. It's possible to sail too far by the lee, which will cause the chute to collapse. Be careful here. Over-trimming can cause an unscheduled jibe unless you have rigged a preventer to the boom (a preventer is a line or block and tackle that pulls the boom forward and prevents the boom from unexpectedly crossing to the other side of the boat). A wild-flying boom is extremely dangerous.

Once you've mastered your feel for sailing by the lee, you can use this point of sail in a variety of tactical situations. For ex-

ample, when you are rounding a leeward mark, you can sail by the lee to break or gain an overlap. You can also accelerate, as previously described, using waves and rapidly trimming the sails as the apparent wind moves forward.

Shifting Gears from Boat to Boat

Many racing sailors compete on a variety of different-sized boats during the season. Being versatile is a key ingredient in improving your skills, but it takes concentration to shift gears from one boat to another.

Anytime you jump into a new boat or class, the first thing to do is look for common denominators. Starting techniques, finding the favored side of the course, and maneuvering are not very different from boat to boat. But to sail at peak efficiency on a boat that's new to you, go back to the basics. Practice your boat handling—even for a short period of thirty minutes—to get the feel of the boat and make sure your crew knows how to handle the sails.

Once you get some practice maneuvering, the next step is to speed test alongside another boat, both upwind and downwind. Make a note of the angles that you tack and jibe through.

One summer, I raced on four different boats and found myself having to shift gears frequently. It amazed me how similarly the boats sailed, even though there were major differences in size. My racing was diverse: Laser, J/22, a 43-foot sloop, and a 62-foot sloop. All four boats performed best when footing for speed and not pinching. Downwind the biggest mistake I made was sailing

Even with a keel, a J/22 feels like a dinghy. The crew must be sensitive to the smallest waves and windshifts.

too low a course. On a Laser you can sail effectively by the lee. But on a larger boat you lose distance rapidly. I had to work to correct my Laser technique for larger boats. The compass was a helpful reference tool in determining my optimum sailing angle.

One of the biggest benefits of sailing different boats is transferring knowledge from one class to another. The Laser and J/22 made me sensitive to the smallest waves and windshifts. I also found my tactical calls to be more accurate because of my small-boat experience. On the larger boats, racing is on longer courses and the strategy is longer term. You are constantly planning your strategy and you see things that you miss on short-course races. These big-boat tactics apply to small boats as well.

On a larger boat, one of the biggest adjustments is adding more crew members. The larger the crew, the more "experts" on board. As I've said before, to be successful it's imperative that one person makes the final tactical call. It is quiet on a Laser, and it should be equally quiet on a larger boat.

Throughout the summer, the biggest mistake I watched many competitors make, on all four sizes of boats, was inconsistent sailing. I frequently saw boats take an early lead and then sail away from the fleet and lose distance. The key to winning regattas is being consistent. For example, it might not be worth trying for the perfect start and risking jumping the gun or fouling out. Be a little conservative. Work so your average

Tips for Championship Sailing

❖ Anytime you bear off in a sailboat, ease out the sheets simultaneously. Sailboats only increase speed when you ease the sails out.

❖ If you are hit by a sudden gust, the first reaction should be to ease sails before turning the rudder. Anticipate wind changes by watching ahead.

❖ Keep an eye on the masthead fly. The wind often changes aloft before it does on the water.

❖ When reaching, move the lead of your jibsheet forward and outboard to maximize power in your sail. Keep the telltales breaking evenly.

❖ When tacking, start turning slowly. Never allow your jib to back. Increase the rate of turning once the boat is head to wind.

❖ If you are rolling wildly when sailing downwind, head up fifteen degrees and the boat will steady out.

❖ Anytime you are approaching another boat, accelerate for speed. Maneuvering is easier when you are sailing fast.

❖ Assign every member of your crew a specific job for times of action. On a well-sailed boat, everyone works in their assigned area. You can tell a well-sailed boat because the crew is always down low and in position.

❖ Before maneuvering, always sail at full speed. Wait until the crew is organized. Make your maneuver two to three lengths after being hit by a puff of wind.

❖ Assign one crew member the role of tactician. This person should keep his eyes outside the boat—watching for changes in the wind and studying the actions of the competition.

❖ Always overshoot the windward mark by half a boatlength to allow for misjudgment, unfavorable current, a bad set of waves, or another boat. When you do round the mark, you will have more speed.

❖ When maneuvering, keep your crew off the foredeck. Weight forward slows a boat down.

❖ Listen for updates on the weather radio while on the water. Thunderstorms can arrive quickly without warning.

❖ When steering with a wheel, stand up so you have a greater height of eye. Angle of heel is your most important reference. Never sit to leeward. Keep two hands on the wheel.

❖ Always carry gloves on the boat, particularly for the mainsail trimmer.

❖ When the day's race is over, reconstruct the race by drawing a diagram and making notes of what went right and what went wrong.

❖ Measure the rake of your mast. Haul a tape measure to the top of the mast and measure the distance to the transom. Use this number to compare with your competitors. Your competitors might be anxious to know your number. This might be good information to exchange.

❖ Your controls should have a wide range of adjustment; i.e., have a long traveler or large distance between inboard and outboard jib leads. The greater the *range* of adjustment in sail controls, the greater the *choice* for adjustment.

❖ In heavy wind, carry the spinnaker pole approximately 1 to 2 feet farther forward than normal and ease the spinnaker sheet the same amount. This makes the spinnaker and boat more forgiving and less likely to broach.

- ❖ Reduce weather helm to keep rudder drag low by doing one or a combination of the following: move crew weight to windward, shorten sail, ease the traveler, ease the sheet, rake the mast forward, or flatten the mainsail.

- ❖ Observe the competition to get a quick understanding of your boat's relative performance. Your first reaction is usually right. Don't wait to make changes.

- ❖ When sailing to windward, immediately bear off 1 or 2 degrees and simultaneously ease out your sails to increase speed.

- ❖ Check your angle of heel. This important speed factor can be corrected with crew weight, sail shape, or wind angle. A balanced helm is your reference. Too much windward helm means you are heeled too much. Leeward helm means you are heeling too little.

- ❖ Are you sailing in clear wind? Disturbed wind or water have a dramatic speed effect on boats of all sizes. If your wind is blanketed or if the water is choppy, maneuver away.

- ❖ In light winds and choppy water ask your crew (politely) to go below to lower the center of gravity.

- ❖ When crews get nervous they often tend to over-trim the sails. Ease your sails out a small amount anytime you are slow. This should be your first action.

- ❖ Only maneuver when your boat is sailing at maximum speed and is in a puff of wind. Be sure your crew is prepared to make a turn.

- ❖ Downwind, the spinnaker trimmer and the helmsman should sit near each other and communicate during every puff. The goal is to sail lower.

- ❖ Be the first boat to jibe in a lift.

- ❖ Keep the crew motionless and quiet during a slow-speed period to allow the trimmers and helmsman to focus on performance.

- ❖ Check to see that your telltales on the jib are breaking evenly when you luff. On the mainsail the top telltale should be just on edge at all times. If the jib luffs at the head first when heading up, move your jib lead forward. If the bottom of the sail luffs first, move the lead aft.

- ❖ When trimming sails, remember that the correct shape is more important than the amount of projected sail area. Sails work at peak efficiency when the draft is normally 40 to 50 percent aft of the luff. To point higher, move the draft aft. To sail faster, move the draft forward.

- ❖ When making changes to your sailing configuration, make one adjustment at a time and then observe for any differences.

- ❖ Have a checklist that includes the sail inventory wrapped in a piece of plastic. Refer to it often.

- ❖ Anytime you are slow, recognize the fact and take immediate action.

scores are near the top and not fluctuating. Avoid taking big chances.

Boats of all sizes are affected by the same things: windshifts, waves, and other boats. So you really don't have to change your way of thinking, even though your platform is different. In one hour you can easily tune up aboard a new boat.

CHAPTER 11

Practice Routines

It was no accident that the *Alinghi* crew was so strong during the 2003 America's Cup. When races were called off due to unfavorable wind conditions, the rest of the fleet headed back to the harbor. But *Alinghi* kept sailing and spent their bonus time practicing. Take note: the best sailors spend time practicing. It takes discipline and desire, but you too can organize your own practice sessions. A typical session need only last from one to three hours. The sailors who work hardest and make the most out of their practice sessions will always come out on top.

There are many drills you can use to practice maneuvers and seamanship. This chapter includes routines you can practice alone, with another boat, or with your fleet. Be serious and concentrate on every move you make in the boat. Execute each drill as if an Olympic medal or an America's Cup victory depended on your getting it right.

Practicing Alone

Many of these drills were adapted from my high school wrestling days, perfected during my college sailing years, and refined as I coached at Kings Point, the Naval Academy, and in hundreds of racing clinics conducted over the years. They are proven techniques, so give them a try.

When you practice alone, you have the steadiest of all competitors: time. Race from Buoy A to Buoy B and clock the time it takes. Then sail the course again and try to beat your own record. The wind will vary but try to make the best of it. You can also look for two channel markers to use as a windward-leeward course (the shorter the course, the better). Make a time trial and, again, work to improve your pace.

Before you head out on the water for a practice session, make a list of what you intend to go over, then go out and follow your plan. In a short time you'll be working to the top of the fleet, making fewer errors, executing faster spinnaker sets and smoother tacks, and reaching your goals. Don't try to practice everything in one session. Combine practicing something you have been working on with something new.

Drills for Solo Practice

In some of these drills, a single buoy or mark can be used as a starting pin, windward mark, reach mark, leeward mark, a reference point for your tacking radius, or a point to judge the set and drift of the current. Here are some sample solo drills designed to help you improve general boat-handling skills and boat control.

SPINNERS

The first drill is a "spinner," a continuous set of 720s. Sail in a small circle as fast as you can four times in one direction, then spin four times in the opposite direction without losing speed. This will improve your 720s; but, more important, it will improve your seamanship and boat handling.

To begin a spinner, sail to windward and then make a fast tack. When you tack, keep in mind that the faster you push the tiller, the faster you will stop. Your tiller action (to quote Graham Hall) should be "logarithmic—first slow, then faster!" That is, slowly increase the rate of your tiller movement as you tack. Trim your main as you round up. This will help you luff while

cutting down on the amount of tiller action, which will keep your speed up. To prove this, ease your sail out until it luffs, let your tiller go, and then trim your sail. The boat will round up into the wind. In a sloop-rigged boat, ease the main slightly but trim the jib as you begin to tack. At the same time, push your tiller slowly at first until the boat is head-to-wind and then speed the tiller up to get the boat on the new tack faster. Speed is lost while heading into the wind, not when bearing away.

Once your tack is completed, pull the tiller all the way to windward while dumping the main out as fast as possible. At the same time, it is extremely important to keep the boat flat or you will have trouble bearing away quickly. Don't jibe the sail until the wind is dead aft. Pre-jibing the main before the wind passes astern can help accelerate your maneuver. When you do jibe, trim the sail rapidly; this will help you round up into the wind faster for your next spin. A series of roll tacks and roll jibes is the key to making good spinners.

Continue spinning four times until you are just about to get dizzy, then reverse your direction. Spinners don't take much time and give you plenty of practice. They take a lot of physical work, but will keep you and your crew in good shape.

TACKING

Other than bad windshifts and slow speed on a windward leg, most ground is lost while tacking. Naturally, it is important to practice. America's Cup crews tack for hours, getting the finest motions down until they reach perfection.

When you practice tacks, do them in a

series of six or more. Make your next turn as soon as you're sailing at full speed. After each set, take a short breather and think about what slowed you down. The biggest problem for the skipper is coordinating weight balance with sheet tension and tiller action. This action varies from boat to boat. As you improve your acceleration after each tack, you can spin the boat around slightly faster.

FIGURE EIGHTS

Find two pilings or buoys that are close together. If there are none, anchor two life jackets about two boatlengths apart. Start a series of figure eights around the marks. This will improve your control of mark roundings followed by tacks and jibes. Go through the two marks one complete time, then approach them from the opposite direction.

HANDLING WAVES

Everyone needs practice sailing with waves and into waves. If a motorboat approaches, stop what you're doing and set yourself up so you'll be in a position to surf the waves. Try to stay on each wave as long as you can, pumping your sails to promote surfing and adjusting your weight to keep you on each wave.

In a race, you normally try to avoid a bad set of waves. But now that you are by yourself, head right into the worst part and try to keep the boat going. Each wave is different so practice steering up and sliding down the back or blasting through them.

ACHIEVE BALANCE

You can work on balancing your boat by tying the tiller amidships and adjusting your sheets and weight to keep your boat on course. If the boat begins to fall off, trim your sails a little or heel to leeward and it will head back up. If the boat begins to head up then flatten it and ease the main.

GO RUDDERLESS

A fun trick to practice in a dinghy is to take the rudder off completely and try to maneuver without it, using weight and sheet tension. Someday you might be forced to finish a race with a broken rudder and you'll be prepared for it.

SAIL BACKWARD

Another exercise is to sail backward by holding your main out. This will teach you how a boat responds when traveling backward. If you get into irons or you want to escape from a foe in a match race, this drill will come in handy.

PRACTICE STARTS

Use a mark as one end of the starting line and make a series of timed runs. To make a timed run for one minute, begin by running away from the mark with your stopwatch at one minute, sailing on a broad reach in the opposite direction away from the line. At thirty-four seconds, tack for the mark, thus allowing eight seconds for the tack and regaining speed. If you hit the line early, then adjust your run so that you tack at, say, thirty seconds. If you find that you are reaching back to the mark, adjust your run on the way down by heading on a broader reach. The theory behind the timed run technique is that a sailboat travels the same speed on a broad reach as it does going to windward.

WINDWARD, REACH, LEEWARD MARK

Use a buoy as a windward mark. Judge your layline as you approach. Once you reach the windward mark bear off, ease your sails, and keep the boat flat. Take the mark both to port and starboard. Approach on both starboard and port tacks. Round and bear away; then try a rounding by bearing away and then jibing.

Use the buoy as a reach mark and practice by jibing around the mark in both directions. This is especially useful when sailing a boat with a spinnaker up.

Use the buoy as a leeward mark and practice making a tactical rounding. Stay wide as you approach the mark and stay close to the other side as you round up. Judge the wind direction before you make the rounding so you have a good idea of the course that you'll be on once you round. Thinking ahead will keep you from stalling out by heading too high or losing ground by falling off too much. Keep the boat flat as you round up so you won't go sideways; trim the sails as you round. When you trim your sheets, grab the line right at the block and make a long pull with your arm extended as far away from the block as possible before grabbing the line for a second trim.

You can see how much room you are taking in the water when tacking by watching the mark as you tack around it. By watching the turning mark relative to the shoreline as you sail toward or away from it, you can also determine the set and drift of the current.

SOLO DRILLS: ROUTINES

Here's a quick summary of drills to practice next time you head out on the water for a solo session:

❖ Four sets of six tacks

❖ Two spinners

❖ Figure eights through piles, two each direction

❖ Four leeward mark roundings, followed by tack

❖ Four sets of six jibes

❖ Four spinnaker sets

❖ Four timed runs

❖ Surf in waves

❖ Look at mast rake

❖ Try sailing backward

❖ Four windward mark roundings

❖ Sail to windward balancing helm

Practicing in Pairs

You can learn a great deal about performance using two boats. A second boat serves as a benchmark and practicing is equally beneficial to both boats. Not only can two boats tune up against each other, but they can also set up match races and an organized series of drills and maneuvers.

As in any sport, it's better to practice with sailors who are more experienced. If you are losing in that practice session, don't give up. Keep a good attitude and remember that the work you are doing will help you later when you sail against the rest of the fleet—and against your practice partner. On the other hand, if you find that you're winning most of the drills, don't get cocky. Talk over what you might be doing that is different—as much to keep your partner's interest up as well as to benefit yourself with a psyched-up partner. To get the most out of each drill, sail as aggressively as you can all the time.

When you practice, simulate conditions in which you'll be racing. Keep notes in a log book about each session. Switch partners often. Trade information you learn with many sailors, keeping track of what you learned in your log as you go. If possible, try to space your partners out so you can judge your progress when you practice with a former partner. The real test, of course, comes when you put it all together in a regatta.

Use this practice method to tune up for your next big regatta. Arrive a day early for the event and get out on the water and tune up with a partner. At the same time you'll get a feeling for the wind in that area.

Drills for Practicing in Pairs

When tuning up against another boat, begin by speed testing. First set the jib leads, traveler, halyards, vang, cunningham, and other controls the same on both boats, and then simply sail against each other, constantly trying to make the boat go faster. This will improve your helmsmanship and give you an understanding of your boat. Top sailors know their boats and how they react in every condition. When tuning for speed, make every attempt to stay in the same wind. Two boats sailing in different wind don't prove anything. Each boat should be even at the start of a practice maneuver, not blanketing the other boat.

The best way to set up a practice session is to balance several specific drills with a series of short races. Practicing in pairs will improve your racing instantly. Sessions are easy to arrange, and provide a variety of excellent drills and practice races. Here are some drills for practicing as a pair.

RABBIT STARTS

One of the best ways to practice starts is by doing a *rabbit start*. Boat A dips the stern of Boat B (the "rabbit") while sailing to windward. Boat B continues on for two or three boatlengths and tacks (see illustration next page). The time spent tacking should be equal to the distance lost when Boat A dipped Boat B, so the boats start evenly.

Once underway, keep trying to sail faster than the other boat. The windward boat has the advantage of watching the leeward boat. The skipper of the leeward boat must look back over his shoulder to catch a glimpse of the action, so he should use the tactician to report this information. Both helmsmen must concentrate on speed. Playing your sheets and traveler alone can make the difference in speed; but typically, the faster boat is being sailed by the better helmsman. As soon as one boat establishes a commanding advantage, start over again. Be honest with the other boat and compare notes about any adjustments that you made.

SPLIT TACKS

Get together with another boat and start by splitting off on opposite tacks. Sail for a certain length of time (e.g., ten minutes) and then tack at the same time, coming back together. You can easily determine the favored side of the course in this manner.

DOWNWIND DRILLS

Most sailors spend time tuning up for the windward legs and often forget about tuning for the leeward legs. Sail downwind and

wind

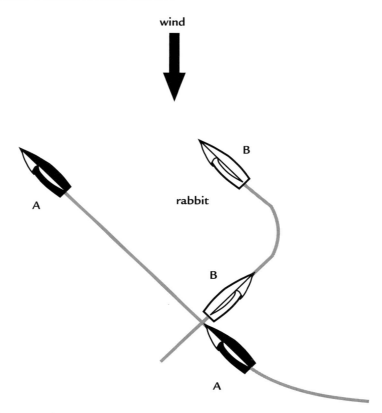

One method of starting when practicing in pairs is to use a "rabbit start." In this start Boat A dips below Boat B (the "rabbit"). Once Boat A has passed Boat B, B sails two or three boatlengths, then tacks. The result is an even start: the time Boat A lost to dipping B is made up by Boat B going two to three lengths, then tacking.

try jibing ten times; see who can complete the ten in the shortest time. At the same time, try to gain distance through the water on your competitor.

TAKE CONTROL IN SHORT RACES

The best practice with another boat is to run through several short races and a series of drills. Set up a short starting line with a windward mark. One boat calls the time and the pair attacks, each trying to gain control of the other. The best way to control another boat is by getting behind and driv-

ing your competitor away from the line.

When tailing another boat, be ready for his actions. If he slows down, so should you. Be aggressive and never give in. Plan ahead while maintaining total control of your boat.

TACKING DUELS

Start with one boat crossing behind the stern of the other. The boat in the lead tacks on the boat, while the boat behind tacks to clear. Set up a drill so that no more than thirty seconds elapse between tacks. At best, tacks will become more frequent. Pay attention to every move you make in the boat. When going through a fast series of tacks, drive the boat off, picking up speed. Don't let the boat heel and stall.

Tacking duels are physically demanding but a lot of fun. At the same time you are watching your competitor, be sure that you're tacking in clear air and in smooth water. Hold on a few extra seconds to avoid tacking in sloppy chop. If you are being covered, throw in some false tacks occasionally to keep your training partner honest. Fake tacks can be very effective in getting rid of a pest who is stealing your wind.

After several sets of tacking duels, switch boats. There is nothing better to even out the competition than switching boats.

720s

One drill that will develop your 720 turns is to go through a set of five 720s and see who can complete them first. You can continue on and do spinners (see section on solo practice earlier in this chapter). As you practice spinners see which boat can execute more spins in one minute.

DRILLS FOR PAIRS: ROUTINES

Practicing with another boat can result in immediate improvement for both crews. Try these maneuvers with a series of partners and document your progress with each:

❖ Four sets of tacking duels, two in each boat

❖ Two sets of five 720s (who is faster?)

❖ Two sets of quick jibes

❖ Rabbit start, sail to windward, tune

❖ Sail on reach, tune

❖ Sail downwind, tune (set chutes; who is faster?)

❖ Four sets of tailing (three minutes each)

❖ Split tacks on the course (switch sides)

❖ Best-of-seven short-course races, windward-leeward

❖ Race to the dock

Practicing as a Fleet

Organized practice sessions help sailors concentrate on specific techniques they might not normally use during a race. These sessions work best if there is a leader or a coach to coordinate the activities. The leader can be one of the competitors in your fleet. Each participant can rotate as the leader of the clinic.

Let regattas be your final examination. While at a practice session, don't be concerned with being first over the finish line; instead, be more concerned with working on specific techniques, such as starts, boat handling, mark roundings, and boatspeed.

A typical practice session includes speed testing, boat-handling exercises, and short-course races. An entire clinic can be run in just one afternoon or evening. But you don't always have to set aside a special day or evening for a training session. You can do some of these exercises with a few boats after a race, while you're waiting for the next race to start. The trick is to concentrate on one thing at a time. All sailors are winners when they participate in training sessions.

With an organized practice session you learn things much sooner and raise the

Coaching is the lifeblood of all sports. This is also true in sailboat racing. Here a coach makes suggestions on the finer points to a fleet of boats.

overall level of all the sailors because everyone at the session is working on a single technique. Collective wisdom speeds the learning process.

Drills for Fleet Practice

In addition to building the skills of your fleet, these drills are also fun. They will also develop comradeship in your fleet. Here are some examples of drills for fleet practice.

SLOW START

From thirty seconds before the start until ten seconds before the start, all sails must be completely luffing. This teaches boat control on crowded lines when you have to get into the "first row" early, hold your position, and accelerate fast.

SPEED START

From thirty seconds until the start you must sail at full speed on a close-hauled course with sails trimmed optimally. No luffing of sails or bearing away is allowed.

PORT APPROACH START

From one minute to thirty seconds before the start you must be on port tack—then you are free to go back to starboard whenever you want.

STARTING WITH NO TIMER

This drill forces the sailor to concentrate on his technique and keep careful time of his own start. The instructor can give signals at thirty-second intervals and eventually expand it to one minute and finally two-minute intervals and make the sailor start at his own time.

AUTOMATIC RECALL

On every start two boats are automatically recalled and have to round the ends regardless of whether they were over or not.

DOWNWIND STARTS

Race downwind to a leeward mark, which forces crowded leeward-mark roundings.

CONE DRILL

The fleet starts normally, but after the start they are confined to a triangle formed by the two ends of the line and the session leader in a motorboat traveling straight upwind. When a sailboat reaches the imaginary wall of the triangle, that boat must treat this as an obstruction and tack. The leader hails those boats that go beyond the cone walls. This drill focuses on tacking skills and the mechanics of ducking a starboard tacker.

TACKING DRILL

All boats start normally and remain on starboard tack until a signal (usually preceded by a short countdown as warning) comes from the motorboat upwind of the fleet. At that point, all boats must tack. After several minutes of this drill, it will become obvious which boats are tacking well. They can be asked to demonstrate their techniques for the fleet.

ACCELERATION DRILL

This is a variation of the tacking drill. All boats completely luff their sails on starboard tack until they stop. On a signal, all boats trim to accelerate. This is a good way to learn proper steering, weight placement, and sail control for whenever you're going less than full speed.

HELM CONTROL

All boats sail on the same tack and make adjustments to their trim (sail, rig, etc.) one at a time on command to determine how each change affects the boat's helm and speed.

360 DEGREES

Boats sail upwind on the same tack and at the whistle each must do a complete 360-degree turn (or two turns, making 720 degrees). This is great for improving execution of turns and 720-degree penalties.

JIBING DRILL

All boats bear off to a broad reach (or beam reach or run) on the same tack and jibe on the signal. Spinnaker sets, trim, jibes, and takedowns can be taught and practiced in a similar manner. It's important for the motorboat to remain upwind of the fleet and repeat the instructions before each signal to ensure that everyone understands what is coming next.

MULTIPLE TACKS RACE

In this drill there are a required number of tacks (ten, for example) that must be made between the start and the first mark. This rewards good tacking, with very little emphasis on boatspeed. Offwind you could require a given number of jibes as well.

TEAM RACING

Start the entire fleet at once and have them race against one another. This is one of the best ways to practice your racing ability and is great for teaching how to control other boats. It is also fun to be a part of a team effort on the course.

MATCH RACING

Split the fleet into pairs and give a separate start for each. You can start two races at once by setting the committee boat in the middle of two buoys. This practice is excellent for one-on-one tactical situations and also for straight-line speed development.

BACKWARD SAILING

On a signal, all boats must start sailing backward. This is good for developing boat-handling control and sail control. But the exercise is sometimes is not as easy as it seems.

CREW RACE

The crew and skipper trade positions for a race or two. This is a perfect way to emphasize the importance of teamwork—and for each person to appreciate the job the other crew member is doing.

DRILLS FOR FLEETS: ROUTINES

Here's a quick summary of drills and techniques to practice for a fleet practice session:

Starting Drills

❖ Slow

❖ Speed

❖ Port approach

❖ Downwind

❖ Upwind

❖ Cone drill

❖ Tacking

❖ Acceleration

❖ Spinners

Downwind Drills

❖ Jibing

❖ Surfing

Racing Drills

❖ Match race

❖ Team race

❖ Fleet race

CHAPTER 12

Thoughts on Performance

You have now learned about the mechanics of boat handling and the mental game of tactics and strategy. But the education of a championship sailor goes well beyond the racecourse. In this chapter are my broader thoughts on performance, from the importance of making sailboat racing fun to what sailors with true grit can teach us.

Mentoring

At a college regatta, I was quick to notice how smoothly the coed teams maneuvered their dinghies. Every dock landing was perfect, roll tacks were crisp, boatspeed was at peak performance, and—best of all—their attitudes were focused. I wondered, "Is talent like this natural or is it learned?" While most every college sailor has mastered the fundamentals, what does it take to achieve that extra margin of excellence that pro-

duces champions? A mentor can begin the process.

Mentors inspire us by setting a high example. We need to encourage current sailing stars to reach out and help others. This is the responsibility of success. Give a protégé a reason to work hard by getting them to set goals. Often a brief talk followed by an encouraging letter initiates the process. At this stage, mention that you will be following the aspiring sailor's progress. Occasional checkups will reinforce the message. When the young sailor starts asking questions you will know that the process has begun. Encourage the protégé to keep records so lessons learned will be remembered.

Once the first seed is sown the next step comes from within. A young sailor must start with the desire and then put in a worthy effort. There is no substitute for

Asking questions speeds up the learning process. Encourage young sailors to place more of their focus on learning as opposed to winning.

scheduling and participating in disciplined practice sessions.

Encourage your protégé to ask for help, read about techniques, and experiment on the water. Use high but attainable short-term goals to measure progress. I define short term as under two months. Offer case studies as examples of how successful sailors have achieved long-term goals.

Many young sailors give up during times of adversity. They take mistakes hard. You can help overcome these problems by pointing out specific problems. During a regatta, ask one simple question at a time to allow a sailor to answer for himself what could be done better on the racecourse. Too much input creates confusion. As a mentor, always be calm, as if you expect

improvement. This philosophy builds confidence. Its okay to be a cheerleader but help flatten out the inevitable roller-coaster ride by not getting too excited when winning or too depressed during defeat. Remember, winning is the elimination of errors. Teach sailors to thrive on working out of bad positions after a slow start, making a penalty turn, or being on the wrong side of a windshift. It takes work to keep one's attitude focused. During the heat of battle a sailor must be calm and never sweat the small stuff when things go wrong.

There is a fine, but dangerous line between helpful coaching and pushing too hard. This problem is frequently found in the Optimist Dinghy Class. If expectations are too high at early ages, a young sailor may reject sailing. For further information about racing Optimists see *The Winner's Guide to Optimist Sailing* (International Marine).

Always balance sailing with other activities. Good grades are the key to opening doors. Make studies a priority. Sailing should never be considered only for young people. The attributes and lessons learned in other sports are often analogous to sailing. The discipline instilled in a team sport is particularly helpful in sailing with a crew. Every one of our America's Cup crew aboard *Courageous* lettered in a sport other than sailing in school.

Once the seed of desire starts growing, organize a purposeful regatta schedule. Sail both large and small boats to broaden experience. Single-handed sailing always sharpens your skills. To prepare for Maxi racing, for example, I sail Lasers to get in tune with the wind and water. Sailing on different waters also builds experience. Sailing today has become too specialized. Maintaining variety keeps interest up and builds skills. One type of sailing supports another.

Rising sailors exhibit many common attributes. They physically match up well with their boat. During a race the body is in sync with a boat's motion. Actions are deliberate. Being in good physical condition enhances performance.

Many sailors try to "over-sail" a race, and make mistakes like tacking too frequently. Teach your sailor to develop a game plan and stick to it. Use common sense. Avoid locking into a match-race battle while you are fleet racing. I like to refer to other boats by sail numbers to keep emotions out. Remember my experience at the Hall of Fame Regatta? (Turn back to page 71.) Referring to boat numbers and not big-time names kept me calm. And remember that it always pays to avoid protests, even if it means occasionally giving a little extra room.

Progress may be slow, and may even regress at times, but keep plugging. As a mentor, if you detect burnout or rejection, let your young sailor know it's okay to take a break from sailing or change boats, crews, or venues.

Young sailors should learn to work with the media. Few sailors are good communicators. Learning to be enthusiastic, helpful, and comfortable with the media at an early age will inspire more people to take up sailing.

Help young sailors by opening doors and providing thoughtful encouragement. There are no limits to the skill level sailors can achieve if they have the desire and put in a balanced effort. Look for young sailors with potential and then help them build the desire to excel. All of you will end up winning.

Take Time to Look Around

Racing sailors are defined as intense competitors. Cruising sailors are supposed to spend time on the water enjoying freedom, adventure, camaraderie, relaxation, and even romance. But I chuckle when I see two boats cruising in close proximity and abandoning this well-grounded philosophy by tweaking their sails to improve performance. I guess human nature does not easily allow one sailor to be passed by another.

Take the time to enjoy the sights. This group of boats has quite the scenic view as they pass Southeast Point off Block Island.

This instinct has driven sailors since the early days of sail. Call it racing while cruising. In contrast, you expect the racing sailor to be completely focused on boat handling, sail trim, strategy, and speed. But can a combination of these approaches make racing more rewarding? Such was my experience on one Block Island Race aboard George Collins's Farr 52, *Chessie Racing*.

Long Island and Connecticut have both had a population and building boom since my first Block Island Race over thirty years ago. Yet the view from the water is remarkably similar. Various islands like Stratford Shoal, Faulkner, Plum, Fisher, and even Block are unchanged.

Long Island Sound is a busy shipping lane. Tugs and barges look businesslike, almost aloof as they pass. But you never see a tugboat captain wave. Then again, few sailors seem to wave in this area.

On this relatively land-closed racecourse, the fleet separates quickly and then magically converges at the turns and gates. I enjoy passing close to buoys and islands to feel the sensation of speed. Every object on the water looks like it's meant to be there.

Sitting on the rail is a great time for conversation. Everyone is upbeat. The metaphysical experience of floating above the passing water erases all problems. When steering, you get into a trance "willing" the boat to sail faster. I notice that helmsmen steer better when they stand because their whole body acts as a sensor. At the helm it seems that you, the boat, the wind, the water, the waves, and the sealife all exist as one.

On the return from Block Island we sailed upwind for 90 miles. Periodic tacks broke the monotony. It's funny how tacking is always popular on deck but unpopular down below. The off watch doesn't like to move.

During the day, sailing is different than at night. In the dark, senses are dull, things seem bigger and faster. This is when most long-distance races are won. In daylight, however, the helmsman and the sail trimmers get into a rhythm. The navigator and watch captains study every element available, searching for clues about what the weather will do next. To me, deciding on strategy is the essence of sailboat racing. Often you can't control your environment. The trick is to set a pace in daylight that extends into the night.

Exiting or entering Long Island Sound through the Gut or The Race is always traumatic. When you sail with the 5-knot current you are on top of the world. But fighting it is painful, like watching your favorite stock fall over several days.

While the shoreline and the regularity of the tides never change, race boats certainly do. An old rule of thumb on this race was it took eighteen hours to get to Block Island and eighteen hours to return. Today twelve hours is a more reliable number. On *Chessie Racing* we averaged 7.7 knots.

There are many creative watch-standing systems today but my favorite is still four hours on and four off. On this race I took a couple turns with the off watch and enjoyed observing the nuances of another group sailing the same boat. The watch captains set the pace. With half the crew below it is nice to race a boat with only six people on deck. Everyone is busy.

It astounds me how much technological progress has been made over the past thirty years. Winches today are light, powerful, and very efficient. Sails are works of art. And the lightweight fabric makes them easy to handle. Navigation is a snap thanks to the accuracy of GPS. And you can continually evaluate performance with laptop computers. The purist misses navigating by sextant. But today's tools are so accurate they help you make better tactical decisions. The end result is that racing becomes more interesting.

Of course weather forecasts on the VHF are helpful. Those computerized voices broadcast in a dull monotone. "The weather this evening will be 22 knots out of the southwest gusting to 30." How about some enthusiasm? "And for you sailors on the Block Island Race, you're going to have a great ride, big winds! Have fun!"

But even with all the tools available it surprises me that boats sail in such different directions heading for the same point. Everyone always seems to have their own idea on how to handle things best. You never know until the end who is right.

Innovation is not always better. One thing I miss today is a real meal. Prepackaged, freeze-dried food does not come close to a roast or an omelet. And I miss bunks with sheets, pillows, and blankets. I think all ocean racers ought to agree that every boat should sail with a hundred pounds of creature comforts.

Thirty years ago, Long Island Sound was filthy. But the increased concern for protecting the environment has made a difference. The water passing by looked (and smelled) cleaner.

The wind can be fickle. Approaching the Gut, a northerly wind was fading and it looked like a southerly would take its place. *Chessie Racing* drew abeam of *Encore*, only five boatlengths to leeward and to the north. After stopping for a few minutes, a light breeze propelled *Encore* into a big lead. She was nearly a mile ahead by the time we got going. That hurt. A half hour later two boats parked in the same spot where *Chessie Racing* and *Encore* were. This time the breeze found the windward (southern) boat and left the leeward boat behind. Darn! What could we have done? The answer? It's just the way it is on Long Island Sound. Timing is everything. And luck helps, too.

The geography of the region is fascinating. I thought back to the days when glaciers covered the area. Long Island was a terminal moraine only eight thousand years ago. In fact, Block Island was actually connected to Long Island. As we rounded Block at sunrise, it made me sad to think that one day this island will probably disappear altogether. But right now it proudly stands 21 miles off Newport, Rhode Island, in some of the finest sailing waters in the world.

The highlight of any race is passing another boat. Sometimes a pass can take hours. We had a good battle with one boat while circumnavigating the island. We started five lengths behind and ended three lengths ahead. Hooray!

I thought about reality television shows and wondered if someday we will be able to observe a boat like *Chessie Racing* on the Internet during a race.

Lying on my bunk I reflected on past Block Island races and it dawned on me that crews from Connecticut always seemed to favor the Connecticut shore while New Yorkers always tend to favor the Long Island shore. Are sailors naturally drawn to their home waters?

As we crossed the finish line race committee officers were happy to see us. It made us feel good that they cared about our safe passage.

One week later on a clear afternoon I was flying over Long Island Sound at 31,000 feet. Below I could see the entire racecourse of the previous weekend. It looked so simple and small from the air. But from the water there was so much to absorb. Looking down I realized I need to do this race again. But cruising would be fine too. Then it dawned on me that a little of each is what makes sailing so rewarding. Take time to look around and experience a little cruising and racing at the same time.

Make It Fun

This particular regatta was going to be intense. Only two boats from the Middle Atlantic District would qualify for the Intercollegiate Singlehanded Championship. The elimination series was held on my home waters off the SUNY Maritime College in a new boat called the Laser. This nifty dinghy was new to all of us. I had only sailed the Laser once. At 6-feet 2-inches tall and 180 pounds I was the right size for the boat. But after two races I was in twelfth place out of

Sailing in a Laser takes great concentration. The key is to pretend that boat, body, wind, and water are one. Gary Jobson sailing in collegiate nationals.

sixteen boats. Not good. Back at the dock my coach, Graham Hall, said in a very calm way, "You look like you are trying too hard and thinking about qualifying." Hall continued, "You're out of it right now so just go back out there and try to make one improvement at a time." "But what about boatspeed?" I asked. "Oh, don't worry about that, just go have fun!" "Fun?" I thought. Somehow Hall loosened me up. It was at this precise moment that I regained my confidence and my sailing career changed dramatically. I went out and had fun, and I won the next race. In fact, I won the next ten races.

Suddenly sixteen years of sailing clicked. Looking back through my college log books (I recorded 2,000 races in four years), there were many fundamentals that I refined through competitive drills and lessons learned from mistakes. Improving is easier if someone helps you. The combination of coaching and practice works in every sport. It worked for me.

At the Intercollegiate National Championship two months later, I again had trouble in the first two races. Now we were racing Lasers on Mission Bay near San Diego. Observing my problem, Graham Hall suggested just one tactical adjustment, "Don't be the first to tack after every start. Wait until you have a clear lane. Use a boat to leeward and ahead to push away traffic." He continued, "Think of a football running back using a blocker to gain more yardage."

The philosophical shift for me was to be more patient and look for good lanes. For the first time I understood how to use competitors as blockers (see the Windward Tactics section in chapter 5). I went on to win ten of the next fourteen races to take the championship.

For me, the keys to getting to that point were goal setting, practice, and good coaching. During my sophomore year at Maritime I wrote down my goals and philosophy:

1. Set high goals

2. Aggressive attacks

3. Take it as it comes, but keep plugging

4. All out—never halfway

5. Never give in

Every single day I worked on boat handling by sailing continuous figure eights, timed runs, and endless tacks and jibes. (Review the practice routines in chapter 11 to learn how to do these drills yourself.) Even to this day I find crisp roll tacks one of the highlights of life. Making figure eights by rounding a pair of buoys lets you practice jibing, tacking, windward roundings, leeward roundings, and acceleration. Precise maneuvering is an essential asset when you are around other boats. These drills gave me an edge. But well beyond the boat handling skills that I honed, the most important lesson was to go out on the racecourse and have fun.

My Favorite Boats

I'm lucky. Over the years I've had the opportunity to race and cruise on a broad range of the world's best sailboats. From Lasers and Sunfish, to giant catamarans and Maxis, and everything in between. I have been there. Wow! What a ride. Someone once asked me, "What is your favorite boat to sail?" A tough question for sure. I didn't have an answer.

A few weeks later I found myself sailing in Sint Maarten's annual regatta. During a one-week period I had the opportunity to steer an 80-foot Maxi in a race, sail a 19-foot catamaran, the 12-meter *Stars & Stripes* (which won the America's Cup in 1987), a Beneteau 42s7, a Corel 45, and a Laser. The shifting of gears got me thinking, what *is* the best boat to sail?

The question is certainly not limited to racing. Cruising is just as important. Although I am relatively new to cruising, over the past years I have spent time on a wooden schooner in Maine, sailed to Bermuda aboard the *Pride of Baltimore II*, and have gone on expeditions to Antarctica, the Arctic, and Cape Horn. Each voyage had a purpose and was rewarding.

I made a list of the sailing experiences I've had over the years to reach a conclusion. Single-handed dinghies are fantastic. You are one with the wind and the water. On smaller boats, it's magic when you can excel with a crew of two, three, or four. The Etchells, the Mumm 30, Melges 24, J/22, Solings, Shields, and E-scows are all boats that have special characteristics. In fact, I'm happy on any of them. But then, thinking deeper, I recalled the many distance races I have sailed: five Fastnets, six Bermuda races, and fifteen SORCs. Camaraderie aboard a big boat, particularly during the heat of battle or in a fierce storm, provides experiences that don't fade away. I can still vividly remember the Fastnet storm of 1979.

The America's Cup? There is no greater thrill than being aboard a boat that has successfully defended the Cup. And what a thrill sailing with Ted Turner and a group of superstars, all of whom have excelled in the sport of sailing ever since.

When analyzing the question further, I wondered if it is the waters and not the boats. The best? Well, Key West is always magic. Honolulu, San Francisco, Fremantle, Newport, the Caribbean, Long Beach, the Solent, and Chesapeake Bay all feature their own special characteristics. Then I considered the races. Come-from-behind victories, speed under sail, and the ballet of a crew orchestrating a complicated maneuver all have special rewards.

Still struggling with an answer, I made a list. Here are my favorites:

Endeavour—the J-class is the most powerful sailboat in the world and a thing of beauty.

E-scow—competitive, fast, and still a dinghy.

Etchells—tactics, tactics, and tactics (and a little speed helps).

Finn—beating 80 boats to a windward mark in a strong blow is the most athletic accomplishment in sailing.

49er—it is about time we had a high-speed skiff.

Interclub Dinghy—you could roll tack forever.

America's Cup Class—it is hard to believe you sail through so much water in such a short period of time.

J/22—nifty little boat providing tight racing; surprisingly quick.

Laser—it is all you for better or worse—and the sensation is magic.

Maxi Class—over 10 knots to windward and twenty-four crew to orchestrate. A real challenge.

Mumm 30—fast, fun, and easy.

Optimist Dinghy—if you can sail one of these well, you can sail anything. The world's best are coming out of this class.

Sunfish—let's go surfing.

Trifoiler—35 knots on top of the water, and no sound.

Megamarans—large fast multihulls. How do you throttle back?

12-Meter—heavy, slow-maneuvering but tactics and boat handling are the secrets to success.

Open 60—sustained 30-knot bursts.

So after my week of eclectic sailing, it suddenly dawned on me that it isn't the boat, the place, or the regatta that is special. It is the people. And for that reason, the people you spend your time with on the water are the reward. But a little variety helps.

Sailors with True Grit

Everyone loves cheering for the underdog. The underdog who prevails when the situation looks hopeless deserves respect. Over the years, three special events come to mind as examples of amazing feats in sailing.

Imagine being expected to win the Olympic Trials, the winner-take-all regatta that determines who will represent the United States in the Olympic Games. The qualifying series is seven races with one throw-out against the cream of America's sailors. The first race ends with a disappointing fifth. In the second race, the mast goes over the side. Now, five races are left and the odds of winning are looking slim. For many sailors the end would come soon. But not for Buddy Melges, Bill Bentsen, and Bill Allen. With a second-string spar and a lot of grit, the trio bounced back by taking five straight firsts. They went on to the Olympics in 1972 but the story did not end there. The Trials were sailed on windy San Francisco Bay with the idea of emulating the breezy conditions expected in Kiel, Germany. But there was a surprise. The winds of Kiel went light. How many times have you been at a regatta where you hear the words, "The winds aren't normally like this here." Melges and his crew trained in heavy winds. But somehow the Americans found one zephyr after another to defeat four-time Olympic gold medalist Paul Elvström. Melges and his crew took home the gold medal. America has never produced a better sailor. Buddy's ability to adapt to unexpected changes sets him apart from all mortal sailors.

By the time he turned forty, Ted Turner had won every major ocean race, the America's Cup, and dozens of small-boat titles. Turner understood comebacks after suffering through a miserable summer on the super-slow *Mariner* in 1974, and he returned to defend the America's Cup in 1977. But that victory wasn't complete since one race still stood out in his mind— the Fastnet. Aboard his Sparkman & Stephens–designed 61-footer *Tenacious*, Turner assembled a crack crew of seasoned ocean racers. The preceding Cowes Week was windy and *Tenacious* won many of the daily prizes. But the magnitude of the 1979 Fastnet Race was not anticipated.

The first 300 miles to Fastnet Rock, 8 miles off the coast of Ireland, were easy. But soon after rounding Fastnet Rock the wind built to 40 knots, then to 50, and finally to a frightening 60 knots. *Tenacious* felt the fury of the storm. Turner kept the crew focused and calm. It was as if Turner actually thrived on the massive waves and powerful winds. With no visibility, feeling the waves and wind proved to be the solution. Turner mastered the storm, and he emerged well into the lead to take the first overall prize out of 303 boats. To this day Turner will tell you it was his most satisfying victory. For me, it is a real thrill to have shared both Ted's America's Cup and Fastnet victories.

Being the first skipper to lose the America's Cup in 1983 would seem like an awful burden to bear. But Dennis Conner actually sailed brilliantly in 1983. The score could easily have been 4–0, advantage *Australia II*—instead the final score was 4–3, advantage Australia. Despite his overall loss Conner outfoxed the Aussies time after time. In one race he actually port-tacked the opposing boat, something that should never happen in a match race. In the end Conner failed to cover on the final run of the last race. The error would have ended many careers. But Conner knew he had the ability to make a comeback.

He and his syndicate head, Malin Burnham, pioneered corporate sponsorship in sailing and developed a fast boat they called *Stars & Stripes*. And they went on to win the Cup back in the next match-up! Overnight, Conner became a national hero. Adding to the pressure was live, worldwide television coverage with onboard cameras. Conner's strongest assets in that campaign were his personal resolve to erase the loss of 1983 and his ability to play the windshifts. Throughout the 1987 series he cleverly chose between covering and playing the wind. It was his finest hour.

In each case, these American heroes knew they had a chance to overcome adversity. Their success was not a matter of luck: it was their resolve.

Winning

In the process of writing *Championship Sailing*, I reviewed my log books, articles, notes, lecture outlines, books, and videos of the past forty years. Many of the racing techniques I learned long ago are still effective today. In fact, my racing career stretches over fifty years. I'm still active and plan to be for many more years. Learning never stops.

As I look back, it astounds me how far technology has developed to improve sailing. Fifty years ago aluminum hulls, inflatable dinghies, fiberglass boats, video, radar on yachts, Dacron, and user-friendly Loran were still a vision on the horizon. Just thirty

years ago, who could have imagined sails being built on molds, GPS, night-vision gyroscopic binoculars, handheld VHF, winged keels, carbon-fiber spars and hulls, Spectra rope, breathable foul-weather gear, laser-range finders, double-grooved headstays, weather routing, or velocity prediction programs on laptop computers?

All these innovations are useful tools for sailors. As a result, racing is more precise, boats are faster, and equipment is more reliable. But even with the availability of advanced technology, winning a race is still decided by determination, careful planning, teamwork, leadership, resourcefulness, and execution.

Everyone has the opportunity to excel. The first step is to set goals and believe you can win. As time passes, keep your expectations high.

Take time to organize and plan your approach. Keep an open mind to new ideas. You can even borrow methods or equipment from other sports and industries.

On the water, be efficient with your valuable time. Schedule both practice and racing well in advance. Extracurricular sailing outside your normal class makes you more versatile. Competitors can give you helpful thoughts. Study the lessons of high-profile regattas like the America's Cup, the Olympic Games, world championships, and round-the-world events. The sailing media likes to write about these events and sailors like to talk about their experiences, so it's easy to learn from these grand-prix contests.

A loyal crew makes a big difference in performance. Most winning teams have been together for a long period of time. Re-

Everyone can excel at racing. Set goals, always strive to do better, and keep your expectations high.

cruit crews for your roster who have the will to win.

Sailing is a sport where common sense rules. The crew that makes the fewest mistakes usually wins. The elimination of errors is hard but if you take the attitude that "you just keep trying to do better," progress will be made.

Excellence on the water is to be savored. It is certainly one of the highlights of life. In reviewing my own career of 5,000 races, I realize there are many lessons that I've relearned many times. By being persistent, difficult tasks eventually become second nature.

The most satisfying achievements arrive when your competitors are happy you won. Inner satisfaction feels nice but remember you are only as good as your next race! Perfection is difficult to achieve. But when you come close and know you've done your best, sailing is most gratifying.

The ideas in this book were learned over many years and from hundreds of others. I'll be reading these words many times in the quest to reach my goals, and I hope you too will use the ideas in these pages to continually improve. Take the time to pass them on to others. Sharing knowledge will help you grow, and it will help our sport grow too.

Glossary

Afterguard—the decision-making group aboard a boat. Includes skipper, tactician, navigator, and occasionally other crew members.

Apparent wind direction—the wind that you feel as a boat moves. The direction changes due to the boat's action through the air.

Apparent wind speed—the strength of the wind you feel allowing for the boat's movement through the air. Upwind you feel more wind while downwind you feel less.

Backwind—the exhaust or disturbed wind caused by the sails.

Barging—passing between a close-hauled leeward boat and a starting mark; or forcing a leeward boat to bear away at the start of a race.

Bear off—to head away from the wind. To alter course.

Bear-away set—to round a mark, steer a lower course, and then set a spinnaker.

Beyond head-to-wind—technically a boat is tacking once it passes directly into the wind.

Blanket/blanket zone—blocking the wind of another boat with your sails; or the area of reduced wind caused by a boat's sail.

Blast reacher—a small sail set forward of the mast to improve speed in heavy wind when the wind is from the side.

Broach—sometimes known as a knockdown. When a boat capsizes on its side due to a strong gust of wind.

By the lee—sailing downwind with the apparent wind hitting the boat from the leeward side.

Cavitation—a vacuum formed when air gets trapped between the hull, rudder, keel, or centerboard. This can cause lack of control.

Center of effort—an imaginary point on a boat's sail plan that represents the center of the force of the wind on the sails.

Center of resistance—the center of pressure on the keel or centerboard underneath the water.

Cover—to stay between the opposition and the next mark; to stay with the fleet

Crossovers—the change in wind strength or direction when it becomes necessary to change to a different sail.

Current shear—a distinct shift in the water flow created by two opposing currents, tides of different strengths, or water traveling in opposite directions.

Draft—the amount of curvature in a sail; or the distance between the waterline and the deepest part of the keel or centerboard.

False header—a rapid change in wind direction that shifts back to its original direction.

False tack—to pretend to start a maneuver by turning a boat but then quickly returning to your original course.

Flyer—to split courses with the majority of the fleet. To sail on the opposite side of the course.

Foot—to head on a lower course in order to increase speed.

General recall—after a false start where a majority of the fleet is over the line, the race committee begins a new starting sequence.

Groove/in the groove—the feeling of speed when the boat is balanced, the sails trimmed properly, and the boat is sailing fast.

Half jibe—the act of pretending to initiate a jibe maneuver. Halfway through the turn the helmsman returns the helm to the original course.

Hand-bearing compass—an instrument used to read bearings on objects such as other boats, turning marks, and points of land.

Handicap racing—assigning a boat "a rating" or "handicap" based on measurement, usually measured in seconds per mile.

Header—a windshift that forces a boat to sail a lower course or away from a mark. Also known as a knock.

Headstay sag—the curve to leeward in the headstay or the luff of the sail caused by the force of the wind.

Head-to-wind—aiming the boat directly into the wind. The sails will luff in this position.

In phase/out of phase—to tack periodically and take advantage of a windshift. You are in phase when you are sailing in a new wind on a course that is closer to the mark you are heading for.

Jibe set—the act of rounding a windward mark, bearing off, jibing, and then setting a spinnaker.

Layline—the course you sail directly for a turning mark.

Lee bow—a tactical position ahead and to leeward of another boat.

Lee helm/leeward helm—the force on a boat to make it bear away from the wind if you let go of the wheel or tiller.

Lift—a windshift that allows a boat to sail closer to its desired course.

Locking up—to match race another boat. To stay in close proximity of a competitor.

Loose cover—to stay between a competitor and the next mark but without blocking the wind of the boat behind.

Luff—an alteration of course toward the wind; or the fluttering action of a sail; or the forward edge of a sail.

Masthead fly—a lightweight weather vane at the top of the mast.

Match racing—two boats racing each other at a time. Format used in the America's Cup.

Maxi—a large racing yacht designed to the maximum handicap rule allowed.

One-minute rule—after a false start or **general recall**, a fleet must stay behind the starting line one minute before the starting gun.

Overlap—a situation where any portion of one boat is abeam of any portion of another boat, no matter if boats are on same tack.

Overstand—to sail past the **layline** of a mark so you have to sail a faster course than desired. This means you are giving away distance.

Peel—to change spinnakers while sailing downwind.

Pinch—to sail too high a course. The boat sails slowly.

Pitchpole—to capsize with the bow running into a wave ahead of the boat. The boat tips over end for end.

Polars—a graph or drawing indicating a boat's predicted speed at different wind angles and wind strengths. A polar diagram gives you the optimum speed your boat can attain.

Preventer—a line used to restrict the boom from suddenly swinging across the boat.

Puff—an increase in wind strength indicated by dark patches on the water.

Rhumb line—the straight line compass course between two points. The shortest course except over long distances where the great circle caused by the curvature of the earth is shorter.

Roll tack—a maneuver that helps a boat accelerate. While tacking a crew heels the boat to leeward and then hard to windward to create wind in the sails. A common technique in dinghies.

Rolled—when a competitor sails to windward, passes, and then blocks the leeward boat's wind.

Shoot the line—a sudden luff when crossing the finish line to arrive earlier.

S-jibe—sailing a boat on an S-shaped course during a jibing maneuver to prevent the mainsail from slamming across the boat.

Slam dunk—a maneuver on a windward leg involving boats on opposite tacks. The boat crossing ahead makes a tacking maneuver directly to windward of the trailing boat to block its wind. The leeward boat is trapped in this position.

Snow-fence effect—the blocking effect on the wind by a large object, point of land, or ship.

Stall—the disturbance or turbulence caused by a break in the flow of air around the sails or flow of water around the rudder or keel. The boat will sail slowly when it stalls.

Starboard tack advantage—the boat that is on the right (starboard side) of another has the advantage under the racing rules. A port-tack boat must always stay clear.

Target speed—boatspeeds that are used as guidelines for obtaining a boat's optimum performance both upwind and downwind. The targets will vary with the strength of the wind, state of the sea, and angle of the wind.

Tight cover—a defensive position in which the leading boat stays directly on the wind of a trailing boat. The leader matches the maneuvers of the trailing boat with every tack.

True wind—the compass heading of the wind direction or wind strength. The true wind direction and speed is not affected by the boat sailing through the air.

True wind angle—the actual direction that the wind is hitting the boat.

Two-boatlength circle—an imaginary boundary around a racing buoy with a radius two boatlengths long used for determining which boat is entitled to room at the mark.

VMG (velocity made good)—the component of boatspeed measured against wind direction. How fast you're heading to or from the direction from which the wind is coming.

VPP (velocity prediction program)—a computer program that analyzes a boat's hull form, weight, and sail plan to calculate a boat's sailing performance. Generates **polars.**

Weather/windward helm—the tendency of a boat to head up when the helm is released. Measured degrees of rudder angle required to steer a straight course.

Wind shadow—the blanketing effect the sails of one boat have on another boat.

Wind shear—different direction and strength of the wind at various elevations.

Windward gauge—the distance between a windward and leeward boat.

Windward hip—the position to windward and behind a leeward boat. The opposite of **lee bow.**

Windwaves—the grouping of ripples on the water caused by the wind. The dark patches indicate a stronger wind usually known as a **puff.**

A Racer's Calendar

There are hundreds of regattas that take place throughout the world each week. Below is a list of major regattas in North America. More information on these can be found in sailing periodicals or on the Web.

	America's Cup (every two–five years)
Summer	Olympic Games (every four years)
January	Key West Race Week
January	Miami Olympic Classes Regatta
February	Miami Race Week
March	Congressional Cup
March	Barcelona Olympic Week
March	Sint Maarten Heineken Regatta
April	Antigua Race Week
June	Santa Maria Cup
June	Long Beach Race Week
June	Newport–Bermuda Race (even years)
June	Block Island Race Week (odd years)
June	Intercollegiate Nationals
July	Cork Race Week
July	ISAF Youth Worlds
July	Monhegan Island Race
July	Marblehead–Halifax Race
July	Chicago to Mackinac Race
July	Port Huron to Mackinac Race
July	Transpac (odd years)
August	Fastnet Race (odd years)
August	Cowes Week
September	St. Francis Big Boat Series
October	Bermuda Gold Cup
December 26	Sydney–Hobart Race

INDEX